THE COLOR CONNECTION:
From a Retailer's Perspective

by Joan Callaway

Illustrations by JoAnn Stabb
Portraits by Tom Deininger,
Impressions Photography

Copyright © 1986 by Joan S. Callaway. First edition. All rights reserved. No part of this book may be reproduced in any form or by any means now known or to be invented, electronic or mechanical, including photocopying, recording or by any information storage or retrieval system without written permission from the author or publisher except for the brief inclusion of quotations in a review.

Printed in the United States of America by
WINTERSPRING PRESS
406 Second Street
Davis, California 95616
(916) 753-2262

Attention: This book is available at quantity discount with bulk purchase for educational use. For information, please write WinterSpring Press.

Quotes from *The Turning Point* by Fritjof Capra, copyright © 1981. Reprinted by permission of Simon & Shuster, Inc.

Seasonal Color Harmonies and Key to Arrangement of Color Chart © 1985. Reprinted by permission of Cheri Joerger.

Quote from Henry Grethel reprinted by permission of Henry Grethel.

Cover Design by Dunlavey Studio.
Cover Photos by Ken Browning and Robert Jaffe.
Typesetting by Graphic Gold, Davis, California.

Book Design by Marilyn Judson.

Library of Congress Cataloging-in-Publication Data:

Callaway, Joan S.
   The Color Connection:
   From a Retailer's Perspective

   Includes Index.
     1. Clothing and Fabric   2. Marketing, Retailing and Salesmanship

     3. Beauty   I. Title

ISBN 0-938651-00-5

*To my mother, who instilled in me
the entrepreneurial spirit by her example;*

to my children, who care;

*to my friends in women's RTW,
Ann, Berda, Jane and Hi, Ed, Heidi,
Hal, Mike, Nikos and Mara, Zeilla, Sid, Delores,
Linda, Beth, and many, many more,
who have patiently put up with me while
I put the pieces together;*

*to Irene Kennedy, who introduced me
to Suzanne and the Seasonal Color
Harmony System, and who helped
immeasurably in many ways in the
production of this book;*

*to Suzanne, Pauline, Cheri, and all
the other color and wardrobe consultants,
without whom the book would not be;*

*to my wonderful, caring staff who
have made it all possible;*

*to Jeanne, Harriet, Florence and all
the others who have painstakingly read
and reread;*

*and to Ed, my husband, whose love,
support, confidence and encouragement
sustained me.*

TABLE OF CONTENTS

	Author's Notes — How to Use This Book	i
Chapter 1.	A Theory Whose Time Has Come	1
Chapter 2.	Fad, Fact or Fiction?	11
Chapter 3.	There's More to Color Analysis Than Color	27
Chapter 4.	The Color Connection — A Continuum	35
Chapter 5.	Winter	41
Chapter 6.	Spring	73
Chapter 7.	Summer	119
Chapter 8.	Autumn	149
Chapter 9.	Yin and Yang	179
	Yin-Yang Questionnaire	182
	About the Author	200
Chapter 10.	People Are a Lot Like Pasta…Or How to Use the Basic Recipe	201
Chapter 11.	"What If…?" — For Designers and Would-Be Designers	205
Chapter 12.	Rags to Riches…or Markdown Madness — A Retailer's Choice	221
Chapter 13.	Want to Be More Than "Just a Sales Clerk?"	239
Chapter 14.	Color and How to Use It — A Review of Some Basic Art Principles	249
Chapter 15.	Illusion Is a Woman's Best Friend	255
Chapter 16.	The Ideal Image — Reflective of the Inner You	263
	Comparative Seasonal Harmony Chart	274
	Index	276

Author's Notes
— How to Use This Book

This book began as a training manual for the staff of my women's clothing shop. As I analyzed, digested and categorized the information that I wished to include, it evolved into a book that clearly discusses the seasonal color harmony theory, as well as its application to the women's ready-to-wear industry. I believe it can become a useful tool for anyone involved in women's apparel, whether they be a consumer, buyer, sales associate, or designer. The theory is applicable for children's and men's apparel, as well, and can even be carried into the home environment — furniture, dishes, sheets, wall coverings, draperies, etc.

In the process of compiling the information, I became aware that, although the book shelves are full of books on style, color, and fashion, none of them includes complete detailed style information related to the seasonal harmony system for the consumer, much less for the retailer and designer.

This is a "choose your own ending" book. Much of the information in Chapters 1 through 10 will be useful to the Consumer, but is also essential to the understanding and application of the theory for the retail buyer, sales associate, and design student.

The style and color information in Chapters 5 through 8 are a composite of the various systems I have uncovered. It is important to note that not every color analyst will agree with everything that I have included, but everything that I have included is advocated by many wardrobe and color consultants.

While it may be a temptation to skip over all but one's own personal seasonal harmony section, for best results it is recommended that all four of the seasons be studied by each seasonal type. In Chapters 9 and 10, the consumer is encouraged to create her own "recipe" for an individualized wardrobe that expresses her inner self; the designer, retail buyer, and sales associate will find much useful information for their purposes, too. A thorough understanding of Yin and Yang and the guidelines of all of the seasons will help the consumer to learn when and how to "break the rules" in order to create precisely the image she wishes to project, consistently and without costly mistakes; it will help the designer, buyer, and sales associate similarly.

The information throughout the book is to be construed as "guidelines" rather than rules. The guidelines 1) have evolved through observing that many, if not most, women who share specific coloring, personality, etc., appear most harmonious when wearing specific styles, fabrics and prints, and, in fact, often independently prefer the styles outlined in the guidelines; 2) are being taught by various color analysts across the nation.

Much of the book is a composite of theories that I have learned through reading, attending seminars, my own color consultations, as well as through my personal experiences of wardrobing women through the years. Credit must be given to color analysts Suzanne Caygill, Dorothy Gietzen, Cheri Joerger, Joan Songer, and Pauline Worth from whom I learned so much; and to Irene Kennedy, who has generously shared with me her understanding of Suzanne Caygill's teachings.

Much of what I have learned about color harmony was originally taught by Suzanne Caygill. It has subsequently been described and illustrated in her book, *Color, The Essence of You* (Celestial Arts, Millbrae, Ca. 1980), an invaluable resource for the study of the nature or Seasonal Color Harmony Theory.

After Chapter Ten, choose your own ending: if you are a consumer, turn to Chapter 14, 15 and 16; if you are a Designer, turn to Chapter 11; Retailer/Buyer — Chapter 12; Sales Associate — Chapter 13, 14 and 15. Chapter 11 is "My Fantasy" of how designers might use the guidelines. Chapter 12 is for Retail Store Owners and Buyers of Women's Ready-to-Wear. However, the information may be applied to children's wear, jewelry, shoes, accessories, and environmental design. While I have not gone into men's style information in great depth, the theory is applicable to them as well. Many color analysts specialize in improving men's personal image through color and line; most also include some information about the importance of using one's colors and style in personal environment whenever possible.

Chapter 13 is specific for sales associates, along with Chapters 14 and 15, which give some basic information about art principles, figure challenges, proportion, and illusion.

You will have views that have grown out of your own experiences. Throughout the book you will

Author's Notes — How to Use This Book

notice wide margins, purposefully left for your own notes and sketches, as well as comments about various clothing and accessory lines. There is a famous personalities listing at the end of each of the four season's chapters, as well as a place for you to add your own friends and/or customers.

It is my hope that you will continue my work; that you will add to this book your own impressions, ideas, arguments for or against the various concepts, any new information that may become available, etc., so that it will become "your book" rather than mine. In this way it will more perfectly meet your needs — whether you are a consumer, buyer, a sales associate, or a designer.

We learn best by doing. We all learn by our mistakes. Hopefully, through the use of this book, your mistakes will be fewer and smaller. The next step is up to you. I hope "the technique" will mean as much to you as it does to me. As you learn more about it, I hope you will share with me your experiences and your impressions. And, of course, please let me know how you feel the book could be improved upon, what additional information you would like to see included in a study guide, etc.

    Joan Callaway
    c/o Tarika, 406-2nd Street
    Davis, Ca. 95616

1
A Theory Whose Time Has Come

The Laws of Color and Principles of Personal Color Harmony in one form or another are being taught by color analysts across this country and many foreign lands, as well; they are being learned by women who are interested in improving their images and simplifying their shopping tasks.

Probably all color analysts agree that everyone's personal coloring — the eyes, hair and skin — is in harmony. The *Seasonal Color Harmony* theorists postulate that best personal colors — ones that are most complimentary to the eyes, hair and skin — correspond to those found in nature in one or more of the four seasons.

While most color systems seem to agree in general with the actual personal color analysis concept, there are several *schools of thought* regarding color harmony in terms of style. Many proponents of the Seasonal Harmony Theory assert that people with similar coloring and personalities have a natural preference for similar design details, silhouettes, and fabrics, as well as color. And, moreover, that there is a correlation, a *Color Connection*, between them: just as each person has her own natural "inner style," each has her own natural "outer style" preferences that are related to her coloring and personality.

This natural inclination to fancy one style and/or color over another seems present in a person even when she has not had her colors analyzed. "Fancy" implies that one takes a liking to something without reason or rational thought processes. According to the theory, it is not caprice that leads a person to accept or reject a color and/or style, but a natural preference.

The principles of the Seasonal Color Harmony theory are important pieces of what has been a great puzzle — important to the consumer, to the retailer and equally important to the designer of fabric, garments, and accessories.

From a retailer's perspective, whether one likes the idea of personal color analysis is not really relevant. Whether one believes in the *Laws of Color* and the *Principles of the Seasonal Color Harmony* is not pertinent either. **It is a theory whose time has come.**

* * *

In color analysis one's "best colors" are found through the *discovery* method. A skillful color analyst or consultant is able to see subtle changes in the skin, eyes, and hair as a variety of colored fabric swatches or paint chips are held up to the face of her client. She is able to discern which colors *enhance*, making the skin appear clear and glowing, and which ones are "sabotage colors", ones that will deepen lines, darken circles, often making the skin appear unnatural in color, e.g., mottled, dull, gray, sallow, or ruddy.

Color analysis almost always verifies this natural affinity. It rarely provides entirely new information for the client. Much of what she learns is merely a validation of what she has known on an intuitive level, even though she may not have consistently applied that knowledge or been able to articulate it. It is not uncommon for a woman to describe her wardrobe purchases as being "hit or miss" prior to color analysis, often feeling that she had made one wardrobe mistake after another without knowing why.

A skillful color analyst will help her discover the reasons for some of those clothing mistakes. For example, she may never have known why a style which she really liked when she bought it is one she rarely wears. She may discover it is in one of her sabotage colors. She will be told which colors are best for her and which ones she should avoid.

She may never have totally understood the whys and wherefores of her disappointment when a garment in one of her very best colors turned out to be an undesirable style. She may discover that while it may have been in a perfect color, the style was inconsistent with her inner style. She will receive style guidelines; some may be new to her, but most will only serve to reinforce what she has already instinctively known.

Rarely will she find wardrobe "mistakes" among the clothing she has really enjoyed wearing. She will discover, however, why some items have not been favorites, e.g., the fabric may have had too much texture or been too bulky; the garment may have been too skimpy or too overpowering for her visual design. With this new information, she should be able to avoid similar mistakes in the future.

Color analysis often provides the rationale for why a person has been attracted to particular styles and/or colors. It provides the explanation of why some styles and/or colors never seemed quite right. It often provides guidelines or principles that are consistent with the individual's already existing clothing preferences. These guidelines replace "fancy" with *reason*. They articulate what she may already have intuitively known, but never been able to put into words. It is not uncommon for a woman to say during a color seminar, "I wondered why I never liked…" or "That explains why…".

From the Consumer's Point of View

From the consumer's point of view, this theory is a godsend. With the color fan in hand and the guidelines in mind, she can wander through a section of a department store or a boutique, glance quickly at the racks to determine whether any of her colors is available. No need to try on and be tempted by styles that may be perfect, if the colors are wrong for her. Even the bargain rack will no longer tempt her unless she locates one of *her* colors.

Once she has found her best colors, ones that are perfect in clarity, shade and value, she can use the guidelines to decide whether the design is her style. She can clearly save a lot of "trying on" time if she knows in advance which styles are going to express at a glance who she is, which will enhance her visual design, and which will coordinate with the rest of her wardrobe.

She is not quite so apt to be influenced by either a friend, a salesclerk or current color and/or fashion trends. If she complies with the guidelines, she will make far fewer clothing mistakes. She will learn when and how to "break the rules" and to what degree she can compromise and still remain true to her "inner style."

From a Retailer's Perspective

From a retailer's perspective the proliferation of this theory can be good or bad. Some hate the idea and can't be bothered. When a recent retail seminar audience was asked, "What do you do when a shopper comes in with her color palette?" one retailer responded, "I show her the door!" That is, of course, one way to handle it.

However, many retailers are finding it worthwhile to learn more about color analysis. Some are offering color classes and wardrobe consulting to supplement the teachings of the color analysts. Many welcome the opportunity to provide a service to their customers that is not readily available in discount or department stores.

Some are discovering that applying the seasonal color harmony theory to their stores in terms of display and sales is giving them just the advantage they need to build a loyal, appreciative clientele. In addition, they find personal satisfaction in helping a customer to grow and to learn to know herself better as she develops her own distinctive style.

The shopper who has had her colors analyzed is delighted when a sales person can help her learn more about her style, how to use her colors, and how to plan a wardrobe around them. She appreciates a call when items that are perfect for her come into the store. She is grateful that someone cares about her and her needs. And, interestingly enough, when she begins to have more confidence in her clothing acquisitions and her personal style, she usually becomes much more interested in her wardrobe and buys more. She seems decidedly more satisfied with her purchases and the store from which she purchased them.

As greater numbers of shoppers learn about the seasonal color harmony theory and become more discriminating, applying what they have learned to their shopping, retailers, too, will need to become more selective in their buying if they are to remain profitable.

For example, I am one of those retailers who has been teaching the principles of the Seasonal

Color Harmony. I have been buying with the guidelines in mind for the past five years. My customers have become very *color* sophisticated. They are more and more often aware when I veer even slightly away from the teachings of the Seasonal Color Harmony guidelines to bring in merchandise that combines design detail from more than one seasonal harmony, sometimes commenting, "Joan, who's going to wear this? It's a Summer fabric and print, but the style seems much too bold and too square — more Autumn-like."

It is probable that eventually even more retailers will be influenced by such consumer admonitions. It is also probable that designers will ultimately be influenced by buyers who seek to better meet the needs of their customers by selecting styles that are consistent with the guidelines of the Seasonal Color Harmony theory.

Designers and manufacturers are no doubt as interested as retailers in customer satisfaction and profitability. The designer-retailer-consumer relationship is a symbiotic one — mutually advantageous. Fashion may begin with the designer, but the consumer always has the last word! The retailer-buyer is in the middle, not in control of either, only able to influence or hope to have had the good fortune to have "bought right".

How Do Buyers Decide What to Order? How do Designers and Manufacturers Decide What to Produce?

Each season the market is filled with an exciting and sometimes not-so-exciting array of fashions. The novice might wonder how designers and manufacturers decide what to produce. They do a lot of "weeding out" before the lines are ever shown at market, of course. But, in the final analysis, it turns out that the middleman, the "retailer/buyer" decides what will be produced.

Designers put forth samples. If buyers place orders in adequate quantities, the styles from the manufacturer's point of view are "successful," and barring unforeseen catastrophes, such as the fabric's not being available, dye problems, quotas, etc. the line is manufactured and shipped. If buyers do not place enough orders, the styles will

Illus. 1 **Design Error**

Illus. 2 **Half Right**

Classic Illus. 3

be eliminated from the line. In some cases, it's back to the drawing board for the designer — before the next market.

And what about the buyers? How do buyers predict which offerings will sell in their stores? How do they know what to order? On what basis do buyers make their selections? Do they select what they personally would wear? What they think their customers will like? What sold last year? What the manufacturer's representative (the "rep") says is "booking" or "checking?" (For the uninitiated, "booking" is wholesale jargon for what other buyers have been ordering; "checking" is what is currently selling well at retail in the stores where it has already been delivered.) Is the predictability of fashion success elusive and shrouded in mystery? Is it dependent on fashion hype?

There are, of course, basic principles of art and design, but what is "good design"? The design — "the look" — is the sum total of all the parts: the silhouette or outer contour, inside design lines (e.g., lapels, collars, pockets, closures,) texture, print, detail (e.g., buttons, embroidery, intarsia, color blocking, etc.), and, of course, color.

For the design to be *good* it is important that there be a consistency of design lines and details. For example, if a jacket has rounded lapels, then the patch pockets also should be rounded; and the blouse that is designed to be worn with the jacket should have design lines that are consistent, complementary and well placed. The illustration shows the shawl collared jacket with design error of square patch pockets and the corrected version with rounded ones. The welt pocket version of the jacket seems the most classic. It would be the choice of most Summer and Winter types.

Other questions that a buyer might ask include:
- Is the overall look harmonious?
- Is the construction appropriate to the weight, the body and the drape of the fabric? Do the pockets sag? Lapels droop?
- Where does the grain line hang? Will the garment move and drape in harmony with the garment design? (In a 4-gore skirt, for example, (see Illustration) if the bias is all in the center front, any extra hip fullness of the wearer will be emphasized, and the skirt will appear tighter along the outline of the hip. On the other hand, if the bias is all at the side seam, the garment may appear taut over the tummy and buttocks

area. While for the very slim, this side bias may promote a desired and somewhat provocative fishtail effect in some styles, it may also pull the skirt in center front between the knees, which is aggravating at best. The ideal, albeit more expensive to cut, would be to have the grain line centered in each gore. This center grainline will be universally more flattering to most figures.)

Those are the some of the obvious design elements (and one important not-so-obvious one) that one consciously or unconsciously looks for when reviewing a line of clothing.

There are "buying errors," such as the buyer selecting the wrong blouse from the group, e.g., the one that had been perfectly designed to go with a notched collar jacket when, in fact, the jacket the buyer purchased from the group is a collarless Chanel type which requires a different collar treatment. Or from a group of jackets and skirts in a line, the buyer might select ones that are incompatible, e.g., a longer jacket with a too-full skirt, one that had been perfectly designed to go with a shorter jacket from the group. Probably every buyer has made a similar mistake at some time.

Did you ever wonder:
...why the same identical **silhouette** is right in one fabrication and wrong in another for the same person?
...why the same **fabric** is right in one color and wrong in another for the same person?
...why the same **color** can be right in one silhouette and wrong in another for the same person?
...why a *good* design is right for one person and not for another?

• **For the design to be "good" — "right" — "appropriate" — for the individual consumer, it must be not only in her best color with design lines and details that are "good" design-wise, but the style must be in harmony with her personality and body type. There is a style or combination of styles most natural for each individual, just as natural to her as her personality or her coloring. And, moreover, there is a relationship between the three. Just as we each have our own unique personality, our own unique "inner style", we each have our own natural "outer style" preferences that are related to our coloring.**

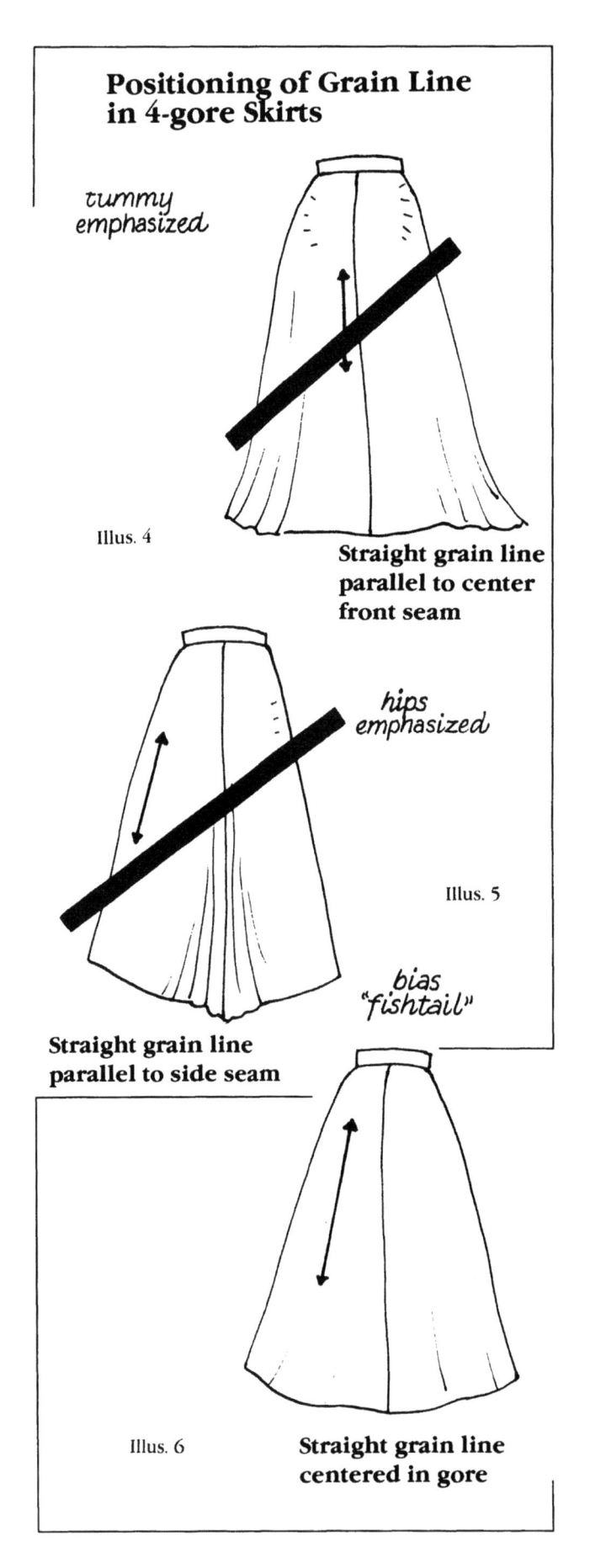

Positioning of Grain Line in 4-gore Skirts

tummy emphasized

Illus. 4

Straight grain line parallel to center front seam

hips emphasized

Illus. 5

Straight grain line parallel to side seam

bias "fishtail"

Illus. 6

Straight grain line centered in gore

This is the basic premise of the seasonal color harmony theory.

This is not an original or new theory. Many of the seasonal color harmony systems utilize the *Consumer Color Chart* (Munsell Color, Macbeth Division of Kollmorgen Corp., Baltimore, Md.), which was developed in 1955 as a visual color relationship reference for personal color and clothing choices, as well as home furnishings. It is an application of the *Munsell Color System,* adapted by Frances Reis Quinn, an Extension Clothing Specialist of the University of California, Alice Linn, a Clothing Specialist with USDA, and W. N. Hale of Munsell Color Corp.

The Munsell Color System orders or numbers colors specifically and relates each color to all other colors in clarity, shade and value. It provides a universal and specific "color language" for color notation. For example, the color name "taupe" can mean different things to different people; it means one thing this season, another the next. It can refer to a variety of values and intensities of the same basic color. *2.5Y 6.8/2.5,* however, is the Munsell number code that would indicate internationally exactly the yellow-beige color being referred to by the much more general and hard-to-pinpoint "taupe". The Consumer Color Chart was a break-through for color analysts —and the beginning of *The Color Connection.*

Suzanne Caygill has been lecturing on *Nature's Color Harmony* for more than thirty-five years; Joan Songer of Oakland, Ca. founded Personal Style Counselors in 1964; as did Gerrie Pinckney and Marge Swenson their Fashion Academy in Costa Mesa, California. These are some of the pioneers in the field. There are undoubtedly others.

In recent years there has been a proliferation (and in some cases mongrelization) of color analysis systems. For better or for worse, I am convinced that designers, buyers, and sales clerks must become skilled in the use of the *Color Connection* in order to keep pace with the consumer. ***It is a growing field whose time has come!***

As consumers more and more often assert their influence by expressing their dissatisfaction and rejecting "design errors", retailers will surely have to re-evaluate the performance of merchandise in terms of markdowns, etc. before ordering from that vendor again. We are in a transition period —

there is time to learn, time to plan, time to survey what is happening as a result of the proliferation of color analysis. There is time to reconnoiter, to be receptive and responsive to new consumer needs.

Clearly, if retailers, anticipating negative reactions from their color-wise customers, refuse to order styles with "design errors" i.e., those styles inconsistent with the principles of the theory, designers will ultimately get the message. It is my fantasy, however, that a more positive, less reactionary approach could make the transition smoother and shorter — and lead to greater acceptance, satisfaction and profitability for all.

Winter

Spring

Autumn

Summer

Illus. 7

2
Fad, Fact or Fiction

Why Is the Field Growing?

As children, we are *socialized* to either wear colors that are fashionable or return, regardless of color trends, to the colors that have gotten us the most compliments.

In the socialization process, a child learns the preferences of her parents, grandparents, or other adults, as well as those of her siblings and peers. These biases, learned early, often influence and sometimes unnecessarily limit her color choices for the rest of her life.

For example, a blond, blue-eyed little girl may always have been dressed in blues because, of course, for her that is a striking combination. As an adult she may continue to wear only those blues because she knows that is a safe combination. Another example might be the redhaired woman who, as a child, was told she should never wear red or pink, and therefore, still always dresses in greens and blues, never realizing that there is a perfect red and a perfect pink *for her coloring*.

Through color analysis, she will discover that if she selects clothing with the correct color base, she can wear most colors and look *all right*. It is a rare person who can wear both blue- and yellow-based colors equally well, and it is virtually impossible to put together a truly workable wardrobe that includes both.

There are cool colors (from red-violet to all the blues and some greens) and warm colors (the yellows, oranges, and reds). It is important at this point to understand that cool colors can have a

Spring   Summer   Autumn   Winter

Illus. 8

warm cast or a yellow undertone or base; and that warm colors likewise can have a cool or blue base. For example, red can be a bluish red or a yellow-red. Both would be considered red and warm colors, but each has an undertone that can ever so slightly alter the color.

It is the *undertones* of the skin (e.g., those very subtle colors peeking through where the skin is thinnest, such as around the eyes), combined with the colors of the eyes and hair that determine the *base* of the colors that will enhance, i.e., yellow- or blue-based.

In the perfect shade, value and clarity of colors in the correct base she will look more than just "all right"; she will look her best! Compliments such as "You look so pretty in that shade of red," as opposed to "That's a great dress!" occur when the color is right. The right colors enhance, making one look vital, healthy and glowing. When one wears colors not in harmony with one's skin, hair and eyes ("sabotage colors"), people will often say, "You look tired today. Are you feeling ill?"

Success-oriented women have been alerted to the importance of "looking good" — not just for their "big moments," but for everyday. This new emphasis on dressing for success has caused many women to seek new ways to improve their appearance. Just as they would consult an architect to design a new house, an interior decorator to assist in the selection of furniture, wallpaper, carpet, etc., many are employing professionals, such as color analysts and wardrobe consultants, to help them with their image.

They are reading fashion magazines and books more than ever before. They are attending workshops. They are unraveling the clues and trying to acquire what for many had previously been elusive, enigmatic and almost mystical — personal style. They are learning a new technique! And when they are shopping they are applying what they have learned.

They are discovering that those people who have a well-defined and consistent "personal style" seem to have a well-defined self image and that more often than not they have come to terms with their bodies. Many are now working to define their own self-images. They are learning to dress to accentuate those parts of their bodies they like the most, often camouflaging the parts they like the least.

Many are looking to those with personal style as ideal examples — those who seem to dress to please themselves, their own self-expression being more important than the approval of others. They are beginning to recognize the role that self-confidence plays in personal style; that it takes self-confidence to ignore current fashion or fads and to express one's self through a unique clothing style.

For some people this seems almost instinctive; for others it is a consciously learned technique. But it can be learned — and is being learned. There is a new all-time high level of interest in personal appearance.

The wealthy, of course, have always been concerned about clothing and appearance; it was a luxury they were well able to afford. Moreover, they always had servants to do their menial and burdensome work. Gardening, sewing, baking, painting, etc., were done by the wealthy as recreational pastimes not as requisites. Not so with the masses, until recently.

As we, at least in this country, have moved into a more mechanized society with convenience appliances and supermarkets from which to buy our food, we no longer must bake our own bread, garden, harvest and can our fruits and vegetables. We no longer need to heat the water to wash the clothes that must later be hung in- or out-to-dry, depending on the weather. We can go to the supermarket and buy eggs, milk and meat. We fish and hunt for sport, if at all. Our lives have at once become physically easier and yet much more complex. We have more leisure time; yet we seem busier than ever. With these dramatic changes, our clothing needs have also changed.

With leisure time has come leisure wear. Because of changes in life style for women from burdensome physical labor from sun-up to sundown, the word "housedress" has become almost archaic and the term "work clothes" has taken on entirely new meaning. Women have become more in control of their lives. No doubt more efficient means of family planning are responsible in large part for that. Even before the advent of women's liberation and the furtherance of greater fulfillment for women, and such a youth-oriented society, women had begun to take a greater interest in their appearance. And now with more women working outside the home, there is an even more heightened awareness of appearance.

These women (and, incidentally, many men) are applying the "Rules of the Seasonal Color Harmonies". And they are learning how to break the rules to create their own unique look. They are learning which fabrics, designs, and colors will enhance their look. They are becoming experts in their own personal style.

Should We Take This New Notion Seriously?

I barely had the doors of *Tarika* open when I began to learn about not just color, but **COLOR** and the proliferation of color harmony systems. Many of my customers had had their colors analyzed and were carrying little swatches of either fabric or paint chips of "their colors" to compare with clothing on the racks in stores.

Many of these neophytes seemed confused as to how to use their color palettes; many were positive clothing had to match these swatches exactly; most were frustrated. I was little help to them because I had little understanding of what appeared to me to be a new *"dogma":* a dogma with increasing numbers of converts who had little understanding of the precepts and who questioned not the preceptor or the preceptor's training and/or talent.

I have come to agree with many of the precepts. I must confess I will have much more confidence in *color consulting* when there is some consistency in training, as well as licensure, such as that required for cosmetologists. In fairness, there are some well qualified color consultants who have studied color and design under an experienced and well trained color analyst, who have a *trained eye,* and, in addition, have worked for a time, initially, under the watchful eye of an experienced mentor.

Unfortunately, however, the well trained ones are outnumbered by a growing number of unqualified who have hopped on the bandwagon. All that is currently needed to start a color consulting business is a large selection of paint chips or fabric swatches and an equal amount of *chutzpah!* Many "color analysts" with as little as three hours to three days of "training" and an investment of a few hundred dollars in a franchise and supplies, are now charging $30 and up for a pre-pack of colors of whatever seasonal harmony they "discover" their client to be.

A skillful color consultant will ascertain the undertone of the skin of her client and in combination with other factors, such as color of eyes and hair, select an individualized color palette that will help her client look her best — a color palette that will open up new color horizons for most people, offering them colors they might never have thought to wear.

Using her trained eye and very often a degree of intuition, the color analyst will determine not only *best colors* but also style, line, and design detail. She will observe the visual image and personality of her client to hone in on what some color analysts call the "dominant harmony" and "secondaries", which are the key to individual style.

The *secondary* concept is one that will be discussed in a later section, but to put it simply one may be what some color analysts would call a cross-season or cross-color type, meaning that her skin tone may be in one category, while her hair color or inner style (personality) are from another; other systems would define the same phenomenon as a *dominant harmony* derived from the most dominant category with one or more *secondaries* from the other categories represented.

Some may think the seasonal jargon "hokey". But it is really just a way of clarifying the colors and the way they are put together. The colors seem to fall naturally into four general groupings, and it's much more fun to be called a "Winter" than a #4. Some color analysts call it "striking", others call it "contrast"; these terms all refer to women who look their best in clear, strong colors or icy pastels when worn in contrast similar to the contrasts found in a Winter scene.

Even the uninitiated can conjure up in their mind's eye an image of the colors of Spring (with its violets, tulips and daffodils), Summer (an English-type perennial garden with its full-blown roses and cascading delphinium), Autumn (gold and red leaves) and Winter (white snow and red berries). It is much easier to think of the colors of the four seasons, which we know from our own personal experience, than to translate into readily assimilated color pictures the meaning of "light/bright," "gentle," "muted" or "contrast"...or #1, #2, etc. I believe it is for this reason that so many color analysts use the seasonal harmony terminology. For the purposes of learning about the theory in relation to retail women's clothing, it is the most useful because it is the most easily visualized.

Whatever terminology is used, I must admit that when I first heard of the "color harmony", I thought "Here we go. It's not enough that we have rules and regulations for various figure types in every woman's magazine on the news-stand; or that our customers are prescribing fashion solutions, often erroneously, for their self-diagnosed figure challenges. Now we will have to cope with the rules and regulations coming down from the color analysts regarding not only color, but style!" I was skeptical. I was concerned about the little boxes I thought people were being put into! I thought it was really gimmicky...not the *color* part, but the seasons, style designations, etc.

But I began to watch my customers, with and without color swatches, and their *"trying on"*, as well as their buying habits. I began to look at the items that ended up on my sale rack. And there seemed to be a consistent pattern.

I began to agree with the color analysts that espouse the theory that people of the same seasonal harmony often have similarities in their personalities — similarities in the quality of their voices, the way they walk, talk, and even look at life. And while this may not be scientific, it is uncanny how often one can accurately *guess* in just a few minutes what colors and style of clothing will appeal to a person by using clues from personality, coloring, and visual design observations. Gradually, I, the skeptic, became convinced that for me and my business there was some validity and value in the theory.

So I had my colors done not once, not twice, but *eight* times over the next few years, by several different analysts using a variety of systems, including:

1) *Color I Associates,* (twice) (individual analysis; a color palette of best colors in paint chips; guidelines include how colors should be combined and the amount of contrast to be worn.) Although this system uses four basic color types that parallel the *"seasons"*, there is no indication that these four types have any specific relationship to style.

2) A pre-packaged type (this was a Winter packet; not personalized. It included a very limited selection of colors);

3) **An all-day seminar with individual analysis by**

Suzanne (Caygill), author of *Color: The Essence of You,;*

4) An individual color analysis by one of her academy graduates, using the same system;

5) A one-hour draping of hair, eye, and skin colors with a determination of my best reds, with the remaining colors determined "scientifically" using the *Munsell Consumer Color Chart System,* followed by a two-hour style conference.

6) Seasonal color harmony analysis *(Munsell Color)* with small swatches of colors held to my face to determine best colors plus a style conference.

7) Same as #6, but including a "Basic Series on Personal Style", fifteen and a half hours over a six-week period. This series was designed to "take the mystery out of the art of dress and replace it with the kind of certainty that develops, grows and lasts a lifetime!" — *Personal Style Counselors,* Oakland, Ca. This alone was well worth more than the price of the color consultation. I had been studying the subject for five years and this series summed up and articulated succinctly what I had been learning.

I absorbed just as much as I could from each analyst. I read everything I could get my hands on. Interestingly enough, I was categorized as a Winter or Contrast type by six of the seven consultants. One proclaimed me to be an *Autumn* type with a Spring and Winter secondary.

There is *similarity* of colors in most of my color palettes, but there is not agreement on the *exact* colors that are best for me. Personal color analysis is not an exact science. Some color analysts will argue with that statement, I suspect.

It is well known and predictable that if you mix yellow and red you will get orange, etc. (see p.249), and, of course, colors can be analyzed scientifically. So, in that regard, color analysis *is* an exact science. But *personal* color analysis is subjective, and the degree of accuracy obtained is totally dependent on the analyst's ability to *see* subtle differences — much the same as the quality of an operatic rendition of an aria is dependent on the vocalist's ability not merely to understand music theory and the intent of the composer, but also to hit the high notes!

In fact, it is no doubt far less important to know the theory than it is to be able to "carry a tune" or hear and reproduce the very subtle variations in melody and rhythm. In the case of the color analyst, it is essential to the task that there be the ability to see the very subtle changes that occur in the skin tone and eyes when various colors are held to the skin.

Certainly, it is an exceedingly rare opera singer who is self-taught or who learned by mail order or in three days. Likewise, it would be an exceedingly rare color analyst who could learn to "hit the high notes" in such a fashion. Unfortunately, many who call themselves "color analysts" are attempting to achieve just such a distinction and, I might add, falling equally short of attaining success. There are computers spewing out pre-packaged color packets and there are even mail order color analysts.

Just as in the case of the vocalist, natural talent plays a great part in the success of a color analyst. Not everyone can develop the eye to see color accurately or to discern the very subtle changes that occur in the appearance of the skin during the color analysis. Moreover, of those people that *do* have the ability color-wise not all have the ability to advise convincingly style-wise. And I would never trust a *computer* to sing *La Bohème*. Would you?

Unfortunately, many wardrobes are being selectively discarded and/or restructured, new ones being planned and purchased, based on these often inaccurate "analyses" at an oftentimes significant expense to the consumer.

Even among well trained analysts there can be variation in the exact colors chosen for a specific individual. The colors selected are often a matter of personal preference on the part of the consultant, who is selecting colors that not only look well on the subject, but look harmonious with all colors on the palette. So it is not surprising or of any concern that all color consultants will not agree on the *exact* colors given for any individual. They should agree, however, on whether the colors are yellow-or blue-based and the general range of colors in terms of clarity, value and intensity.

Just as we each have our own unique coloring, our own unique personality or *inner style,* we each have our own natural *outer style* preferences.

Just as there are design lines said to relate to each of the seasonal color harmonies; there are design lines, colors, personality and physical characteristics that are considered *yin* or *yang.*

Yin and Yang, according to oriental philosophy,

are two opposing forces, neither good nor bad in and of themselves: yin representing the *feminine* and yang representing the *masculine*. Everyone has a blend of both yin and yang characteristics. All physical and social developments are said to be influenced by the *interaction* of these two forces, and it is this interaction that produces harmony (See Chapter 9).

You may wonder why color analysts don't just say "masculine" and "feminine." Unfortunately, we have been socialized to have little respect for masculine qualities in women even though they are found in *every* woman; nor do men like to acknowledge their feminine qualities. So many color analysts have elected to use yin and yang to describe the various characteristics, with yin being equated with *soft* and feminine, while yang is aligned more with *striking* and masculine.

It is important for those in the clothing industry to know and understand the terminology in current usage by the color and wardrobe consultants and, of course, by the consumers. But, in addition, I have found an understanding of yin and yang an extremely helpful aid for individualizing design for each person. For example, a person that has coloring predominantly from Spring or Summer harmony, which relate to yin, may have physical and/or personality characteristics that are more yang in nature than a typical Spring or Summer; she can add yang effects to more accurately express her personality (See Chapter 10).

Just as there are personality and physical characteristics, as well as design lines and colors that have been designated for the seasonal harmonies and have either yin or yang qualities, there are print patterns designated for each of the harmonies. Similarly these prints may also be considered to have either yin or yang qualities. This *system* permits and encourages individualization of design.

While it seems obvious that the designers, both of fabric and of garments, should be taking these theories seriously and integrating them into their designs, each clothing market that I attend is replete with thousands of examples inconsistent and in conflict with the color harmony theory. Needless to say, many of these *"design mistakes"* end up on our sale racks and/or are unsuccessful purchases that can be found unworn in our

A Winter in Spring's Clothing

Illus. 9

Spring

Illus. 10

customers' closets. Thus, the frequently heard comment, "I've got a closetful of clothes and nothing to wear!"

I have noticed repeatedly that designs highly successful in one color and/or print pattern may be failures when translated into others. The *prairie dress* of a few seasons ago is a good example. It was charming in crisp calico prints in bright colors (perfect for Spring types), soft and lovely in blended or muted lavenders, turquoises, and pinks, often with embroidery or lace inserts (just right for the Summer seasonal harmony), but somehow never quite came off for the Autumn and Winter seasonal harmony types even if in their correct colors. Those types may have purchased one prairie dress just to have a current, trendy dress in their closet, but not many of them ever felt truly comfortable in the flounced, ruffled, buttoned and bowed prairie dress. If you talk to them a bit, most will say they didn't feel soft, feminine and romantic; some reported that they felt more like "floozies" or ready for a costume party or a square dance. Perhaps this was not true of every Autumn or Winter type but it certainly seemed so for most.

I have come to agree that the style guidelines of the color consultants are not arbitrary rules. Their *rules* have no doubt evolved over time through observation, not unlike the way scientists discovered the natural laws of the physical universe. I have come to believe through my own observation *that there is a correlation between not only coloring and style, but personality, as well, and that it is predictable WHICH "season" will buy WHICH "silhouette" in WHICH "print" in WHICH "fabric" and in WHICH "color."*

It is predictable WHICH "season" will buy WHICH "silhouette" in WHICH "print" in WHICH "fabric" and in WHICH "color."

The very first Fall that *Tarika* was open, I purchased camel corduroy "hacking" jackets, somewhat fitted, with a high back waistband and leather patches on the elbows. As they say in the *"rag biz",* "they blew right out of the store!" The next season when they repeated this highly successful *proven* body the color selection was expanded. I ordered it again; this time in a new shade of camel and a very pretty rust, thinking: "Those Autumn types will love this wide-wale cord, this very Autumny russet, and the leather trim."

Once again, the camel sold right out. The rust was tried on many times, but not a piece sold. I started analyzing, watching carefully just who was trying the rust jacket. Sure enough, the Autumn types were attracted to the color, but when I asked them what they didn't like about it, they unanimously articulated that it was "too constricting," "too fitted," "too skimpy." Even though they agreed that the jacket fit perfectly, they were not comfortable in the cut of the jacket. As I came to find out, Autumn types, as a rule, like oversized or ample cuts that do not fit closely to the body.

This little bit of enlightenment led me on a quest to learn more about color, personality and style. Contrary to my early misapprehensions about "more rules and regulations" interfering with sales, ***an awareness of what is being taught by the various color and wardrobe consultants across the nation has improved my buying and increased my sales. A knowledge of the very strong connection between visual design, personality and style has also greatly enhanced customer satisfaction.***

This *"Color Connection"* theory is useful not only in the designing and buying process, but in the selling as well. A sales associate can train her eye to quickly recognize seasonal harmony (or at least guess with a high percentage of accuracy) by correlating coloring with yin/yang qualities. She can assess yin/yang qualities by observing visual image, voice, walk, mannerisms and personality. And with this combined knowledge can often then guide even an "unknown" potential customer to designs suitable for her particular harmony. The secret is, of course, that if you learn to use the generalizations of this theory, no one remains "unknown" for long.

At the end of each of the sections on the seasonal harmony guidelines, I have included a list

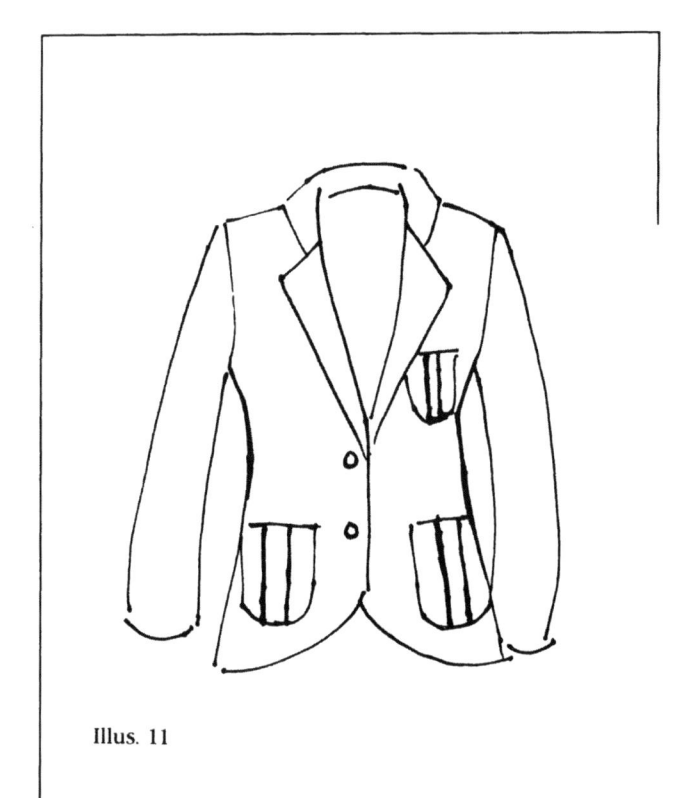

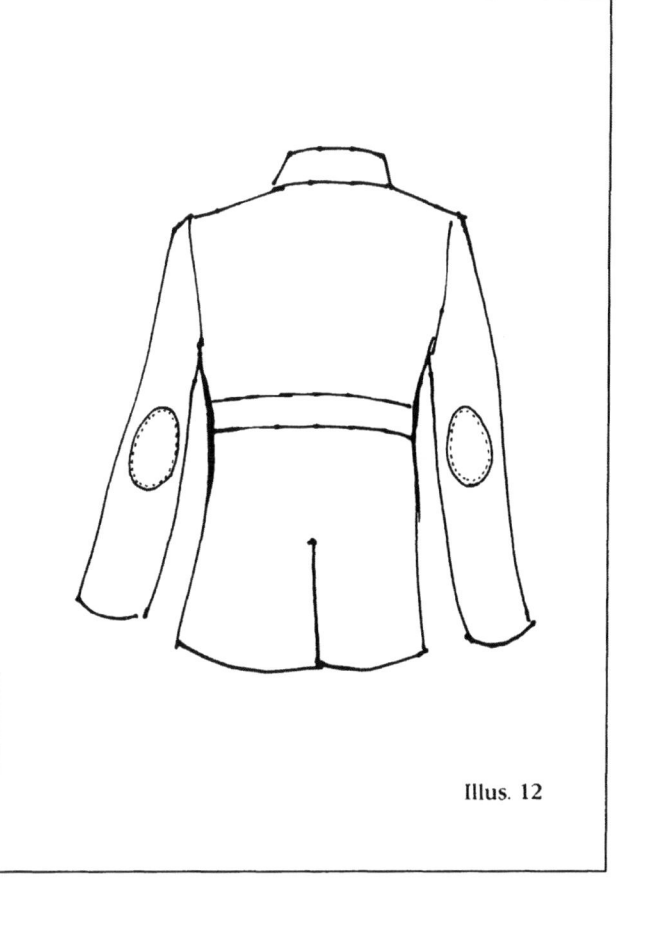

Illus. 11

Illus. 12

of famous persons, who I believe are representative of each of the four seasonal types. They are public figures, past and present, whose faces can probably be conjured up by most readers, selected mostly from the theater, T.V., etc., for that reason. These are educated guesses, similar to the ones a sales associate would make when someone walks into her store. Observing these personalities over the years in movies, T.V., newspaper and magazine photographs, etc. lead me to these *guesses*.

Incidentally, I find watching television an excellent way to practice and have even developed a video for teaching the technique to my staff members. Frequently when I watch television, I do so with the remote control in hand and the VCR connected. When a particularly interesting person or a perfect example of a seasonal type or style comes on the screen, I record the segment. These videos are then incorporated with voice-over comments and/or later discussed with staff members. Seminars are also videotaped for subsequent staff discussion. These composite videotapes help sales associates to quickly learn the technique of recognizing the seasonal harmony types, enabling them to be more helpful to shoppers, known and unknown.

The technique is especially helpful in assisting a customer in the selection of a gift: the sales associate can ask a few key questions about the prospective recipient's coloring, personality, life style, etc. and apply the *technique*. Our returns on clothing gifts this past holiday season were less than half a percent.

Greater customer satisfaction usually means increased loyalty to the store and even to individual sales clerks, leading to valuable word-of-mouth advertising. And, as a result, greater profitability, not to mention satisfaction, ensues for everyone — from the sales clerk to the retail store owner, the manufacturer and, ultimately, the designer.

An increasing number of our customers are consulting color and wardrobe analysts, attending dominant harmony or personal style seminars and learning how to put themselves together harmoniously. It may only be a matter of time until *design errors* will be recognized almost universally by consumers.

Unfortunately, because the marketplace is not keeping pace with the consumer, the consumer must often compromise when she does recognize a design error. "This is the perfect color. Too bad the lines are wrong for me." Or "Great dress. Perfect Summer cascading lines. Can you get it for me in one of my colors?"

Designers may be skeptical of this theory. Perhaps they will even resent anyone's interfering with their artistic expression by suggesting colors for a particular design. In the case of the aforementioned corduroy jacket, although it had been perfect in the original color selected by the designer, when that *winning* design was translated into other colors either dictated by current fashion trend, or perhaps even by acceding to the Autumn seasonal harmony color, it became a *design error*. (Color, alas, is not the only criterion!) I suspect this happens all too often.

There will always be some design errors. As buyers and consumers, we always need to be alert to that. Obviously, as in any field, there are good designers and not-so-good designers. I'm referring to good designers — ones who otherwise apply the principles of art and who design with skill, but who have not yet become convinced of the validity of the Seasonal Color Theory or who have not become aware enough of the intricacies of its precepts to be able to apply it with precision.

Over the past few years several Tarika interns, as well as full time employees, have studied at and/or graduated from the University of California, Davis, with a Design Major. Interestingly, almost without exception, they have indicated that they were drawn to the field of design through a sense of frustration at not being able to find ready-to-wear styles that suited them (and their seasonal harmony, even if they didn't know to call it that at the time!) Their first designs were ones with which they could personally identify in terms of their own seasonal harmony.

Their fashion sketching styles continued to reflect their personal seasonal type even later when they were following the dictates of fashion trends in designing for others. Their best designs seemed to be true to their own style. Most designers probably instinctively create best for their own personal season or for a particular type of woman that they admire, perhaps because they feel so intensely what would be *right*. I wonder if many seasonal harmony *design errors* don't perhaps result from the designer yielding to the dictates of fashion color trends or perhaps the mandate of an employer.

Frequently I find myself commenting to manufacturers' representatives at market: "That's a great style. What other colors is it going to come in? Oh, too bad! The person that will wear that style isn't apt to wear those colors." or "Great color, but the fabrication is too . . . (soft, crisp, textured, shiny, etc.) for the person who will wear the color." For example, the soft, drapable, rayon/linen blend cricket cloth is typically a Summer fabrication. A garment of this fabric in the rich earth tones of Autumn would be viewed as a design error because the fabric would not be firm enough to satisfy the Autumn types nor would many of the colors of Autumn be on a Summer palette, although there could be some overlap in the blue-greens.

Every designer will probably agree that not every design can be translated into all fabrications. For example, to be successful a draped design requires a soft, pliable fabric, certainly not a heavy stiffened one. This theory goes a step farther to suggest that those soft, draped designs should be cut in Summer or Winter colorations, with additional discrete design detail determining which of those two season's colors would be most appropriate. If the feeling is more romantic with cascading lines, the colors should be soft and somewhat grayed (Summer); if the styling is elegant, striking or dramatic, the colors would be clear and vibrant (Winter).

Just as the lines of a design dictate which fabric should be used or just as a fabric will suggest a possible style to a designer, the style *and* the fabric dictate the colors in which that style and fabric will be successful. Not every design should be translated into a color suitable for every seasonal type even if those colors are deemed most fashionable in today's marketplace. If the style, fabric and color are in harmony with a seasonal harmony type, the item will be more successful at retail, as well as for the consumer.

It is for this reason that I am putting my energy into this writing. As customers become more discriminating in the styles and colors they will accept, then so must retailers. Designers may resist this concept, as many retailers have. There may be reluctance to sacrifice or seemingly compromise creativity by yielding to the dictates of the seasonal harmony concept. It would seem, however, that within the constraints of the concept there is still much room for artistic expression. (See Chapter 11.) The time has come for retailers and designers to catch up with the consumers.

Even the skeptics or disbelievers have little to lose. It is not essential that a retailer or designer be convinced of the credibility or authenticity of the theory to profit by its use in his/her buying or designing practices. There is irrefutable and confirmable evidence that variations on the theme are being taught throughout the country.

Providing styles in colors that conform insofar as is possible to the guidelines of the seasonal harmony system can certainly do no harm. Surely merchandise more compatible with the current prevailing teachings can only assure increased profitability and fewer markdowns for the merchant and greater satisfaction for the consumer. Even the consumer who has not yet had her colors analyzed should reap the benefits.

To summarize:
1. Personality and physical qualities have been attributed to the seasonal color harmonies.
2. Design lines have been ascribed to each of the seasonal color harmonies, undoubtedly because of the consistency of personality characteristics found in people with similar coloring.
3. There are design lines, as well as personality and physical characteristics, that are considered yin and yang, a distinction which further refines the system.
4. There are fabric qualities, as well as color and design, that best suit each of the seasonal harmony types.
5. There are "experts" out there teaching consumers these theories.

THEREFORE, it behooves consumers, retailers, and designers to learn as much as possible about the *"Color Connection."*

Illus. 13

3
There's More to Color Analysis Than Color

The theory has been named *seasonal color harmony* or *nature color harmony,* by many color analysts because the colors in each of the four major color types are similar to those found in the four corresponding seasons. It has nothing to do with one's birth season or with the season of the year in which clothes are purchased.

As has been noted before, there are many schools of thought about color harmony. To describe the color harmony types some color consultants do not refer to the seasons, but instead use other terms which correspond to the seasonal type shown in parentheses below:

1) striking or contrast (Winter).
2) animated or light/bright (Spring);
3) soft, gentle or muted (Summer). (Some color analysts use the word "muted" for Summer, others use it for Autumn, which can be confusing. In the case of Summer, the usage of the word "muted" means grayed down or softened with gray, or sometimes with rose or blue.)
4) rich, muted, or earth tones (Autumn). (For Autumn, muted refers to colors mixed with brown, referred to as "earth tones.")

These terms refer to one's *overall appearance* (animated, soft, etc.) and/or a description of a person's *colors* (light/bright, muted, etc.).

For the color analysis to be accurate it should be done in natural daylight. The client should wear a neutral top or be draped with white. And, of course, since it is the natural coloring of the individual that determines the seasonal harmony type, no make-up should be worn; and colored or tinted contacts should be removed. Best results will be obtained if the hair color has not been altered.

All of the color analysts whom I have observed and/or read about have used some form of *comparison* as their primary method, comparing one color with another against the skin to determine colors that will be most harmonious with the skin—colors that enhance the individual's coloring and minimize shadows, lines and dark circles. It is through this process that they decide whether their client will wear cool, blue-based colors (Winter/Summer) or warm, yellow-based ones (Spring/Autumn).

Winter and Summer seasonal harmony types have blue undertones in their skin and will wear *colors* that are blue-based (colors to which blue has been added). Some of the colors to be worn by these two seasonal types will overlap. Light to dark olive skin with a blue undertone that is almost purple is the most common Winter type skin. Since olive skin is thicker than others, it has a tendency to look yellow and the blue undertones are therefore often very difficult to detect. It is for this reason that Winters are often misdiagnosed as Autumn types.

If yellow-based colors are worn by a Winter type with olive skin, her skin will look yellow, even sallow. Whereas, if blue-based colors are worn, her skin will look natural and vivid.

Winter types will look best in all values from *dark to light* of either true basic colors or colors that have had blue added to them. The intensity should be clear—not muted or dusty—in either true or blue-based colors. Winter types will wear their colors with strong contrast, e.g., black and white or gray and red.

> **Winter colors are true or blue-based, clear and worn in contrast.**

Summer types will wear *medium to light* values in almost true colors or ones that have been gently softened with gray, rose or blue (some color analysts call this "dusty" or "muted"); but when their colors are *medium to dark* in value, they should always be soft, dusty, or muted tones. Summer types will wear their colors with much less contrast and with a soft look, either analogous (the two colors found on either side of a specific color on the color wheel are known as its *analogous* colors, see page 252 or monochromatic combinations.

> **Summer colors are soft and romantic looking.**

Spring and Autumn types have yellow or golden undertones in their skin and will wear yellow- or golden-based colors. As was the case with Summer and Winter, some of Autumn's and Spring's colors may overlap. The Spring skin is a part of the light/bright picture, as it is most often bright with a rosy glow to it. The Autumn skin tends to be somewhat sallow; the yellow undertone is much more noticeable than in the Spring type. Rich yellows and golds enhance the Autumn and Spring skin.

Spring types will wear clear colors or light and bright colors with a yellow base (e.g., they will wear red that is either clear or yellow-based). Spring types will often wear combinations of three of their colors, e.g., red, white and blue or yellow, green and purple. They will wear contrast, but it will be lighter and brighter, fresher looking than that of the Winter type. They will wear their darker colors in combination with lighter and brighter ones.

While Spring and Autumn types share the same yellow undertones, Autumn types will wear stronger, richer, more intense colors with *gold* base; their *medium to dark* colors will be dusty, muted, blended earth tones worn in analogous or monochromatic combinations with accents of contrast. Their colors will be blended one with another rather than clear, e.g., blue-green, yellow-green, yellow-red, etc.

As I watched Suzanne analyze the colors of several people one afternoon in her studio, I became aware that unlike the many color analysts who use pre-packaged color systems, she did *not* decide upon the season of the client and then give her predetermined colors belonging to that season. She mixed paints to exactly match her client's skin tones in all its varying shades. Next she separated out all of the colors found in the eyes, using a magnifying glass if necessary. The hair, skin and eye colors determined the basics or best neutral colors. The best reds were determined by lip color and by colors found in the palm of the hand and by squeezing a finger to bring the blood to the surface of the skin.

It was only after these basics had been determined that she began to add colors to the palette — colors that were complimentary to the skin and to the other colors already on the palette. At the very end of the process, Suzanne would announce the name of the season and explain how the colors should be worn together.

It was a *process,* and one that required an

> **Spring colors are worn in light and bright contrast with a fresh, young look.**

> **Autumn colors are blended, rich and flamboyant.**

Illus. 14

The Winter Cocoon

objective, trained eye. (I suspect a bit of intuition is also helpful!) But it was the coloring and the way the colors combined that determined the season.

I was only one of several Winter types the day Suzanne analyzed my colors. Each of those Winter palettes had its own distinctive look. My palette was that of an *onyx Winter*. My colors seemed dark — grays, black, an almost mossy green (my eye color), berry, and teal. The only light colors on the palette were my light grays and my skin tones. Suzanne said that I could wear icy pastels, but she thought my light grays and light skin tone colors were better for me. She said that they were more enhancing to my skin than the icy pastels, so she was going to leave the pastels off my palette, although of course I could wear them.

I remember being more than a little envious of the brilliant colors given to two *dynamic* Winters that day. My colors seemed dark; theirs seemed vibrant. The truth is, of course, that I never get so many compliments as when I wear black and gray with a dash of my best colors. Or when I wear my skin tones with a splash of teal. I can wear the vibrant, electric colors and look fine, of course, but Suzanne knew that I look my best in the colors that she gave me.

Each of the palettes that day were individually selected with great care. We each had a blue, but the one on my palette was *my blue*. We each had a red, but they varied, depending on each individual's coloring. Several were Winters, but each Winter palette was distinctive and personal. We each had a blue-green.

Some form of blue-green will be found on all palettes, as it can be worn by all types, although there will be shades or tints that are better than others for each individual. Blue-green is what is known as *a universal complement* as it intensifies and enhances the personal coloring of all types. The individual's personal coloring determines which blue-green is best. The perfect blue-green for an individual usually will be found directly opposite his/her skin tone on the color wheel.

Unfortunately, the *universal basic dress* has yet to be found inasmuch as each seasonal type, as well as each body type, has her own preferred neck styles, skirts, etc. There are very few, if any, designs that will be worn equally well by all of the seasonal types. However, I have found that a rather simple classic style, whether a blouse,

A Shirtdress for All Seasons

Winter

Illus. 15

Spring

Illus. 16

Summer

Illus. 17

Autumn

Illus. 18

dress, suit or sweater, in a middle value teal will often be purchased by all types. Because the color is flattering, they seem willing to compromise a bit on style. However, the four seasonal types may prefer to accessorize the same item in different ways, and given their *"druthers"*, they would each probably have individual style preferences:

1) The Winter type might prefer a very classic, uncluttered style or perhaps a very high fashion exaggerated look or one with a single focal point, in a fine gabardine, a silk broadcloth, a smooth silk/wool blend or some other fabric that will not wrinkle too much or perhaps one that has a bit of lustre.

2) The Spring type will like her teal dress brightened with white or yellow or some other light/bright color, perhaps in a sporty look. She will want it in crisp fabric and with small details, such as tucking, little white or contrast color buttons, or a Peter Pan collar or perhaps all three. The sleeves may or may not be gathered. She often will roll them or push them up to give a rounded silhouette if the garment does not already have it. In addition, she will like a closer-to-the-body fit.

3) The Summer type will prefer a soft, pliable fabric with a more romantic quality to the design, e.g., some shirring off a yoke and at the top of the sleeves perhaps, and like her Winter sister, will want uncluttered lines and detail. She may like a softly shaped notched collar. She perhaps will add some lace, pearls or a cameo; she won't want a lot of little detail, such as patch pockets, little buttons, applique, etc. to interfere with her own design statement.

4) The Autumn type will prefer a looser fitting garment than the spring type and in a rich combination of colors, such as teal with russet or orange or even green or blue and preferably fabric that has a firmness to it as well as a texture that can be seen as well as felt. She will like larger detail and a V-neck, banded, or notched collar, probably with a squared effect at the shoulders as opposed to softness. She will enjoy the military or safari look with pleated pockets and even a pleat in the sleeve.

And then, each of the four will choose different types of accessories to make it even more distinctively her own.

34 — The Color Connection

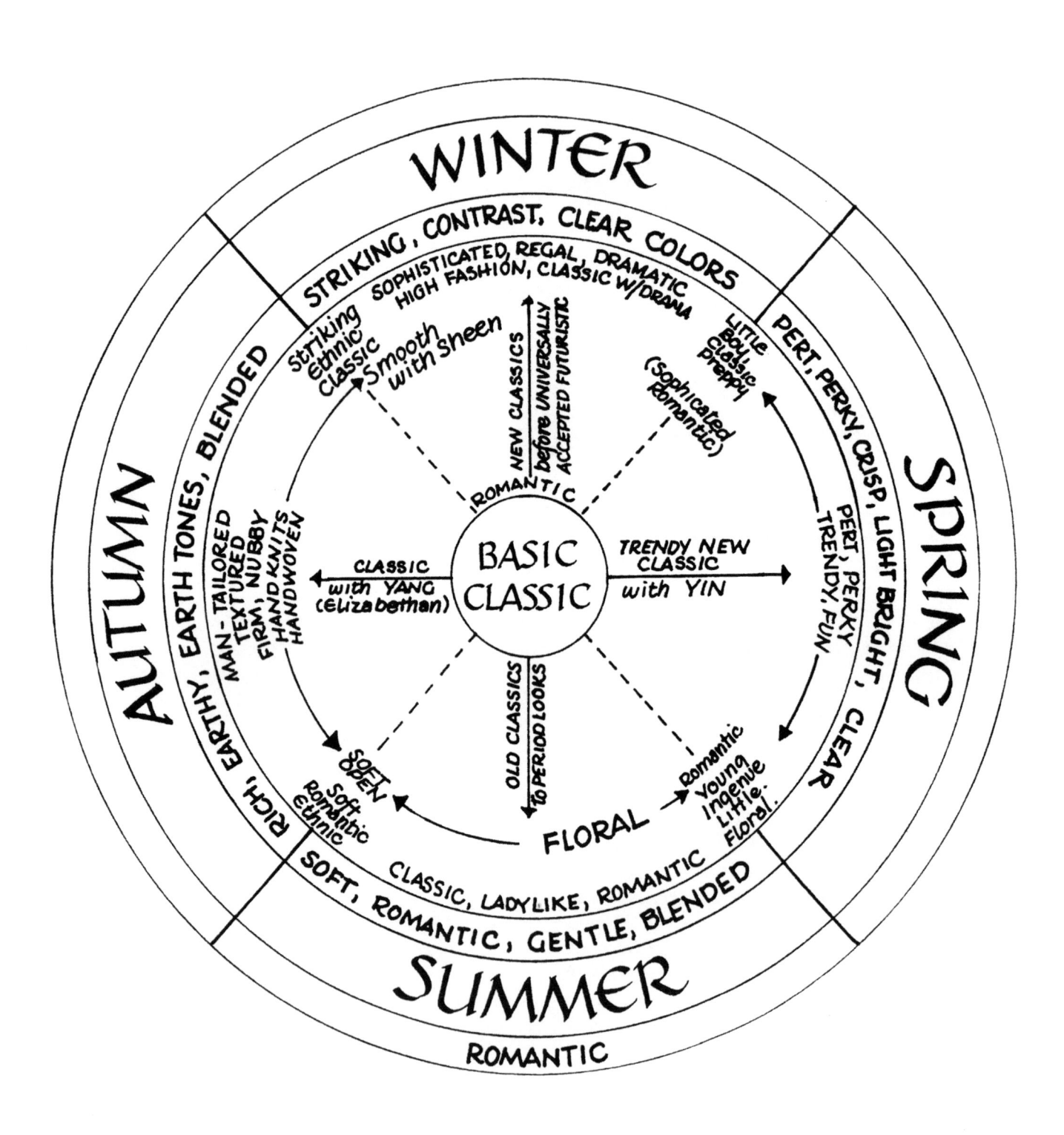

Illus. 19

4
The Color Connection — A Continuum

Just as the four seasons are on a continuum I like to think of the seasonal harmony types on a continuum. Think of the seasons — from the late autumn/early winter when there are still a few autumn leaves around and the weather can't quite decide what it's going to do; mid-Winter alternating between persistent gray fog or rainy days to crisp snowy days that seem to encompass all the shades between white and black with very little color, perhaps a few red berries. And then, there is late winter/early spring when new leaves are beginning to appear on what had been dead-looking branches of deciduous trees. The days are a little longer, a little brighter, a little crisper and fresher looking. So it is with the seasonal harmony types in terms of coloring, in terms of style.

It seems to me to be a logical way to explain the variation in coloring and best personal colors, as well as why some people within the same season will prefer one style over another. Some systems use classifications such as natural/town & country; youthful-natural/preppy; ingenue/or eternally youthful feminine; feminine/romantic; dramatic or classic sophisticate to describe the personality types and therefore styles. Probably one system is as good as another. I personally find the continuum idea the clearest way to explain the range of styles within a seasonal type.

In terms of style, the Winter type just coming out of Autumn (Winter/Autumn secondary) has more yang characteristics, is more naturalistic, sporty or town and country-looking. She may enjoy more texture, more asymmetry, less conservative looks than the target Winter type. The

A Continuum of Style

Illus. 20

Illus. 21

Illus. 22

Valentino type jacket of houndstooth plaid (See Illustration 20), with the much more yang angularity in the squared shoulder treatment, is an example. In an Autumn color it would be considered an Autumn design line; in the black and white it will work for the Winter going into Autumn, but needs the softened effect achieved with the ascot and the softer, rounded version of the fedora. The Winter type will want to be careful to keep the accessories softer when wearing this very yang type of jacket lest the image become too strong a statement.

The late Winter type (Winter/Spring secondary) has more yin characteristics, than either the Winter/Autumn or the target Winter. She is often petite with a balanced figure, and may prefer the softer, more refined, more feminine, conservative styling, perhaps with fine dressmaker detail. The black and white Glen plaid suit with the black velvet collar in an elongated Chesterfield-type jacket might be an example of a Winter/Spring look, a bit more dramatic looking than the traditional shorter jacketed Chesterfield, which is considered early Spring, Vital Spring or Spring/Winter (see Illustration 22). It is still sophisticated, but with a touch of *"pert!"*

The black and white herringbone Valentino-type jacket (Illustration 21) features oval lines. The black mouton collar's rhythmical pattern is suggestive of drifted snow. It would be typical of a dramatic target Winter design. It offers more texture than the Glen plaid, yet more softness than the houndstooth. It is strikingly dramatic, especially when worn with the contrasting smooth kid gloves and sleek close fitting perfect-for-Winter hat.

Think of the seasonal harmony types on a continuum just as the seasons of the calendar are on a continuum. You might even consider that winter will mean different colors and climate in some parts of California than it does in the midwest or the New England states. So just as there is variety in the seasons, depending on geographical location and current year's weather patterns, there is variety in the seasonal harmonies, depending on personality, life style, figure challenges, and how each individual wishes to be perceived.

To add to the continuum idea, think also of the colors as on a continuum with the late Spring/early Summer type wearing soft combinations of colors, being considered perhaps a *gentle* Spring.

The contrast worn by this type might be less; her teal, for instance, might be slightly softened and she might wear it with a light coral. The early Summer might wear lighter and brighter color combinations than the target Summer. The early Autumn type would wear richer colors than that of the Summer type but perhaps less so than the target Autumn, etc.

You might also think of Spring as a smaller, younger version of Autumn, with the Spring type wearing the little boy looks — a baseball cap or jacket, the Little Lord Fauntleroy look, a middy blouse or sailor pants with double rows of little buttons, or a U.S. Navy pea coat.

The Autumn type wears grown-up styles. She wears man-tailored jackets and trench coats with big lapels, perhaps with epaulets and big brass buttons — the military look of the officer rather than that of the enlisted man.

Autumn type women have frequently been described as of the earth or even *earth mother,* as they tend to be very natural, active, mature, well organized, and usually devoted homemakers and/ or care givers, (e.g., nurses, doctors, psychologists, etc.). If Autumns are the *earth mother,* then one might think of the Spring type as the *earth child,* in that she, too, is natural, active, casual, but seems eternally young and sometimes may even appear scatterbrained and/or dependent. (Do not let appearances deceive you!)

And just as Spring is a younger, more yin or petite version of Autumn, Summer is a younger, more yin, modest, and less sophisticated version of Winter. The Winter type may be willing for her necklines to be draped lower, her dresses showing more cleavage; and for her styles to be more sculpted and body-revealing with bolder prints and designs and, of course, with much greater contrast than will the Summer type, who tends to be much more demure and ladylike than her elegant, striking, and often sophisticated Winter sister.

The style guidelines found in Chapters Five through Eight are a composite of the recommendations of many Seasonal Color Harmony wardrobe consultants. These guidelines seem to have evolved over time as it was noted that harmoniously well-dressed women who had similar coloring, physical and personality traits, etc., seemed to choose similar colors, design lines and design detail. They seemed intuitively to follow similar basic unwritten patterns of dress. There were individual differences, of course. But there seemed to be a recognizable pattern that could be broken down into four distinct groups, corresponding to what has become known as the Seasonal Color Harmony.

Each person is encouraged to use basic silhouettes from her dominant harmony guidelines, adding bits and pieces from her other secondary harmony/ies, if any, in order to express her own uniqueness or, in some cases, to enhance the observer's perception of her. She is also encouraged to remember, however, to keep the amount of those secondary seasonal details in proportion with her dominant harmony or, in other words, in balance with her visual image and her yin and yang qualities. Even if she wishes to project a stronger or more feminine image, her look should still be consistent and compatible with her dominant harmony. Note particularly the *professional* and *formalwear* sections of each of the harmony chapters.

For example, a very striking Winter woman may wish to appear more friendly, a little softer, a little less threatening. She could add a little lace hanky to the pocket of her very simple jacket to achieve this softening effect. To add a cascading lace jabot with a cameo might be too much unless she has a very strong Summer secondary.

The same Winter woman might in the course of the same day, wishing to appear more fun-loving, choose to add some playful Spring effects to her Winter casual outfit, which is still quite elegant by a Spring's standards. Again, she would want to keep the amount of Spring effects in proportion to the amount of her Spring secondary. She can vary the amounts, depending on how she wishes to be perceived, as well as on the varying activities of her day. One of the primary goals of packaging, however, is to give clear messages of what's inside.

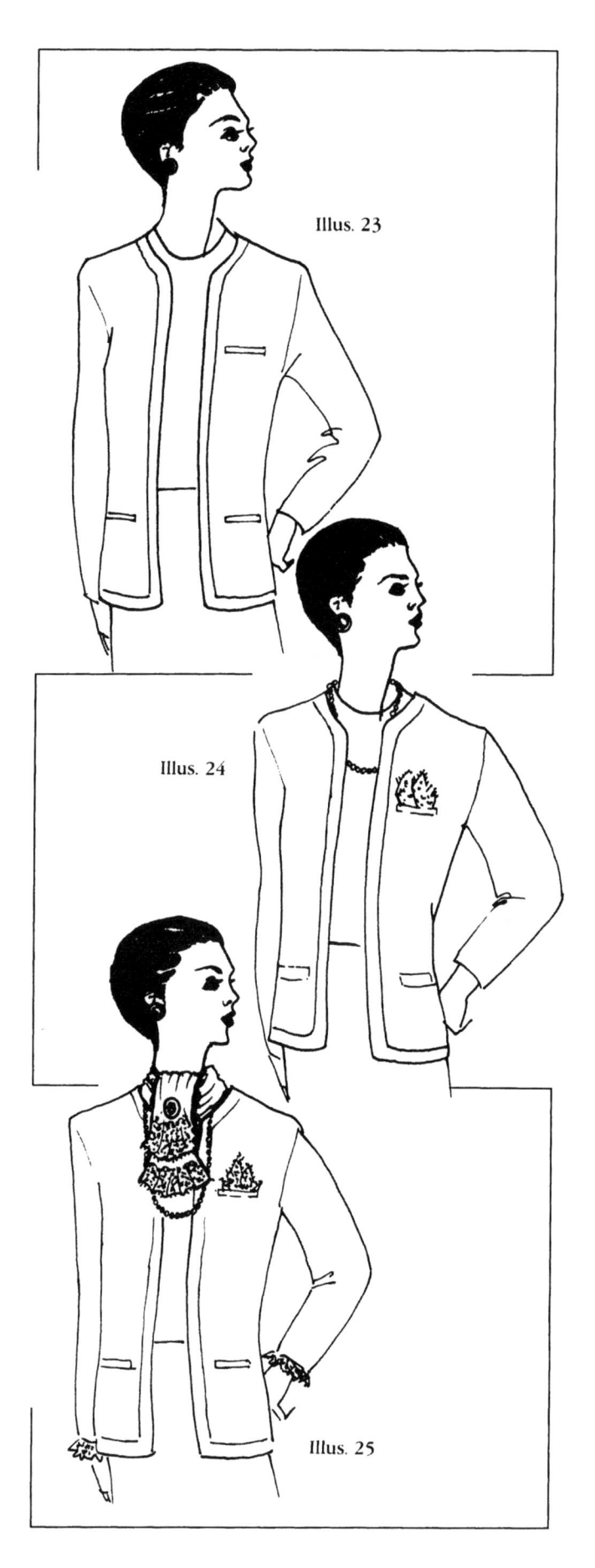

Illus. 23

Illus. 24

Illus. 25

Illus. 26

5
Winter

Shakespeare often wrote about the seasons of the year; he compared them to the seasons of one's life, beginning with spring and comparing it to childhood, midsummer to middle age and winter to old age. Perhaps because the day I write this it is snowing outside my window, I choose to start with "winter", when everything appears to be asleep under a blanket of snow, awaiting the kiss of the sun to raise it (and us) from the doldrums.

As I sit this morning at my writing table, looking out the French doors toward my back garden, I am struck with the quiet drama of a winter day. It snowed during the night — a light covering. I can see the green of the pine, spruce and fir trees; the lighter green of a protected spot of lawn; the white snow in contrast with many shades of gray, black and dark brown.

The deciduous trees and shrubs are free of leaves. Their branches are graceful, uncluttered and stark against the sky. Some leaves left on berry bushes at the back of the yard are shades of burgundy, as are the few buds remaining on the yet unpruned rose bushes. The sky is electric blue with scattered white clouds. This may change any minute to clouds of gray to almost black; it did yesterday. The only touches of brilliant color outside are the bright red on the head of an acorn woodpecker, the deep intense blue of a Steller's jay at the bird feeder, and a profusion of red berries on the photinia hedge bordering our driveway.

Inside I have a Christmas poinsettia, adding a touch of color. Some gray-green pussywillow branches, being forced to bloom a little early, are a promise of what's to come.

My winter garden is well groomed, stark, and carefully cut back. Leafless branches of lilac and flowering quince, that memory tells me will soon blossom, now look like so many dead sticks rising gracefully from the ground.

• The **colors** of winter are pure, deep, intense and brilliant or pastels icy as barely tinted snow; there are few middle value colors. The contrast is dramatic. The colors of the Winter type are those of the season.

The winter scene looks stark, subdued, serene, cool — aloof! Winter types are said to share these same inner characteristics. These words describe not only winter, but the Winter type, as well: quiet, dramatic, contrasting, graceful, uncluttered, well-groomed, stark, subdued, serene, cool, aloof, refined and still.

The Winter woman wears all of the blacks and grays of a winter scene with accents of color: electric blue, cranberry, scarlet or poinsettia red, or icy pastels. She can wear large amounts of pure, undiluted color. She wears the greens and blue-greens of the evergreen trees, as well as that of the eucalyptus, peacock and emerald. She might wear electric, cobalt, sky, royal and Persian blues; purples such as royal purple, blackberry, blueberry, midnight blue, eggplant, thistle, plum and magenta.

Most Winter types do not wear yellow, but, if one does, it will be in the very light ivory, vanilla and pale lemon range. Depending on an individual's coloring, she may be assigned any of several whites, such as: snow white, frosty white, silver, chalk, pearl, ivory, oyster, or white with a blue cast to it. Her reds are clear or blue-based, ranging from true red to medium and deeper values of cranberry and burgundy. Her neutrals are taken from her hair, eye and skin colors and serve to dramatize her own contrasts.

One color accent at a time is enough for a Winter type. For greatest enhancement, she will wear one or two shades of a dark color with the addition of a contrast color near her face; or one or two shades of a light color with the addition of a dark or bright color near her face.

Winter types are not necessarily beautiful in classic terms, but they are striking in appearance with high contrast physically. They may have black or almost black hair and, in contrast, what often appears to be nearly white skin as in the

Snow White look. The Winter skin may be, in fact, porcelain white, light to dark olive, champagne or alabaster, or even light peach, pink, or black brown.

- (Note: Some color analysts categorize all **non-Caucasians** as Winter types. Others find variation in the skin tones of these other races also. It is theorized that these variations have a relationship to the seasonal types similar to that of Caucasians. Suzanne Caygill suggests that if the non-Caucasian *skin is peach the individual is probably a Spring; if it is rose, she is a Summer; if it is apricot, she is an Autumn; and if it has a violet cast, she is a Winter.* I have found that the personality verification tests also apply.)

The Winter type will often have even and well-defined features with high cheekbones and eyes that may appear almost black, although they may be gray-green, green, light blue-green, pine green, deep evergreen, lapis blue, navy blue or pale, misty or icy blue. Even without make-up the eyes and eyebrows of the Winter type are prominent and distinctive. The eyebrows are usually arched, symmetrical and may be distinctively dark and heavy. Winter types may gray early. They are usually slim and refined looking — at least when they are young. (To compare with other seasonal harmony types, see Comparative Chart, page 274.)

(Note: I have noticed and Suzanne also mentions in *Color, The Essence of You* (page 112) that as the hair of other seasonal harmony types turns gray or white and their own look gets a little softer, they may prefer to wear the more classic Winter styling, often favoring the brighter, deeper and richer colors on their palette.)

Additional words used to describe the Winter type range from regal, statuesque, elegant, and luminous to commanding, well defined, expensive, frosty, and restrained.

The Winter woman's walk, voice and speech reflect these attributes. Her walk is somewhat regal and serene, almost a glide; her diction tends to be precise, well-defined and sometimes dramatic; her tone of voice (often alto) is in the lower yet still feminine range.

The Winter type tends to be a perfectionist, and just as she wears black and white, she is apt to make black and white decisions, too. She seems to need more alone time and silence each day than those of the other harmonies. Some people stand

Personality traits for the Winter seasonal harmony type, as well as those of the other three seasons, are generalizations. Not every Winter type is going to have all of these traits. Suzanne suggests that personality traits be used as verification of the seasons in the final analysis. However, for the purposes of the women's ready-to-wear retailer, personality in combination with visual design is the most expedient and practical indicator that we have. I have found these two elements to be an effective indicator and verification of seasonal color type and, therefore, a very useful tool.

Illus. 27

Illus. 28

in awe of the Winter type and often even consider her to be aloof. The Winter woman is usually highly disciplined and considers punctuality and organization very important in herself and others.

• **Design Lines:** Winter types express themselves best with the oval form, such as that found in the cocoon shape. The lines are relaxed, smooth, and released as in hills and valleys or weeping willows, and are found in the falling lines of the unstructured look of a Grecian gown or a Roman toga design; or in relaxed S-curves, as found in a sarong — no abrupt beginnings or endings.

Other examples in fashion include draped or cowl necklines, Indian saris, capelets, or monk's robes. Other Winter styles might include simple abstract or geometric shapes such as those found in tent dresses, straight skirts, modified princess lines or other fit and flare styles; exaggerated, modern or even futuristic shoulder and sleeve treatments; slim pants or skirts.

Not all Winter types will wear extreme styles in vibrant colors or in black and white. But it is safe to say that many of the extreme elegant styles with oval silhouettes, such as cocoon shaped coats, sweaters and dresses, will best be worn by Winter types and should therefore be purchased by the retailer in the colors of Winter.

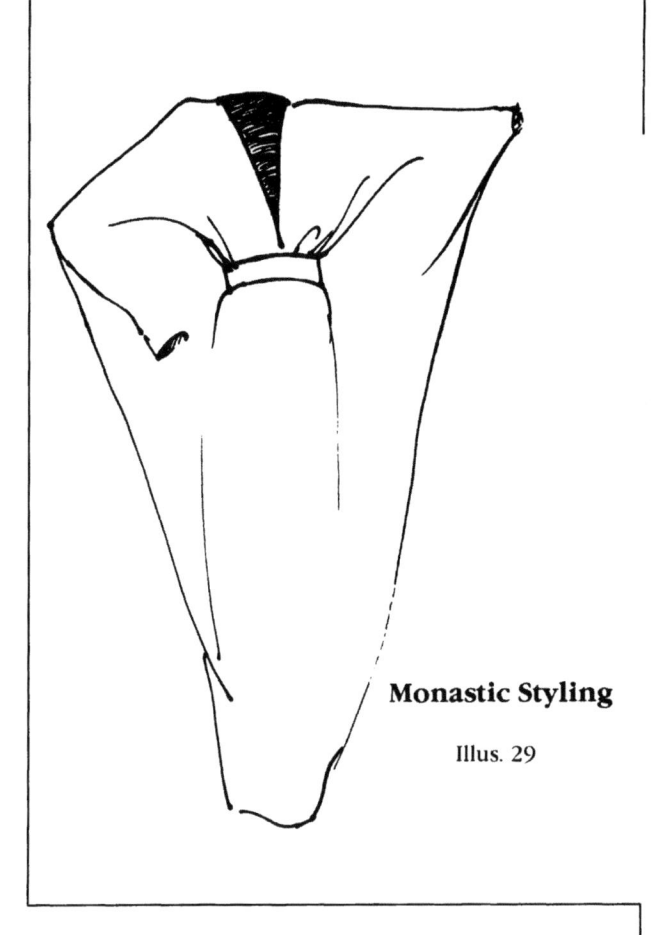

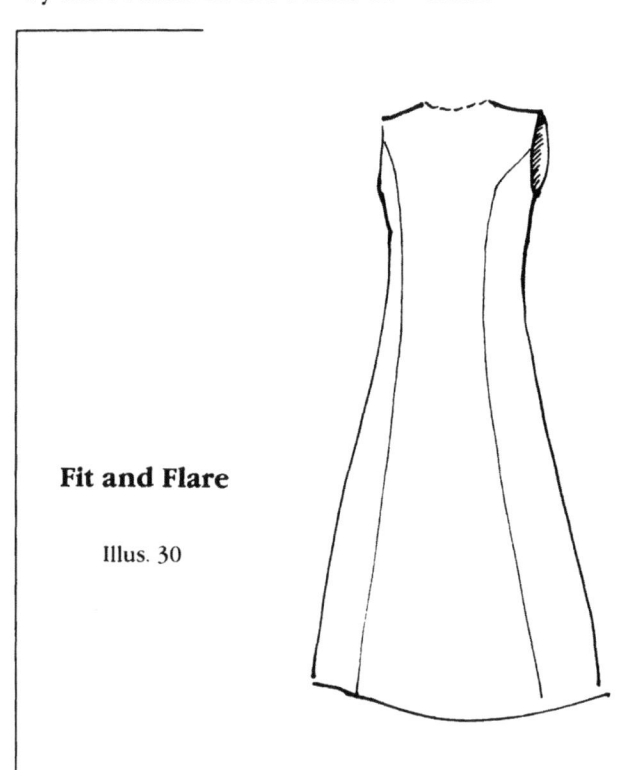

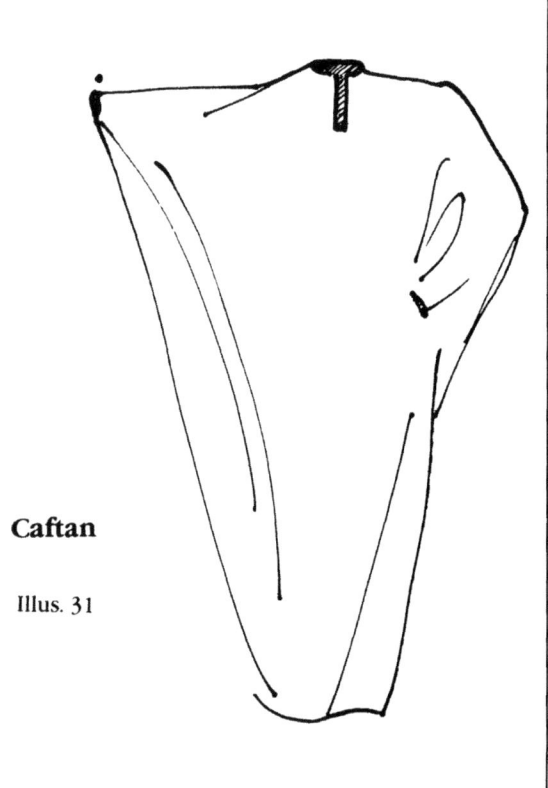

Monastic Styling

Illus. 29

Fit and Flare

Illus. 30

Caftan

Illus. 31

Illus. 32

Classic styles, those simple tailored lines that are basically in fashion year after year, will be worn by all seasonal types in their own best fashion colors, even if the design lines are not quite right. The illustrated knit turtleneck is an example of such a classic style. By replacing the Summer belt (knots and twisted) with one more typical of her own season, each of the other three seasonal types would also wear this design if in her colors. A classic notched collar jacket in a perfect Winter color will be worn by almost all Winter types, even with what for a Winter would be considered a *design error,* such as patch pockets. It has been noticed, however, that in neutral colors that same classic style will often be passed over in favor of styles that contain the design lines most appropriate for her season.

In a neutral color, given a choice, the Winter type would probably favor a less cluttered classic, a shawl collar or the collarless cardigan with welt pockets or concealed side pockets rather than the pointed notched collar version. In other words, each of the seasonal types may be willing to compromise a little on style if the color is *perfect!* In a neutral, each will prefer her own flawlessly harmonious design lines.

Illus. 33

Illus. 34

A Grecian Gown for All Seasons

Winter
Illus. 35

Spring
Illus. 36

Summer
Illus. 37

Autumn
Illus. 38

It should be noted that all seasonal types can wear a grecian gown and, in fact, the appropriate one can be worn during one's entire lifetime with a timelessness that few styles afford:

- The *Winter Grecian gown* will be one with released lines and will be in a shimmery or lustrous fabric.
- The *Spring Grecian gown* will perhaps be in a crisper fabric and will be tucked and secured with braided cords or it may have floating panels.
- The *Summer Grecian gown* will be in a soft drapable fabric and will have cascading lines or the suggestion of knots, which will create S-curves in the fabric.
- The *Autumn Grecian gown* will be full, pleated, tucked and controlled, perhaps with a knot, and either in a chiffon, a crystal pleated fabric, or a homespun or handwoven fabric that is nubby and somewhat textured.

Illus. 40

Illus. 39

Illus. 41

Winter 51

- **Specific wardrobe design detail** of the Winter type would include:
- specific focal point on each outfit;
- extreme contrast;
- an uncluttered look with stylized, pure and simple lines;
- modern or futuristic lines as in many high fashion looks;
- a sleek and/or shimmery look;
- a stark and well-defined look;
- diamond or harlequin shapes or color blocked designs;
- extreme bouffant top, skirt, sleeves, or bows.

Illus. 42

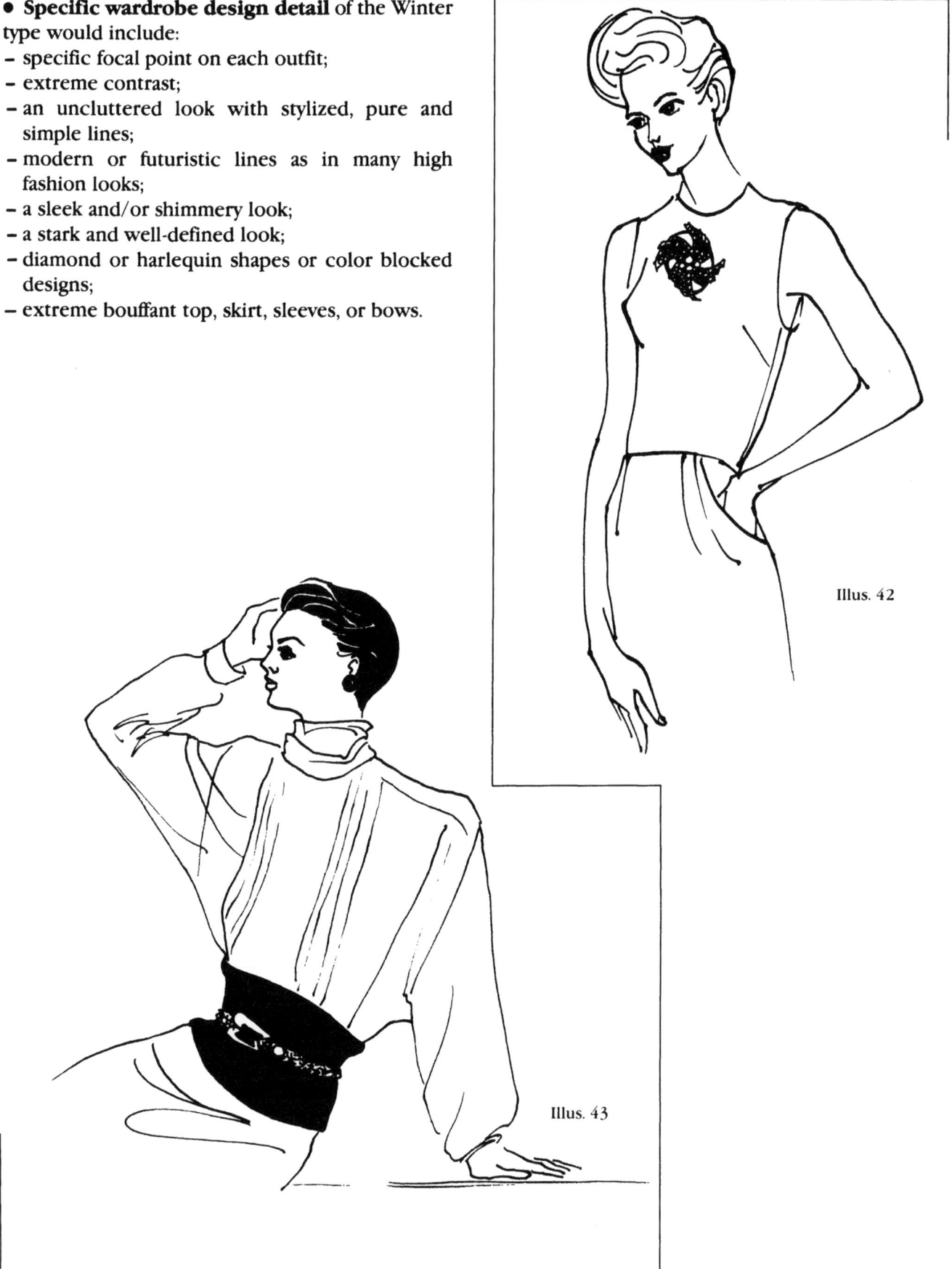

Illus. 43

Illus. 44

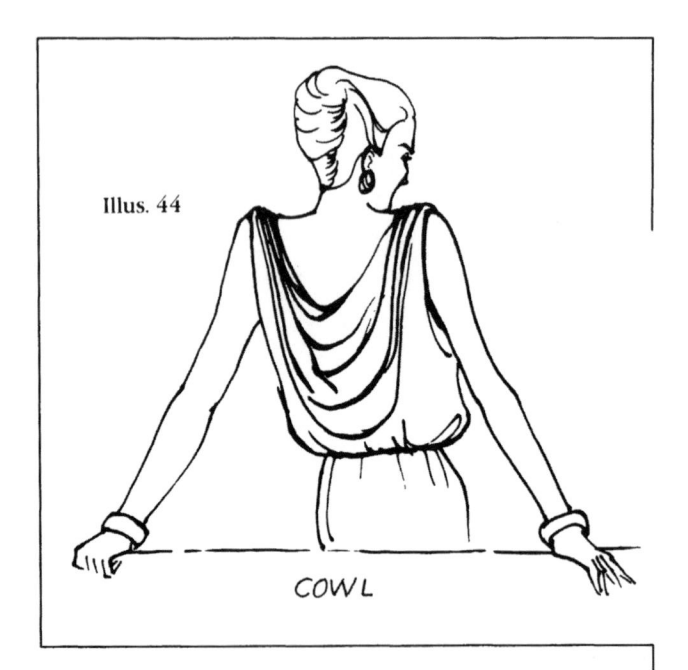

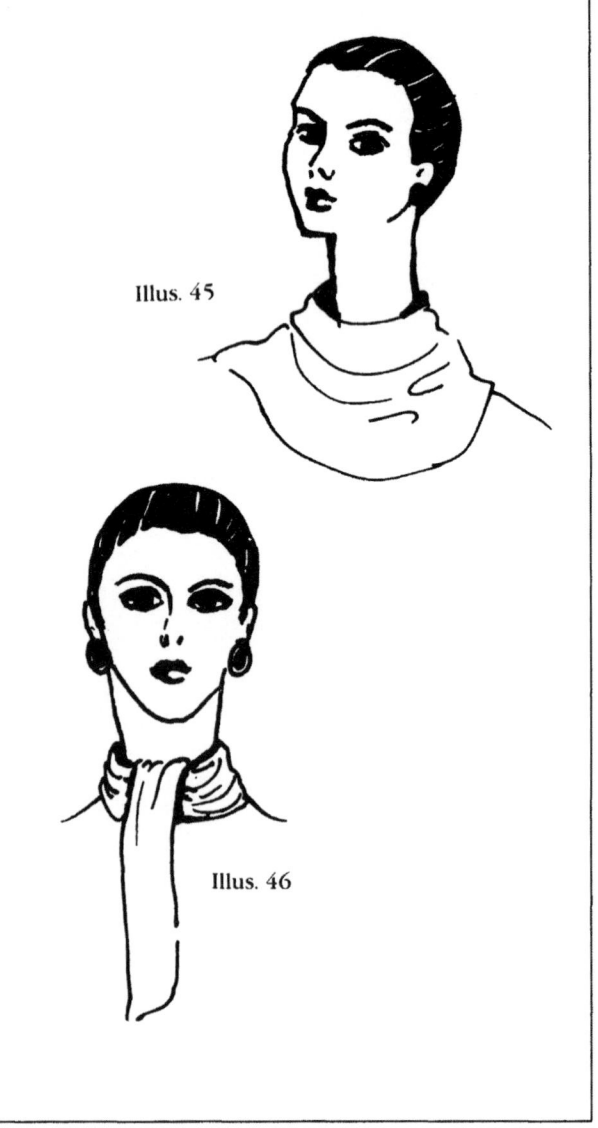

COWL

Illus. 45

Illus. 46

- **Inside design detail** might include a stock tie, a jabot, draping, or oval shapes created by draping. Winter detail will not be small in scale or *cute* looking. Most Winters will prefer to just loop their stock tie into an ascot rather than a pussycat bow. If the stock tie is too long, they may wrap it around their neck twice, giving the illusion of a draped turtle neck with an ascot. Those with short or wide necks may prefer to wear the scarf looped low onto the mid-chest area. Simplicity or stark drama is the key to the Winter design.

Think uncluttered and clean lines, e.g., no pockets, buttons, or collar probably means that a garment is a Winter design if it is in the right color.

Striking, smooth, severe, luminous and/or lustrous are words associated with Winter styling. The models in perfume and deodorant advertisements in the fashion magazines are often shown wearing dramatic and draped Winter design lines. If the designs are so distinctive you can't imagine the gowns on anyone but a very dramatic looking woman, they are probably appropriate for a Winter woman and should therefore be in Winter colors. In fact, many of these very dramatic designs would overpower the visual design of another seasonal type, causing the observer to see primarily the outfit rather than the person wearing it, even if it is in an appropriate color.

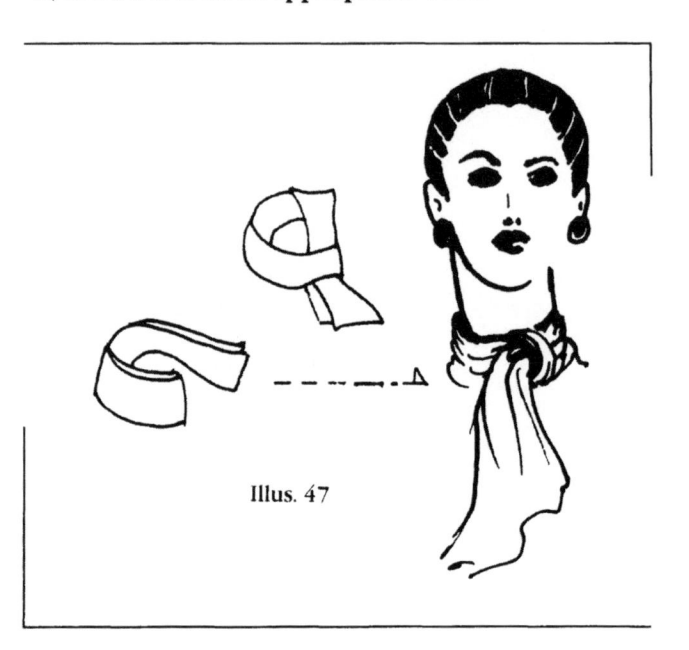

Illus. 47

- **Fabric choices** for the Winter type are lustrous, smooth, and/or refined — as in satin, satin crepe, silk, silver lamé, Qiana, chiffon, crepe de chine, cashmere, velvet, panne velvet or satin, smooth wool or knits, gabardine, very refined and smooth handknits and handwovens or uncut corduroy. She may choose smooth and refined cottons or wools with a bit of Dacron or polyester added to prevent wrinkling, since the messy, wrinkled look is not consistent with the well-groomed look of winter or the Winter type. Winter fabrics should always be very smooth and preferably with a bit of sheen, although a Winter with more yang characteristics (Winter with an Autumn secondary) may choose to wear a bit more texture. A Winter may enjoy a coat of a fabric with a glossy sheen, e.g., oil cloth.

- **Surface prints and patterns** of fabric for the Winter type include spaced abstract or stylized designs, tone-on-tone combinations, black and white houndstooth (or any high contrast combination of her colors), black and white with or without touches of color, simple stripes or unevenly spaced and sized bold stripes, relaxed S-curves or ovals in the pattern, and even some very bold checks and dots — all with contrast and, of course, in the colors of Winter.

It should be noted, however, that not every Winter woman will be attracted to or enjoy wearing prints even if the retailer is able to find the perfect stylized prints in her colors. Many seem to find prints, in general, too busy for their simple taste.

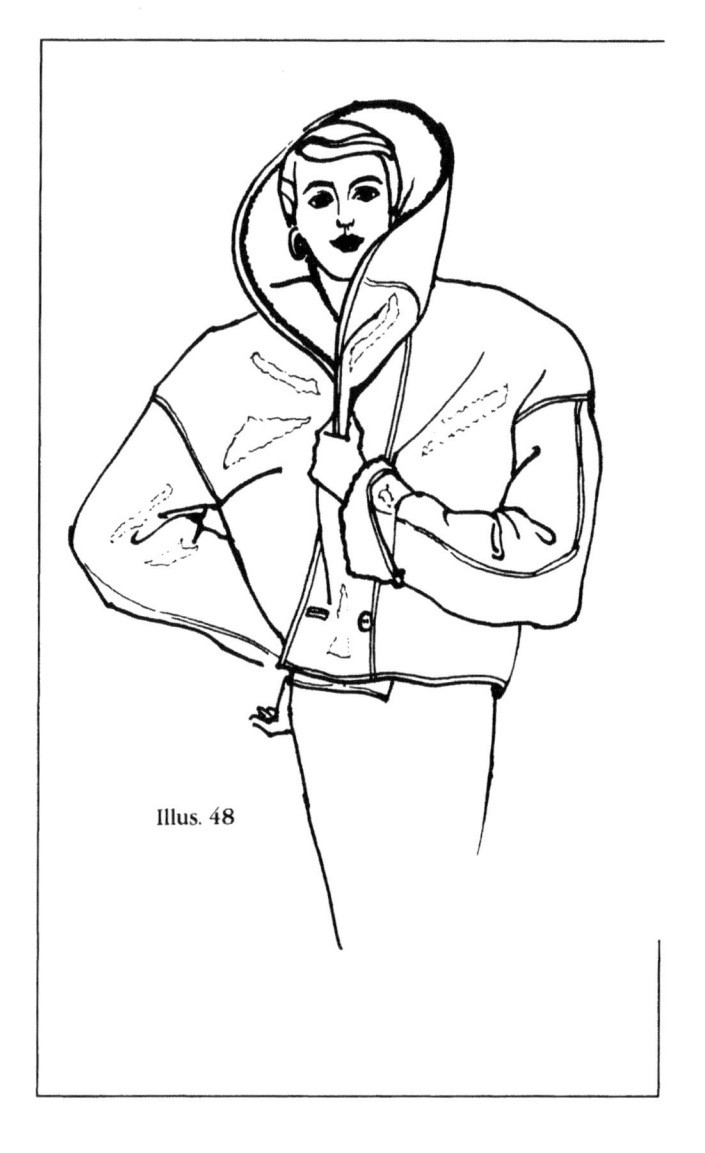

Illus. 48

Illus. 49

Illus. 50

- **Hair Styles** are apt to be sleek, smooth, stylized, asymmetric and sophisticated as in a chignon, French twist, or page boy, blunt cut, smooth waves, a smooth brow (as a rule no bangs), always striving for an oval shape and control. The messy look is rarely suitable for the Winter type. Remember some of the descriptive words of the Winter type: controlled, elegant, dramatic, regal, sophisticated, smooth, etc. Hair styles should be in harmony with the personality, as should all other aspects of her appearance.

- **Hat** shapes can be pill boxes, turbans, hoods, extreme perfectly aligned bows or futuristic looks. Her hat is striking and exotic rather than cute and perky (Spring); soft, romantic and undulating (Summer); or angular and somewhat masculine looking (Autumn). Some will wear a large picture hat, but it will have more body and definition than the undulating fluid lines and softness of the Summer hat. When the Winter type wears a fedora-like hat, it will usually be a softened version. The Winter hat may be decorated with sequins, crystal beads, or rhinestones for her evening or holiday look.

- **Bags** for Winter types are best in oval shapes or at least with rounded corners, in soft, smooth leather or lustrous fabric. Clutches may be preferred by many Winter types as they appear more elegant than shoulder bags. Brocade, silver or crystal beaded bags would be appropriate for evening.

- **Jewelry** preferences of the Winter type tends to be medium to large, stylized, smooth and simple. Metals are preferably silver, platinum, or white gold. A single focal point on an outfit is usually enough for the sophisticated, elegant look of Winter; she will often prefer one piece that is oversized and dramatic. Her jewels will be ones that sparkle (as opposed to ones that glow), such as diamonds, rhinestones, crystal, jet, black onyx, rubies, sapphires, emeralds, zircon, amethyst, alexandrite or aquamarine, although she will wear pearls or white jade as well. She may enjoy dramatic large silver earrings or ceramic ones that appear almost luminous or vibrant. The more exotic types may wear old jewelry from the Orient, Africa or Afghanistan or even bizarre, futuristic or contemporary looks.

- **Necklines** should always be well suited to the shape of the face, of course, but stand-up collars, shawl collars, cowl necklines, narrow lapels, flowing draped effects, hoods, and exposed backs are all Winter designs. Winter types usually will avoid contrast colored top stitching or other decoration on their collar treatments.

Classic lines and pure lines are the all-time favorites for most Winter types for everyday wear, e.g., a collarless cardigan jacket with concealed, besom or welt pockets and unobtrusive buttons, while the more extreme, sleek and sophisticated high fashion looks provide the theatrical and exciting, exotic look that they may prefer for evening wear.

- **Buttons** should be integrated into the uncluttered or specific focalization concept of Winter design. One, two or three medium to large interesting buttons might be effective; concealed, unobtrusive or innocuous buttons promote the uncluttered look usually preferred. In any case, they should be without fussy detail and usually not in contrast with the fabric, although they may be pearlized or made of rhinestones for a shimmery effect. Frog closures (no beginning and no ending) are, of course, suitable for the Mandarin styles.

It is worth remembering that if all else is perfect, incorrect buttons can, of course, be quite easily replaced.

- **Sleeves** may be either sleek and classic, tailored and set-in, or dramatic and high fashion. They can include sleeves that are tapered from hem to shoulder, full drop shoulder detail, modified kimono sleeve, a dolman (good for those with narrow to average shoulders), a simple raglan sleeve or even an exaggerated raglan (good for the top-heavy woman, but not for one with sloping shoulders or one who is extremely thin — even if she is a Winter!). Sleeves that help to create an oval silhouette are, of course, the ideal. The Winter type may like the drama of a flange shoulder detail, which is feminine and yet gives the futuristic effect of the space age. While she often likes some softness in her sleeves, she will always strive for chic, rather than *cute,* so her puffed sleeve, for example is going to be bouffant and extreme rather than *sweet* or *cute* such as a Spring type might wear.

Illus. 51

56   The Color Connection

Illus. 52

Illus. 53

Illus. 54

- **Skirts** for Winter might include straight, gored or perhaps full bouffant skirts, or ones with draped or sarong effects, especially for evening wear. The Winter type prefers either the very sleek look or the extreme — not often anything in between, although as figure challenges dictate so goes the skirt. Thus, even a Winter type will move from her straight skirt to a modified dirndl or one with soft pleats if she has a protruding tummy and/or larger hips. She will wear a skirt that will provide the illusion needed to disguise her own particular figure challenges.

- **Pants** for the Winter type are classic in style with concealed pockets, zippers, and stitching lines. The look of the mature Winter woman seems too refined and elegant for jeans, although they are probably worn for hiking, camping, gardening, painting, and other very casual occasions. She particularly will not be interested in the five pocket, top stitched variety, however, even if they *are* in the perfect color. (I noticed, however, that some Winters seemed more comfortable in jeans during the era when the silk blouse, blazer, jeans and heels look was an in-vogue fashion statement.)

Winter's *harmonious* look is one of elegance and simplicity. Her sleek, often sophisticated hair style and her natural elegant look are not consistent with blue jeans, shorts and camp shirts, and she therefore often seems somewhat out of harmony in that sort of casual attire. She will, however, usually like trousers, although she will want a relatively trim fit. Again, she may like the newest high fashion look — but rarely the trendy junior fashions.

Illus. 55

58   The Color Connection

Illus. 56

Illus. 57

Illus. 58

Illus. 59

Winter 59

- **Dresses** for the Winter type are classic and flowing: tent dresses, wedge shapes, modified princess lines, tunic styles, sarong styling, Grecian or Roman effects, caftans, floats with concealed pockets, backless or halter dresses; ones with exaggerated details, flowing drapes, or even a cape or the hooded effect of a monk's robe. Asymmetrical closures such as those found in Mandarin styles or the no-endings and no-beginnings styling of the cocoon are perfect for a Winter dress.

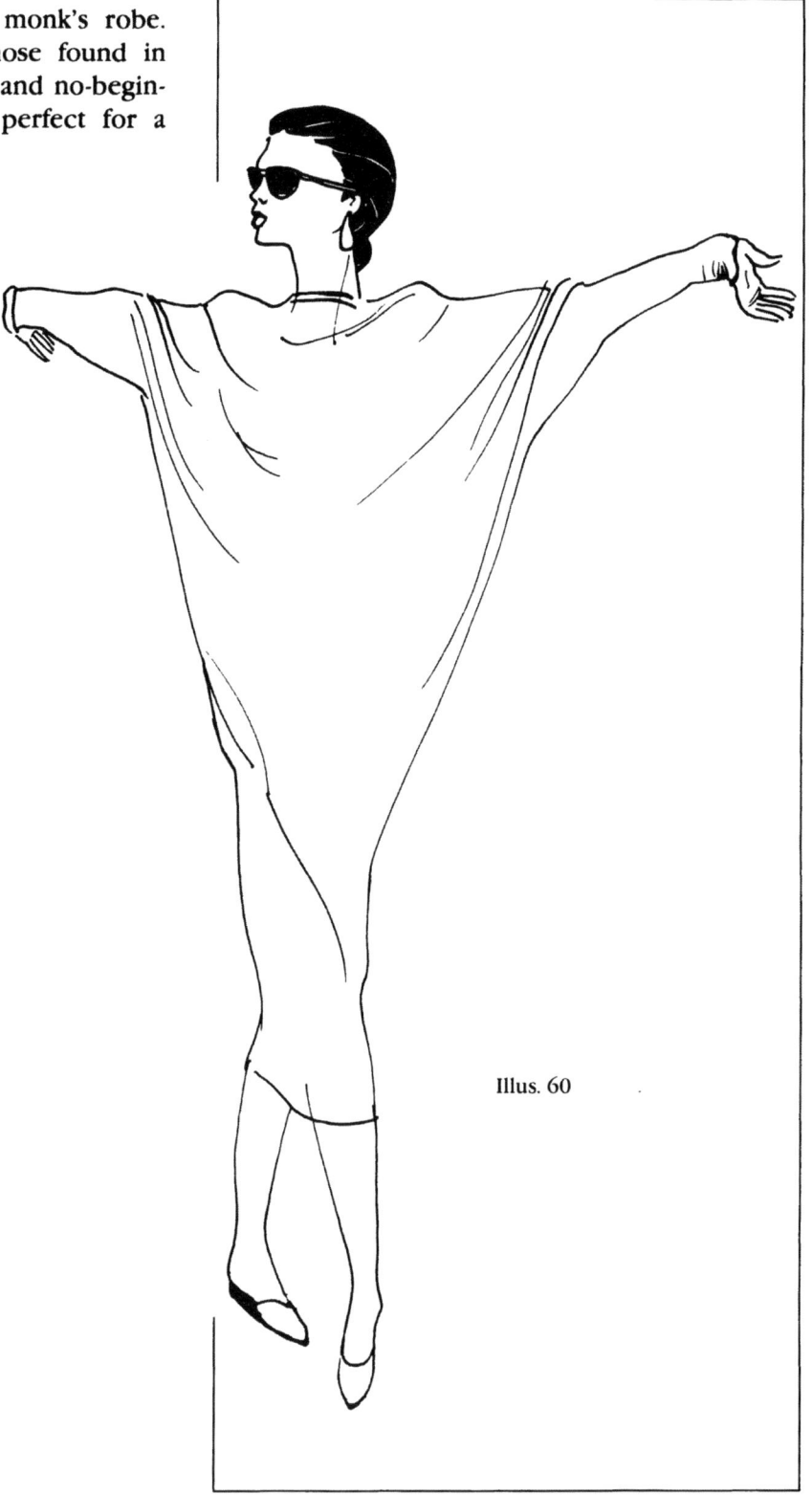

Illus. 60

60 The Color Connection

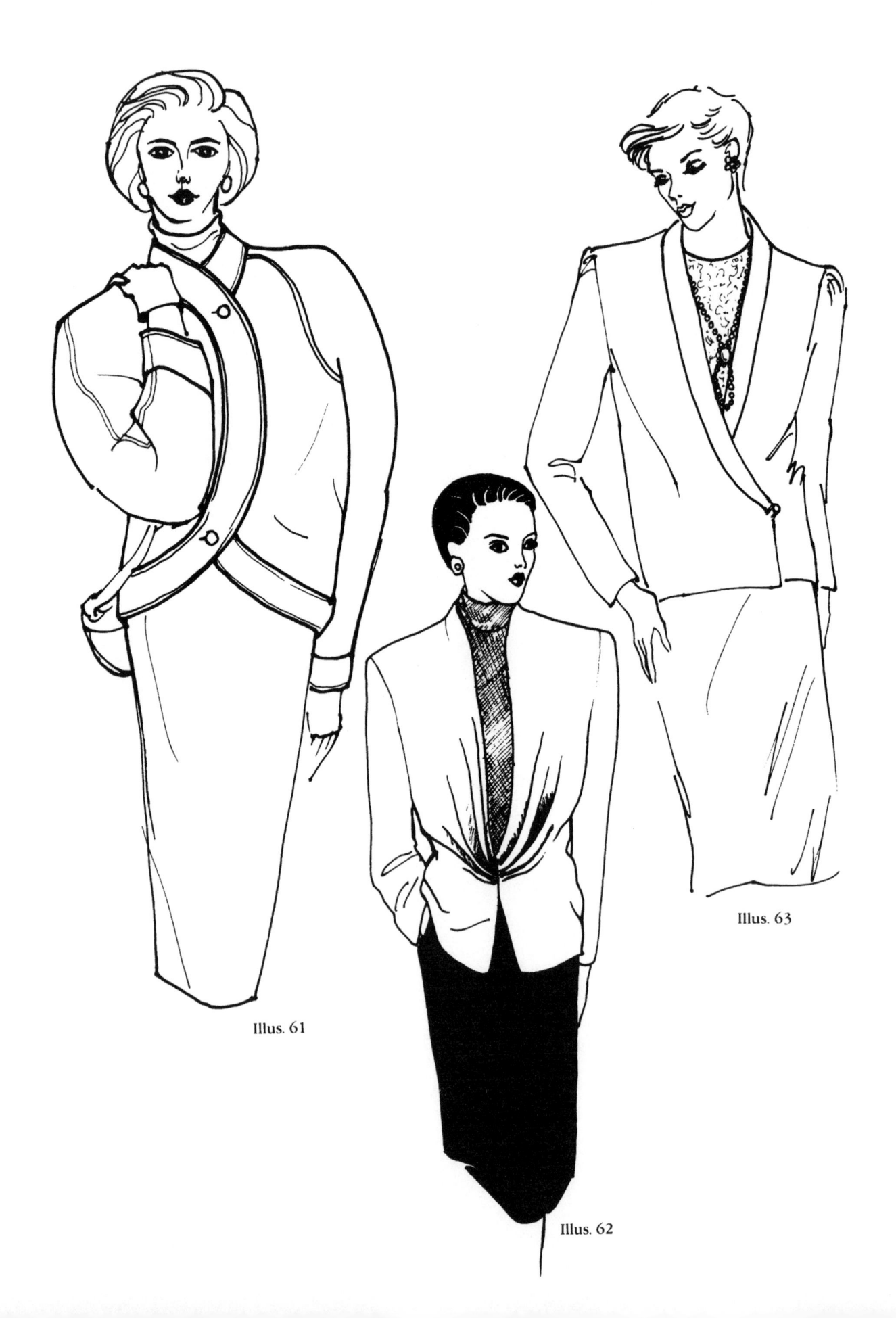

Illus. 61

Illus. 62

Illus. 63

- Her **professional look** would be finely tailored, classic suits or dresses with unfussy details in gabardine or smooth wools. She especially will not want fabrics that wrinkle badly, often preferring a bit of poly with natural fibers for that reason. Again, she seems to prefer besom, welt or other concealed pockets rather than patch pockets for an uncluttered look. She will like a shawl collar, a collarless cardigan, the Chanel look, or a rounded notched collar, i.e., one that would be a shawl collar were it not notched. She tends to retain her need for simplicity and will usually opt for accessories limited to at most a single focal point in the form of a dramatic pin or pendant.

She will wear a scarf, but not usually in the form of a bow unless it is a formal bow or extreme. She may tie it in an ascot or loop a long scarf hacking-style and pull it toward the center of her neck loosely; or perhaps tie a large square to form a draped cowl effect. She may tie a knot in the center of a large square (See Illustration) and drape it inside her blouse, dress or jacket.

Professional dress is simple for the Winter type. Her look is naturally simple and uncluttered, neither cute nor soft. (See page 36.) Even her shirtdress looks elegant in comparison to that of the other seasons. (See page 32.) She perhaps needs only to guard against looking too elegant, too striking and sophisticated, or so perfect that she may appear unapproachable. It is perhaps one of the reasons that she is often accused of appearing cool and aloof. In her professional dress, she may wish to compensate in some way to neutralize that impression if it appears to be a problem in her work.

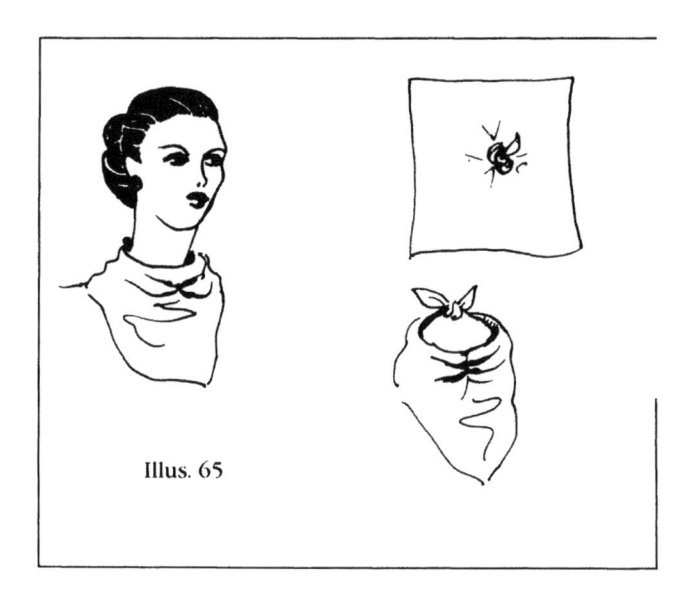

Illus. 64

Illus. 65

Illus. 66

62   The Color Connection

Illus. 67

Illus. 68

• **Formal Wear** never seems a problem for the Winter type. Much of the formal wear seems designed just for her—from all of the black, exotic looks to the alluring, theatrical high fashion evening statements of an Academy Awards evening, ranging from the sleek, stately luminous satins and velvets to the taffeta or moiré bouffant styles—almost all Winter styling.

Black, of course, is always perfect for the Winter type, and on a Winter woman even a very simple black dress can look more than basic, particularly with the addition of a sparkling single piece of jewelry. Red is always considered sensuous and romantic, and therefore appropriate for evening wear, but the skin tone is also an excellent dinner dress color because it is soft and also very feminine.

Lustrous refined fabrications, as well as all of the silver, white, clear, or electric blue metallic sequins and meshes for more dramatic occasions are all especially for the Winter type. Any effects that simulate snow or ice are effective for the Winter type, such as white or silver fringe, crystal or iridescent beading, sequins, etc.

A Winter rarely feels uncomfortable or too elegant in her formal wear. She should strive for looks that are regal, refined, classic, or sophisticated and at all costs avoid *cute* looks. The *kicky* short little black dresses with net, sequins, and froufrou that are often shown in *Vogue* and *Women's Wear Daily* are not refined enough even in black and/or white for the Winter type, but have the buoyant qualities that are perfect for Spring types. (See Illustration 69)

Illus. 69

64 The Color Connection

Illus. 70

Illus. 71

Illus. 72

Illus. 73

Illus. 74

Winter 65

- **Knits** should be smooth feminized knits that are soft and drapable. Some of the abstract and geometric intarsia looks are excellent for Winter types, providing the needed contrast as well as a specific focal point. Color blocked knits are perfect for a Winter type if done in her colors.

Illus. 76

Illus. 75

66　　　　　　　　　　The Color Connection

Illus. 77

Illus. 78

Illus. 79

- **Shoes** likewise should be classic, refined and uncluttered, although some draped effects, especially those that create oval shapes, are desirable. The Winter woman seems to think that the classic oval pump in her best neutrals is all she needs for all of her outfits. (This may be another example of the serenity and simplicity found in the personality of Winter women. Having a few perfect things seems all she ever needs or wants.) The Winter boot will be sleek, smooth, unwrinkled, unornamented, and, of course, always perfectly groomed.

- Winter's **Coat** should be finely tailored and distinctive. A style that would be particularly good would be one with cocoon styling, an ample fit, with draping from the shoulder, fullness in the middle, and tapering to finish the oval at the hemline. Capes and capelets, even the Sherlock Holmes Inverness cape look, are excellent for Winter types in that they have the oval silhouette that a Winter enjoys. Other styles might include princess lines or futuristic styles with clean, classic and uncluttered lines. To be avoided is a too-masculine look.

Illus. 80

The Color Connection

• **Contrast** is worn by all Winter types, but the amount of contrast varies depending on the strength of her visual image and personality, or to put it another way, on where the woman is on the continuum of the Winter seasonal harmony. An early Winter (Winter with an Autumn secondary) might choose to wear less contrast, for instance, than the mid-Winter (target Winter) who would wear strong contrast, such as black and white together in large amounts. The later Winter (Winter/Spring) perhaps would wear fresher contrasts, such as her medium or dark value colors with white in smaller quantities.

The Winter type of all the seasonal types has the most contrast in her personal visual design and can therefore wear the most contrast in her clothing, but she must keep that contrast in proportion to her own visual image. Rarely will she wear more than two distinct colors. For example, she may wear a monochromatic combination of one color, adding a second color for contrast or as an accent. Interestingly enough, the target Winter will usually prefer even her prints and stripes in only two colors if, in fact, she will wear them at all.

> **The overall effect of Winter is one of sophistication and dignified elegance. The dominant quality is one of serenity, refinement and contrast. Think specific focalization, uncluttered, stylized, sleek, modern, extreme and striking for a Winter type.**

Illus. 81

The Winter Man

The Winter Man seems the most dramatic and elegant of all men — classic, high fashion looks will work for him, too. He enjoys his clothes. He appears self-assured and in control, has definite coloring and well defined features.

Envision him in European styled suits, double breasted jackets or one with a tuxedo shawl collar, cashmere sweaters, and slacks rather than jeans even for casual wear. He will prefer plain fabrics, a subtle herringbone or glen plaid, or perhaps a chalk stripe. He will probably like tone-on-tone shirts. His very best look may very well be white shirts with dark suits.

He naturally looks elegant. Even his most casual looks may appear dressy to a Spring or Autumn man. The tuxedo appears to have been designed with the Winter man in mind.

His ties would perhaps be stripes or dots with contrast in lustrous fabrics, e.g., navy blue silk with an icy blue stripe or a black ground with a tiny red pin dot.

His hair is controlled. He always seems neat and well put together, probably sending his cotton broadcloth shirts out to the laundry, since he prefers the starched look to the wash and wear dacrons or poly blends. His shoes are polished to a sheen. Even his jogging shoes are immaculate. (The same disclaimer about generalizations holds true!)

The Winter man would wear his suits in his neutrals, which might include dark navy blue, medium gray, slate gray, charcoal, a grayed taupe, light gray, maroon, and, of course, black. His bright colors, such as true red, a blue-based red, royal blue, pine green, or teal would be used as accents or perhaps in active wear. His shirts and sweaters, as well as summer-weight suits, would be in his light colors, which are all in the icy range. The best colors for his shoes and belts would probably be black or cordovan. He, too, will wear silver jewelry best.

(Author's Note: While my area of expertise is, of course, clothing and style for women, The Seasonal Color Harmony Theory is also applicable to men, as well. So I have decided to include a brief description of how I believe the theory is applicable to men. I discovered, however, as I was writing the book the need for a new singular pronoun — a new unisex singular pronoun. I know I'm not the first to notice or mention this. "Them" and "their," are exceedingly useful, but they are, of course, plural. So until someone invents the new pronoun, please be aware that in many instances where I have used "her," you could substitute "him.")

Some Famous Winter Women: Cher, Joan Collins, Veronica Hamel, Audrey Hepburn, Lena Horn, Jacqueline Kennedy Onassis, Marie Osmond, Suzanne Pleshette, Jaclyn Smith, Elizabeth Taylor, Debra Winger.

Some Famous Winter Men: Harry Belafonte, Yul Brynner, Clark Gable, Richard Gere, Cary Grant, George Hamilton, Ricardo Montalban, Gregory Peck, and Sylvester Stallone.

Some Winter People I Know: (Add your own friends, relatives, clients, etc.)

The following words have been attributed to the Winter Seasonal Color Harmony. (Using this list and the ones at the conclusion of each of the other seasons, **make a word portrait** of yourself by listing the words that relate to you in any way, such as your personality characteristics and/or physical attributes, your affinity for what the word describes, e.g., abstract designs. This word portrait may be an aid in discovering your percentages of each of the seasonal harmonies. Some words appear in more than one season.

abstract designs	dramatic	luxurious	smokey
alluring	duskiness	magnetic	smooth
aloof	elegant	magnificent	sophisticated
ampleness	enticing	majestic	sparkling
beautiful	exotic	moonlit quality	stark
black and white definiteness	expensive	opulent	stately
calm	explicit	pearly	statuesque
captivating	exquisite	polished	still
chic	extravagant	precise	striking
classic	extreme	pure	stunning
clear	formal	quiet	tempting
clearly expressed	frosty	refined	theatrical
commanding	glistening	regal	tranquil
controlled	gracious	restrained	undisturbed
cool	high fashion	romantic	unrelieved
costly	icy	scintillating	urban
crystalline	important	sense of fullness	urbane
defined	imposing	sense of mystery	velvety
dignified	impressive	self-assured	vibrant
distinct	incisive	serene	vivid
distinctive	lavish	silky	well-bred
distinguished	luminous	soigné	worldly

Illus. 82

6
Spring

Soon my spring garden will be a joy to behold! The daffodils will begin to appear, as will a bright new spring green in the lawn. The little meadow in the uncultivated back garden area will be dotted with a few golden poppies. A profusion of crocuses, hyacinths, and tulips will fill the flower beds and the wooden tubs on the patio; iris will border the side of the house; rhododendrons, camellias, azaleas, and bleeding hearts will flourish in the shaded areas. Previously dead-appearing *sticks* will suddenly appear fully laden with the blossoms of lilac and flowering quince, and the liquidambar tree will be fully dressed in its new green leaves. All will be lit by the spring sun with no shadows and no darkness.

It is no doubt because of the winter doldrums that we appreciate so much the lightness of spring. After many months of fog, cold rain and snow, we are only too eager to get out of doors, go on a picnic, take a hike, fly a kite or otherwise enjoy the warmth of a radiant spring day. We feel light, gay — alive!

Spring types wear all of their **colors** in light, medium and dark values. Many can wear black to good advantage, but usually with light accents near the face, with organza, net, or other sheer fabrics to simulate airiness and buoyancy, or with much skin showing, e.g., low neckline or bare arms. Spring's darker colors are almost always worn with light, fresh contrast in the form of jewelry or white collars to give these types the light/bright look that they need. Their beiges and browns are based on their skin and hair color, usually golden beiges and browns.

Illus. 83

They may wear white, natural or bleached white; all of the colors found in a spring garden (tulip red, daffodil yellow, violet, hyacinth blue, etc.) or in a meadow (lupin, poppy red, etc.), as well as those we associate with fruit (lemon, banana, lime, peach, apple yellow, cherry, tangerine, apricot, etc.)

Sometimes not all the colors on a Spring palette seem to *go together*. More than one color analyst whom I talked with suggested that in the case of the Spring type it really didn't matter that the analogous colors were not so pleasing to the eye as on the other seasons' palettes because, in order to get the light bright effect that most Spring types would like, they would rarely wear their analogous colors together anyway (see page 252). They will usually wear a triad of colors (any three colors that form an equilateral triangle on the color wheel) or one or more of their colors with white, e.g. peach, aqua and white or the nautical look of red, white and blue.

As you can see from the list of Spring colors above, Spring types can wear many *different* colors — more perhaps than the other seasons. Whatever a Spring type wears, it should look fresh and crisp! Fresh prints; fresh colors. A new look. Young, light, active — never heavy or burdensome looking.

There is a lightness to the feminine Spring type, too. She can appear golden and radiant with her hair highlighted with gold (flaxen, blonde, brunette, or lighter values of red) and her eyes sparkling blue, green, blue-green, blue-gray, turquoise, green-blue, purple-blue, yellow-green, or occasionally brown. (Note: Brown eyed blondes, who tan very readily and have a more exotic (Autumn) look as opposed to the animated (Spring) look are often Autumns. The determining factor is the skin tone, which seems less translucent than that of a Spring and is enhanced by the richer colors of the Autumn season. The eyes of this tawny Autumn type have a different quality, too. In the Autumn type the eyes may appear exotic looking rather than predominantly twinkly and bright-eyed, as in the Spring type.)

The skin of the Spring type appears almost translucent and is usually lighter and brighter than her Summer and Autumn sisters; it is ivory, light peach, or light golden in tone; freckles may be obvious; she may or may not tan easily. Her hair often gets lighter with exposure to the sun.

Spring

The **personality** of the Spring type is much the same — radiant! (Remember my disclaimer about generalizations on page 43!) She is effervescent, open, outgoing, wholesome looking, and has lots of energy. Some say she is "like a breath of fresh air." Her body motions and her walk, as well as her speech, tend to be quick and light. She meets people freely, smiles and/or giggles easily, and has a lilt to her voice. She is often described as talking fast and of sounding like a little girl.

The Spring type is often thought of as bubbly and bouncy and sometimes is perceived as fragmented and a bit scattered, perhaps because of her lightness, her gaiety, or her quickness. The stereotypical *dizzy* blonde of the movies and TV is usually a Spring type. The Spring woman is perky, pert and eternally young in spirit. She may even be considered feisty. And it has been said that "a party without a Spring is like a balloon without air." She likes people to drop in; she entertains easily and usually with informality. She is willing, even eager, to try new things for the fun of it — for the adventure.

Her face expresses animation, sometimes with dimples, rounded cheeks, and wide-open eyes. She may have a shorter, even slightly upturned nose, or she may have a heart-shaped face with a pointed chin. Or she may even have an almost square face shape. She is often first thought of as *cute* rather than sophisticated, beautiful or chic. Her body contours are also often rounded. Even when a Spring woman is tall and slender, she is not usually what you would call angular.

She will be the first to buy trendy clothes — probably because of her fun-loving nature and sense of adventure. Wardrobe planning does not seem a high priority for her. She seems to replace her old clothes quickly when something new and fresh-looking appeals to her. She tends to be an image shaker and maker!

If you are shopping for a Spring type, it is a good idea to ask to see what has just come into the store — what's really hot! The Spring type likes the new and fresh. It is for this reason that the trendy clothes produced in Spring colorations will sell to Spring types, even though they do not have perfect Spring design lines or if the print is a little too large or the design a little too exaggerated, etc.

Illus. 84

The Color Connection

Illus. 85

Illus. 86

Illus. 87

Illus. 88

Illus. 89

Carole Little produced a floral print woven-angora group, including a long, shoulder-padded cardigan, a trim pullover top, an ankle length pant and a body hugging trumpet skirt for holiday '85. The floral was too large for a Spring stereotypically and too distinct and contrasting for most Summer types. In my store, I noticed that a few Summers bought one piece, which most wore with winter white as an "item." Springs, on the other hand, loved the entire look of the flippy trumpet skirt and the long slouchy cardigan in that scrumptious fabric that we hadn't seen before. It was so fresh looking, so new, so light/bright that Spring types snapped it up. They bought the whole outfit!

Another example of *design error* that undoubtedly sold to Spring types is the large distinct cabbage rose prints in light bright colors in blazers, dresses, etc. of Summer '86. While a rose print typically would be considered the perfect Summer surface pattern, these seem too distinct, too bright and dramatic and in styles with bold shoulder treatment, that is far too much visually for the average Summer type woman to wear. They are fresh, new and pretty, though — and, while the Summer woman will probably resist, knowing they are wrong for her, the Spring type will buy them and wear them for one season because they're fun. It is not something that she will treasure forever as a *perfect-for-her* item.

The spring '86 jungle motifs in bright, bold primary colors are another example of trendy designs probably purchased by Spring types. Were the colorations of those bold, naturalistic jungle animal statements in blended earthtones rather than in the overly contrasted primary colors of Spring, these would be perfect for Autumn types. Again, many of the jungle prints of this season seem to be in Spring primary colors and, even though they are too strong visually, will probably be purchased by Spring types anyway.

Please note that I am not advocating or encouraging the retailer to purchase *design errors* on the basis that if they are trendy, at least the Spring types will buy them if they are in their colors. I have merely observed this to be true of many Spring women. I would caution retailers to be wary of such *design errors* and not buy too heavily. Just as a knowledge of the rules of the seasonal harmony theory help the consumer to avoid expensive clothing mistakes, the ability to know when and how consumers will be willing to

Illus. 90

78   The Color Connection

Illus. 91

Illus. 92

Illus. 93

break the rules will help the retail buyer to prevent unnecessary markdowns.

The Spring type can wear all of the little-boy looks (striped T-shirts, jeans, baseball cap), the nautical look or that of Little Lord Fauntleroy, as well as casual, sporty, active wear and still look chic. She does the clean-cut, All American, Ivy League preppy, or *girl next door* look far better than any of the other seasonal types.

Not *every* Spring will identify with all the *small detail* that will be mentioned in the style guidelines, although many will. *Most,* however, will enjoy small detail to some degree, depending on their percentage of yin characteristics. Almost all will like some dressmaker detail, such as tucks, pleats, top-stitching and shirring, although perhaps in varying degrees and in varying amounts. Small prints and small detail do not always need to mean *cute.* (See Illustration # 94)

Again, it helps to remember the continuum concept. As the Spring *season* is on a continuum, so is the Spring *seasonal harmony:* from early spring when some days feel so cool and crisp yet with spring blossoms beginning to appear; a touch of winter still in the air yet more spring than winter (Spring/Winter secondary). This usually darker haired Early Spring type, with more

Illus. 94

Illus. 95

The Color Connection

Illus. 96

Illus. 97

Illus. 98

Illus. 99

Illus. 100

yang characteristics than the target Spring type, will probably wear the more classic or even preppy look, while the Late Spring or most yin Spring will have softer features and a more ash quality to hair. She will wear more romantic styles in prints that are perhaps a bit larger, with detailing, contrast and colors a bit softer, but, of course, still within the Spring guidelines. I suspect that a Summer with a Spring secondary would wear the same garment. The target Spring will have the most pert light/bright look.

• The **outside contour or silhouette** of Spring is circular in shape, contributing to the effect of buoyancy, light heartedness, etc., e.g., puffed sleeves or gathered dirndl skirts as in the Gibson Girl look. Gathers, shirring and ruffles create rounded effects and express animation. Other details might include piquant lines, which can best be described as curved lines that curl to a point, as in collars unfurling like the petal of a flower or petal shapes. Petal shapes are especially flattering to a slim person with a pointed chin.

Illus. 101

Illus. 102

82   The Color Connection

Illus. 103

Illus. 104

Illus. 105

• **Design Lines:** Spring or Animated, Light-bright types express themselves best with the circular form and with curved lines, which are feminine and reflect the natural roundness of the Spring woman's body. An exception to the *circular form* rule is the pert and youthful looking square collar so often used in the nautical look or the perky little points on the little boy shirts that are worn so well by some Spring types.

Illus. 106

Illus. 107

Illus. 108

- **Inside Design Lines** such as Peter Pan collars, scallops, petal shapes, ruffles, pleating, buttons, *cute* effects, stand up ruffles, or collars with tuxedo pleats are always small in detail. Ribbing on sweaters and cuffs on shirts are narrow.

Buoyant lines with uplifting qualities, as if held up by air (as in puffed sleeves or bishops sleeve), collars that are rounded or rolled, circle or half circles, scallops, petal shapes, fluted edges — all express gaiety, youth, vigor, and animation, while adding decorative touches.

The more feminine Spring type will want to select slightly curved jacket lines and rounded patch pockets, while the more yang Spring will wear the more preppy look, creating the roundness required by pushing up her sleeves and lifting the collar of a more masculine-styled jacket.

- **Spring harmony design details are small.**

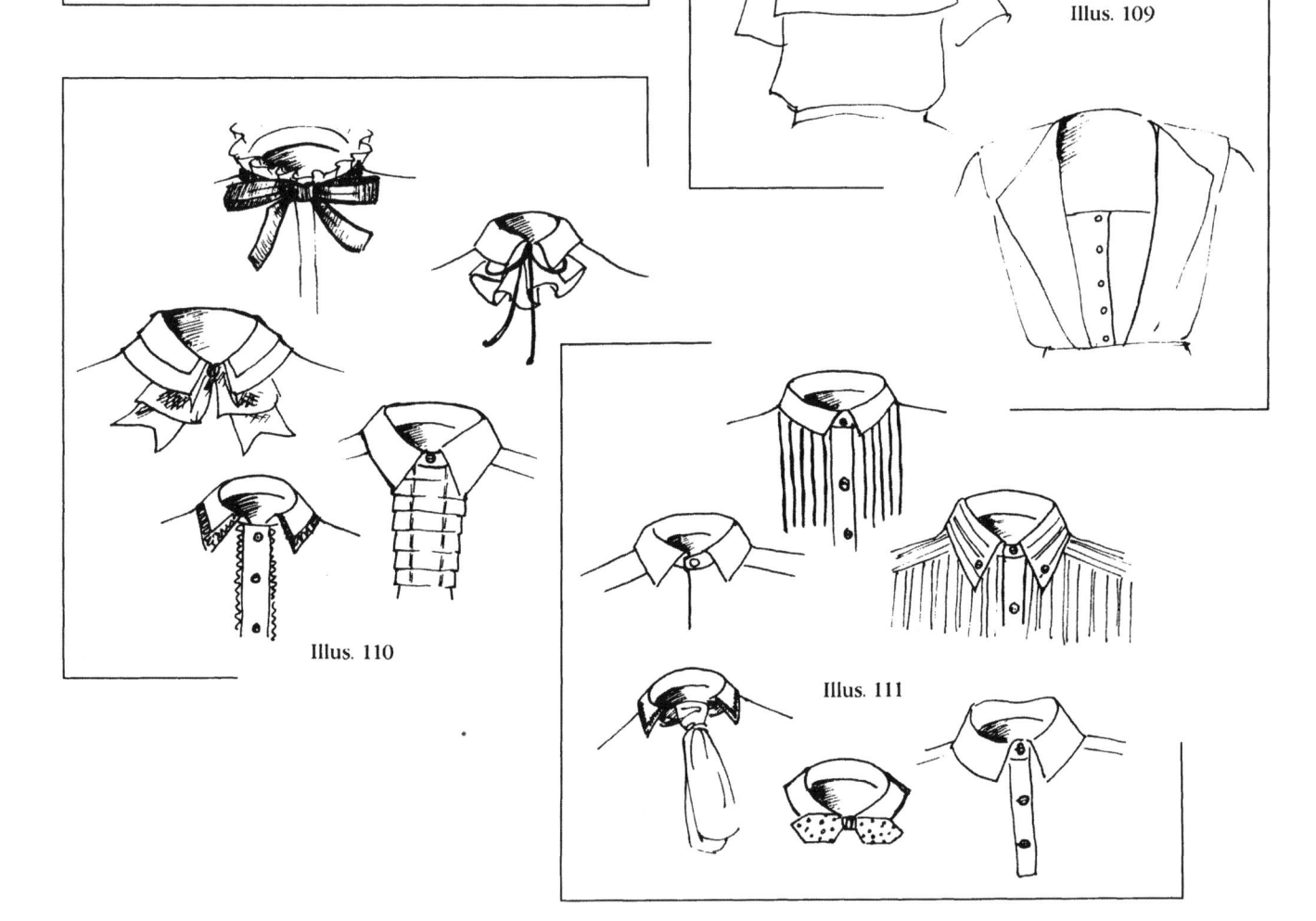

Illus. 109

Illus. 110

Illus. 111

The Color Connection

Unusual Combinations

Denim with Pearls

Illus. 112

Lemon Yellow Plastic Discs

Illus. 113

Illus. 114

Zipper Skirt

- **Fabric choices** for the Spring type are smooth-surfaced fabrics with body. **Think crisp and small detail!**

Cotton: twill, pique, organdy, organza, gingham, chambray, chintz, seersucker, plissé, net (because of its feeling of airiness), dotted swiss, eyelet, and refined gauze. (Dotted Swiss and eyelet seem most appropriate for very yin Spring types.)

Silk or polyester: broadcloth, gabardine, satin, taffeta, crepe de chine, poplin, sheer tissue fabrics. The more *yang* type Spring may wear raw silk or even silk tussah, although purists will assign these fabrics to Autumn. In my experience, if the colors are perfect and the design lines correct, all of the seasonal types will wear silk in almost all of its forms.

Wool: gabardine, smooth flannel, and classic or feminine knits.

The pert Spring image shaker will often combine materials and/or items in unusual and sometimes interesting ways, e.g., lace and leather; or stockings worn with lace trimmed ankle socks and little pumps.

- **Surface prints** for Spring types are fresh and small scaled, as in the distinct and scattered flowers of provincial or calico prints, polka dots, foulard prints, neats, bandana prints, nautical motifs, or windowpane plaids. Teddy bears, lambs, butterflies, hearts and flowers, or other animated effects and amusing ideas suggesting childhood, translated into nursery colors and prints, will be worn by many Spring types. Just as the flowers of Spring are distinct and usually single blossoms (e.g., daffodils and tulips), the prints of the Spring harmony are distinct and scattered.

88 The Color Connection

Organdy with Chambray

Illus. 115

Illus. 116

Illus. 117

- **Hair Styles:** Curly, wispy, fluffy, loose curls, the windblown look, flipped, with tendrils, and wavy are all examples of Spring hair styles that are buoyant and repeat roundness. The current wash and wear tousled look or the playful pixie look of pigtails and ponytails are perfect for the fun-loving Spring type. She usually will prefer a look that is playful, easy care and suited for her active life.

Illus. 118

Illus. 119

- **Hats:** The trendy Spring type gains sudden impact with the surprise of a hat. It might be of light straw, brightly colored or multi-colored with a little brim and rounded lines or decorated with crisp bows, small flowers or clusters of flowers, such as violets. The brim might be turned up to create an uplifted perky look. Her hat is typically perky and pert rather than dramatic or soft and romantic looking.

- **Bags** in all of her bright colors should be somewhat rounded in shape or with scallops and/or cute or whimsical ideas, e.g., a bag in the shape of a watermelon slice or a stuffed toucan perched on the shoulder with a bag below. A brightly colored shoulder bag, bouncing on the hip, is totally in character for a bubbly Spring type.

- **Jewelry** should be light, open, and small in scale for the Spring type. In addition to yellow gold, she will enjoy all of the new fun looks, including colorful enamels, cloisonné, ceramic, plastic, handblown glass, etc. She will wear everything from computer chips to the finest crystal — whatever the current fad and in whatever trendy material. She often seems to enjoy animated, whimsical jewelry, as well, such as bunnies, teddy bears, cats, frogs, etc. Her stones are determined by her colors, e.g., turquoise, opals, moonstones, diamonds, emeralds, yellow topaz, coral, and aquamarine.

92 The Color Connection

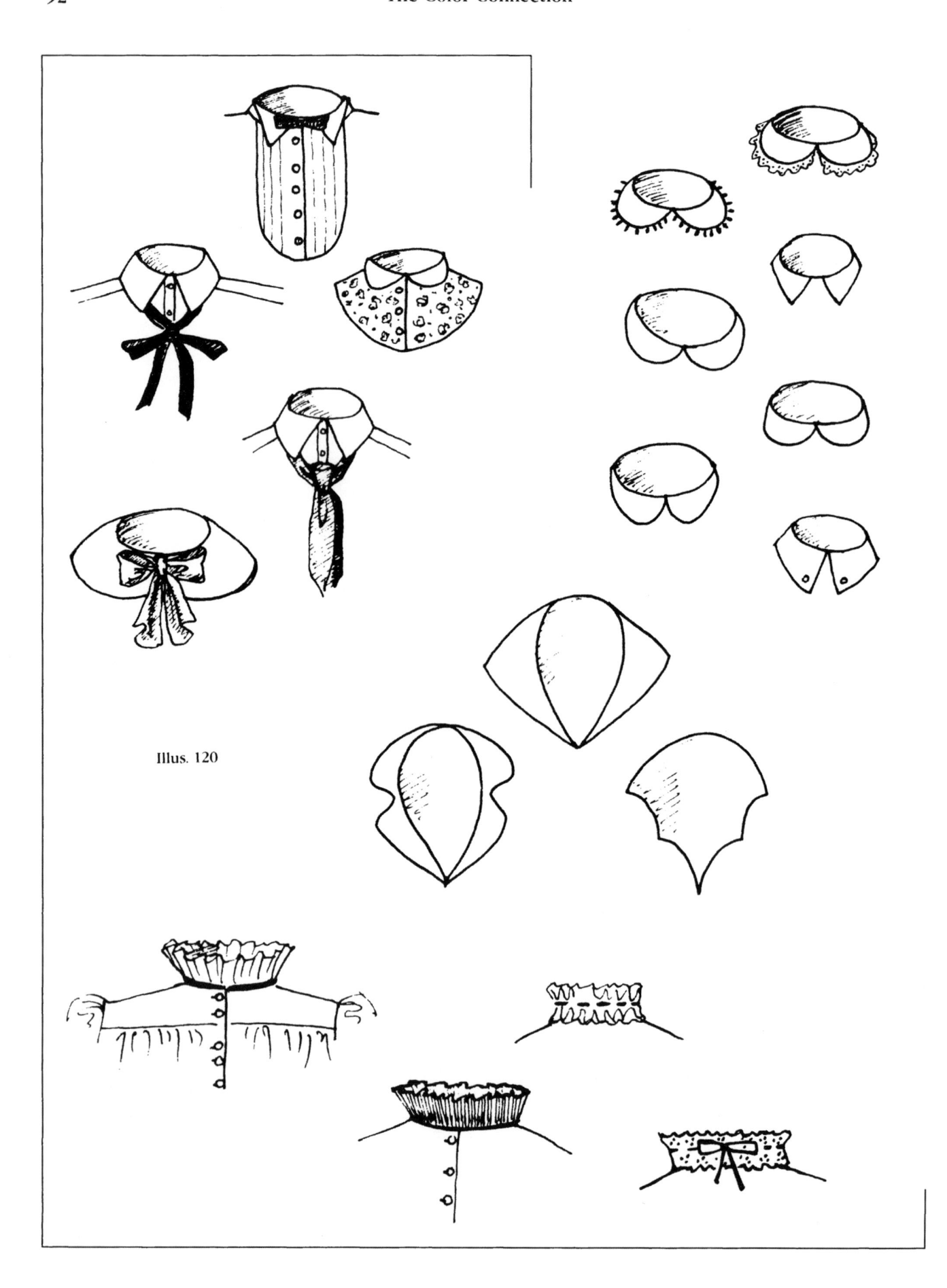

Illus. 120

- **Necklines** should, of course, always be well suited to the shape of her face first and foremost. The square nautical collar, for instance, although a Spring effect, should not be worn by an individual with a square jawline. Other examples of neckline detail most appropriate for Spring types include: little pressed pleats, eyelet, stand-up crisp ruffles, small collars with tuxedo pleats, Peter Pan collars in all of their variations, narrow notched collars, cricket and button-down collars, bateau, jewel, scooped, or turtlenecks. She will add lacy collars, little pert bows of fairly crisp fabric, or narrow velvet or grosgrain ribbon.

Her collars may have tatted edges, scallops, eyelet with narrow ribbon run through, embroidery, or applique trim. They may have beadwork or embroidery in shapes of flowers, hearts, insects, or other animated figures.

Spring detailing includes contrasting top stitching, rows of little buttons, little pressed pleats, contouring, gathers and shirring. The preppy or traditional sporty casual collar treatment found in active sportswear are good looks for the active Spring type.

- **Buttons** should be *small in scale*. They may be round or in shapes of flowers, hearts, teddy bears, etc. These may seem too casual or cute for some occasions, but for a more elegant look the flowers and even heart shapes can be made of jade, ivory or mother of pearl. Buttons provide light/bright contrast: e.g., colored buttons on white ground; white buttons on colored ground; or gold metallic trimmed colored or white buttons. Brass nautical looking buttons are Spring effects.

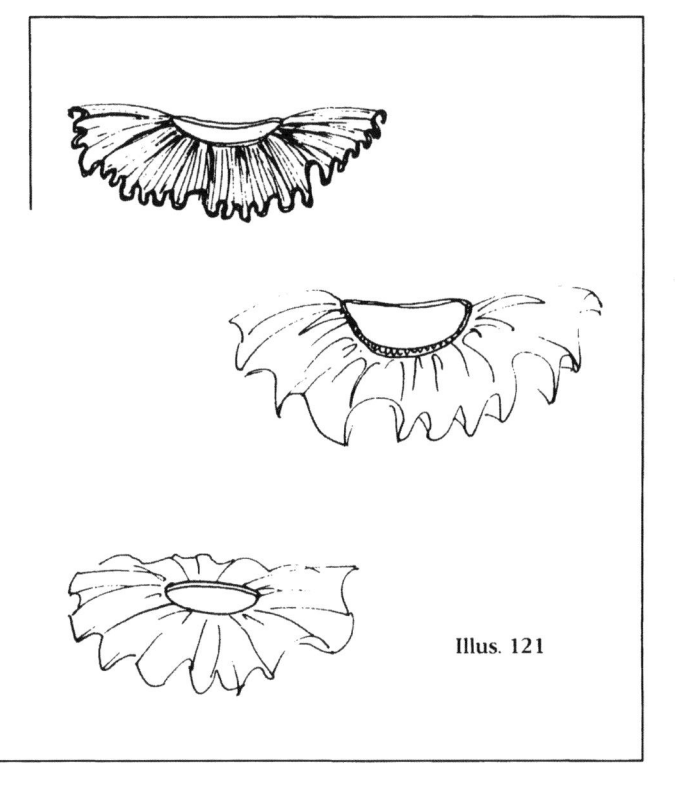

Illus. 121

The Color Connection

Illus. 122

Spring

- **Sleeves** may be softly gathered or fully puffed as in a puffed, bishop or bouffant sleeve. Petal shapes on sleeves are excellent for the Spring type, too. Her short sleeves may be pleated with little button detail or even that of the camp shirt. The camp shirt sleeve may seem a little too squared off for a Spring if it is too full. Most Springs will roll a too-full camp shirt sleeve to give it an uplifted look.

The Spring type will often roll or push up her long sleeves too — again to give that buoyant feeling by creating a rounded silhouette. At the same time, she will probably lift her collar to give an unfurling petal effect, so typical of the Spring season.

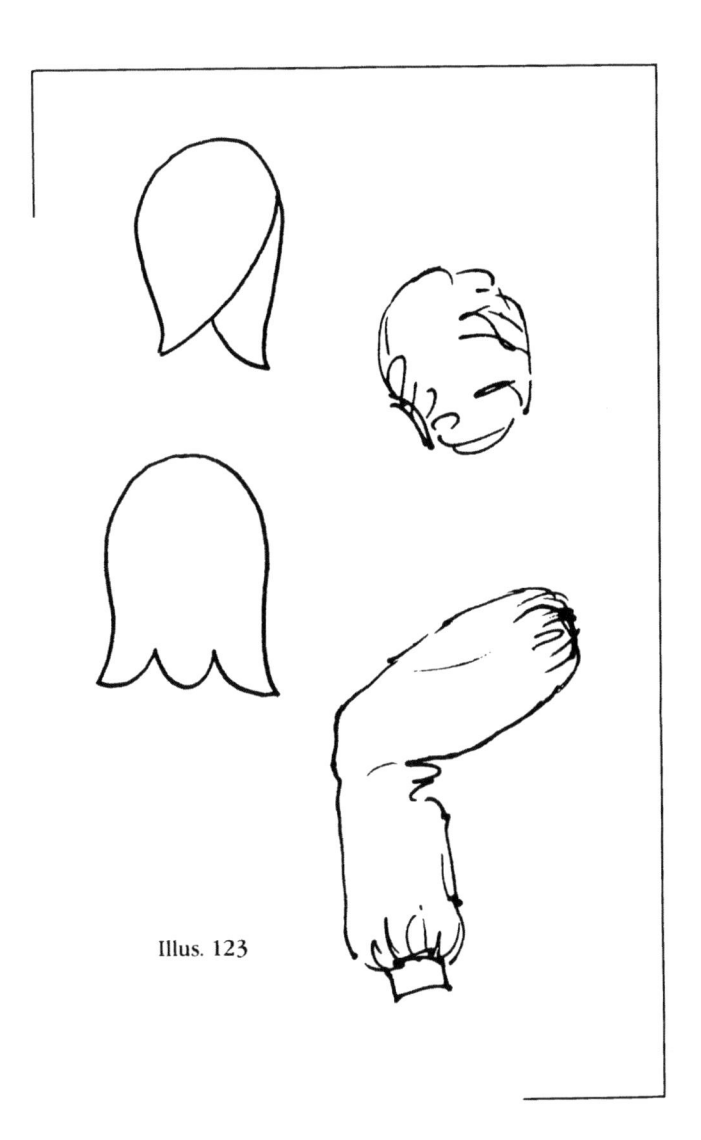

Illus. 123

96　　　　　　　　　　The Color Connection

Illus. 124

Illus. 125

Illus. 126

Illus. 127

Illus. 128

- **Skirts** may be dirndl, gored or shaped gored as in the trumpet skirt, A-line, or any that express the animation, flippancy or buoyancy of Spring. Scalloped, petal or tulip hemlines are perfect for Spring types. Petal and tulip shapes are often created by the overlapping of wrap skirts. Occasionally extra gusset-like detail (godet) may be used to make a trumpet skirt even more *flippy*.

Skirts with top-stitched yokes, little pocket details or tiny buttons are perfect for the Spring type. Yokes, either V-shaped or rounded, might be top-stitched over either pressed pleats or shirring.

Gathers, ruffles and shirring create natural rounded effects, expressive of Spring types. Skirts may have exposed zipper treatment, multiple pockets or pockets in unusual places, with contrast top-stitching or little buttons. Additional Spring details to watch for are: scalloped hemlines or tucks with scallops, embroidered flower details, round shapes or print motifs.

Illus. 129

98 The Color Connection

A Continuum of Style

Illus. 130

Illus. 131

Illus. 132

- **Dresses** should be in solids or well defined small-to-medium scale prints of animated motifs, such as those often found in children's rooms or in their drawings; the country or provincial look; chambray, stripes or plaids in combinations of their colors, e.g., red and white; pink and blue; pink, blue and white; aqua, pink and yellow; rainbow colors, or rainbow colors with white.

Dresses should not be too soft, drapable or romantic looking. Fabrics should be crisp and natural, such as cotton, linen, small scaled basket-weave in wool, wool gabardine, raw silk, silk broadcloth — and always in the colors of Spring with a light bright effect. Whatever the fabric, the style should include some feminine detailing.

Remember that the very feminine Spring type (one with a high percentage of yin characteristics) will wear dainty designs, dotted Swiss, eyelet, embroidered collars, e.g., the provincial or prairie look. A less feminine type may prefer the *preppy* look.

The latter Spring type will often wear shirtwaist dresses, but with pleated fronts, tucked and pleated sleeves, little buttons, Peter Pan or cricket collars, in her colors and in small prints. She will usually like this dress cut fairly fitted, sometimes with a shirttail hem or vents to provide ease for walking.

The Spring shirtwaist dress might typically have little pleats down the front of the bodice with many small colored buttons in contrast, roll-up sleeves and a small top-stitched collar. It could be in a madras that is not too faded looking, chambray, denim, or any other crisp, fresh looking fabric.

Other dress detail might include: petal shapes, piping, applique, crisp bows, crisp ruffles, scallops, embroidery, top-stitching, ribbons, smocking, shirring, rickrack, or tucking.

The Color Connection

Illus. 134

Illus. 136

Illus. 133

Illus. 135

- **Pants** for the Spring type would include almost all of the casual or active sportswear looks. Jeans seem made for her, especially the ones with appliques, floral prints, top-stitched designs, etc. I have noticed that she is the only seasonal type who wears jeans as an adult in public without apology. Other pant styles might include those with rolled up cuffs, crop pants, knickers, sailor pants or bell bottoms, the reversed silhouette or baggy look. All of the fun fashion pants with little button details and/or multiple pocket arrangements in fashion fabrics and trendy colors are typical of Spring expression. The pull-on pant with elasticized back or little yoke with pressed pleats is also favored by many, especially if it has other *fun* details, such as animated motifs or little pockets, maybe in rows or in unusual groups or in strange places.

Illus. 137

Illus. 138

Illus. 139

Skiwear for All Seasons

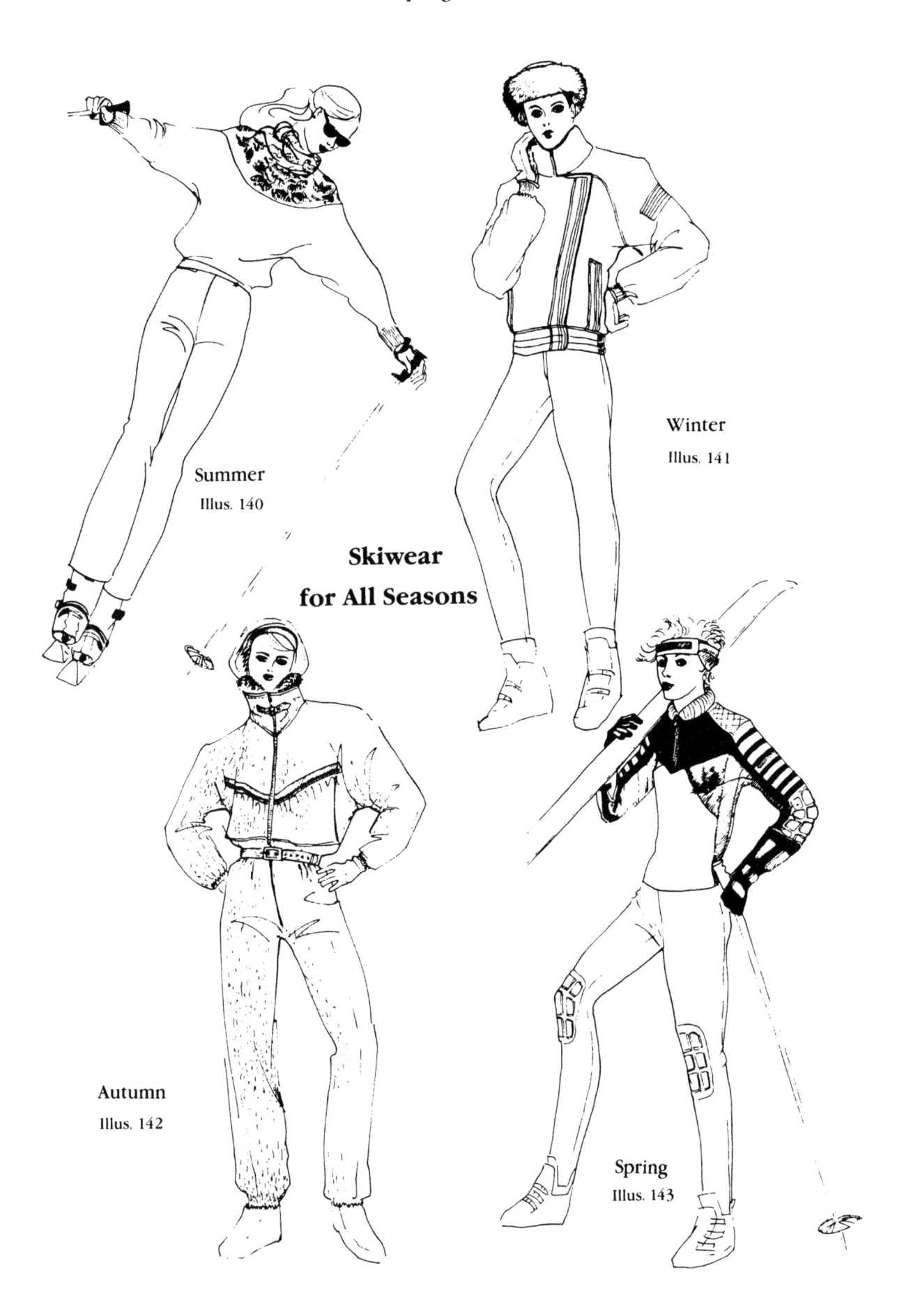

Summer
Illus. 140

Winter
Illus. 141

Autumn
Illus. 142

Spring
Illus. 143

104 The Color Connection

Illus. 145

Illus. 146

Illus. 147

Illus. 148

Illus. 144

• The Spring **professional look** would typically be a tailored or dressmaker suit. Although other seasons may find tailored dresses suitable for their professional look, most Spring types will find it difficult to appear authoritative in a dress. The Spring type tends to look younger than she is and often can appear somewhat scattered because of her animation. So it is vitally important to her professional look that she not look too cute. She should, however, avoid *overcompensating* lest she end up looking as if she is wearing her father's clothes. There is a happy medium that must be reached for the Spring type's professional image: not too cute and yet not too masculine for her young-looking yin visual image.

Just as the Winter suited look varies depending on her place on the continuum of the Seasonal Harmony scale, so does that of the Spring type. She might prefer a crisp look in a jacket with either a narrow pointed or rounded notched collar. She would even like the dressmaker look of a shorter jacket, perhaps one having pockets decorated with piping or with little buttons.

Or she might favor the classic preppy look with brass buttons on the blazer. The jacket can even have the current oversized shoulder treatment or the longer look. The Spring woman will probably *create* a pert look by pushing up the sleeves of this jacket and lifting the collar, simulating an unfurling petal, a Spring symbol.

Another example would be a medium bright blue suit with a white blouse or one with a windowpane plaid of the white and blue, with a Peter Pan, cricket or button down collar, little buttons, and with a besom pocket with a button and button-loop, accessorized with a little crisp bow, a grosgrain ribbon tie, or even the man-styled four-in-hand knot. Whichever she chooses, it will always be worn with a light-bright, fresh look.

She might add a whimsical vest. The jacket might be trendy, such as the current big shouldered, almost man-tailored styling or it might be a Spencer jacket or a hacking jacket. The Spring type will also layer blouses with vests, roll up sleeves, even roll blouse sleeve up over jacket or sweater sleeve and push the whole thing up.

Her jacket might have small, even slightly rounded narrow lapels, buttons on the sleeve or a little pleat with a button. The one essential is that it must be pert looking — not masculine. Little

Illus. 149

Illus. 150

The Color Connection

Illus. 151

Illus. 152

Illus. 153

Illus. 154

Illus. 155

stand up collars, polka dot or foulard ties, stick pins, rainbow groups of colors in beads or other jewelry, flowers, and narrow or shaped belts complete the animated look.

• To **formalize** her wardrobe, the Spring woman should apply all of the characteristics of the rest of her wardrobe. For a conservative look she might try a shirtwaist dress in a silk broadcloth or silk-like fabric, with pleating, tucking or shirring on the front of the bodice, perhaps off a yoke, with a little collar or contrasting collars and cuffs, and in her more sophisticated colors.

A peplum (a short overskirt) on a dress of taffeta or moiré ribbon stripe or a shirred dropped waistline dress in a Monet-like water print would be suitable to formalize for a Spring type. Small rows of pearlized or self-covered buttons would be appropriate Spring detail, as would a lace or tatted panel in the yoke. A gold mesh belt might be a dressy addition as would an appliqued belt in a fresh look.

Scale and color must be correct. Scale still must be small — no exaggerated bows or too dramatic effects. The Spring type might choose her more understated, elegant or sophisticated colors for her formal wear. She can use sequins, especially in designs such as butterflies, flowers, or any that show animation and perkiness.

The Spring woman frequently bemoans the fact that her Winter friends always look so elegant and sophisticated: "Why can't Springs ever find something like that in their colors?" The truth of the matter is that if she *did* find those kinds of styles in her colors, she would probably not be comfortable with the look. It might seem overpowering and too dramatic-looking for her pert looks, personality and life style. Many Spring types seem much too fun-loving and adventuresome to be concerned about formality. Sophisticated, dramatic elegance in clothing style and typical Spring "life-of-the-party" behavior are not always compatible. She will often look for the more *kicky* pert looks for her night life.

Illus. 156

108 The Color Connection

Illus. 157

• **Shoes** may be strappy sandals, a narrow strap with a little button, small woven effects, tiny buckles or bows, spectator pumps in contrasting colors, plain pumps, open toed pumps, shiny patent leather, smooth leather, or colored cloth shoes. The straps or her sandals should be thin straps; many of the heavier luggage brown sandals are too heavy looking for a Spring and, in fact, are for Autumns. Spring's shoes may have straps of many colors, rope soles on rainbow colored canvas (rope is also an Autumn effect, so care should be taken that the look for Spring is kept light, not heavy or burdensome), small heels, stacked leather heels in contrast with the tops, or rainbow colors.

Unless her basic neutral is black, the Spring type should avoid black leather as a basic. Frequently a college-age Spring type will come into Tarika, looking for a black belt to wear with a brightly colored dress. I usually ask why she wants a black belt, which I find to be deadening the whole effect. Her reply usually is something like "The only shoes that I have to wear with it are black." In the interest of economy, her mother has advised her, "We can only get one pair of dressy shoes for you to take to school, so they had better be black. Black goes with everything." Of course, that is true.

Black does go with almost anything, but not always harmoniously. It doesn't necessarily create a well put-together look for the light/bright Spring type unless it is repeated elsewhere in the outfit or unless they are black patent leather, which is quite appropriate for the Spring look.

She was on the right track in looking for a way to repeat the black in the outfit. But the look she was creating was anything but harmonious. The black belt gave a heavy look to her bright Spring dress, as would the black shoes — especially for a Spring.

If the Spring (or any other type, actually), can afford only one pair of shoes, a better choice in my opinion would be either her hair color or her best taupe. Taupe shoes literally will go with everything — black, brown, blue, pink, red, etc. They will not look heavy or out of place if they have to be worn with a light or bright color and there will be no need to repeat the truly neutral and innocuous taupe elsewhere in the outfit.

In addition to her best neutrals, the Spring woman should turn to her colors for her shoes,

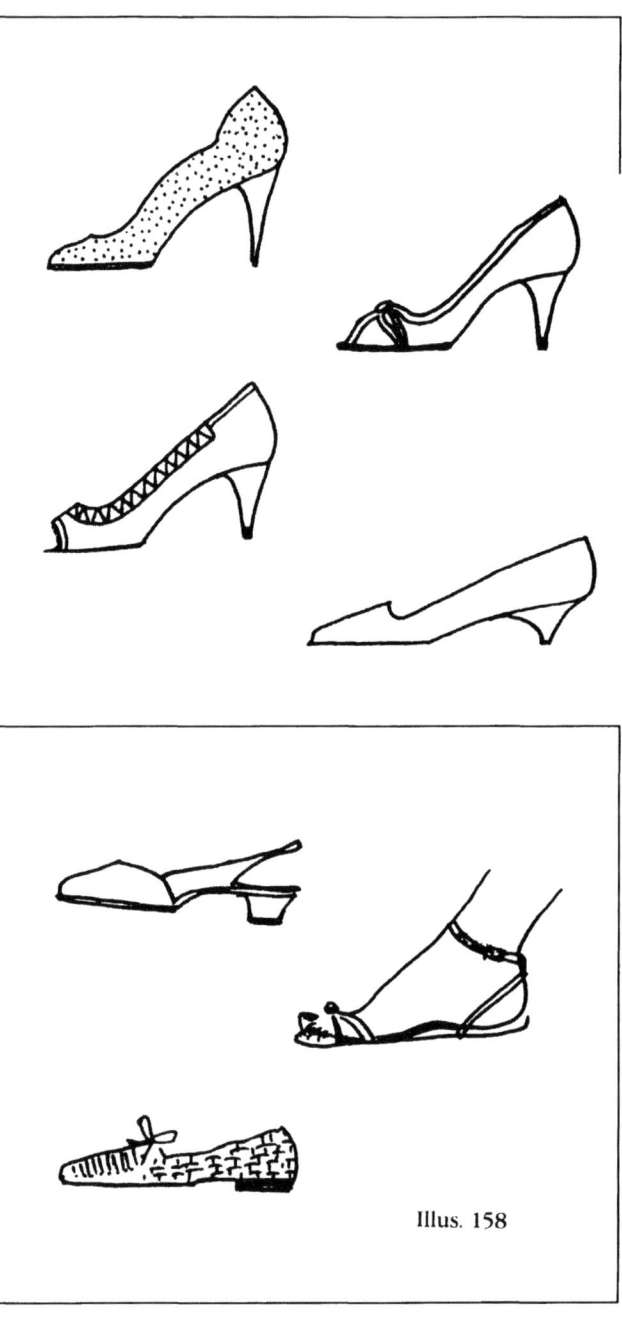

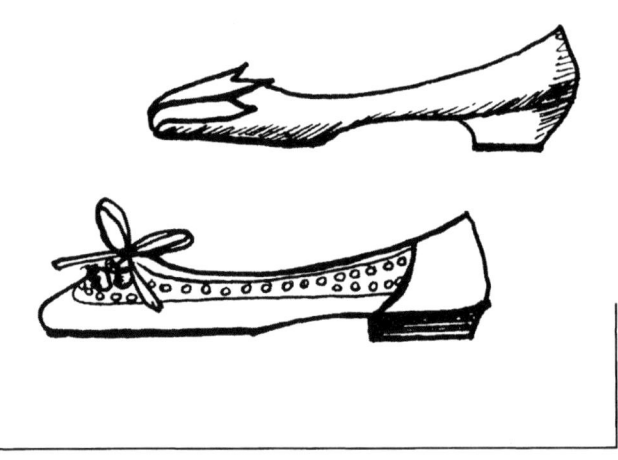

Illus. 158

Illus. 159

Illus. 160

Illus. 161

Illus. 162

especially her related reds. Whether a Spring type will enjoy using all of her colors in her shoes depends somewhat on whether she wishes to draw attention to her feet and/or legs. In any case, if a bright color is worn on the feet, the color should be repeated elsewhere in the outfit.

• Her **coat** should have feminine tailoring qualities and be softly pleated, have shirring from a yoke, or have the preppy or nautical look. She should avoid the trench coat or too masculine look, however. A Chesterfield is considered a Spring design, as are the pea coat and the jean jacketed look.

And for the cooler climates, the polo coat could be worn, but it should not look too bulky or burdensome. A cape with contrast trim, top stitching or braid detail is appropriate for a Spring if in a Spring color and with enough small detail — not too bold a statement. Shiny slickers or oilcloth-type coats are also perfect for the Spring type.

Illus. 163

Illus. 164

112   The Color Connection

Illus. 165

Illus. 166

Illus. 167

Illus. 168

- **Knits** should be feminine in character or have the preppy look. Watch for boucle, pointelle, scallops, little patterns in the knit, as well as animated designs, such as windmills, butterflies, little animals, and/or flowers, hearts, etc.

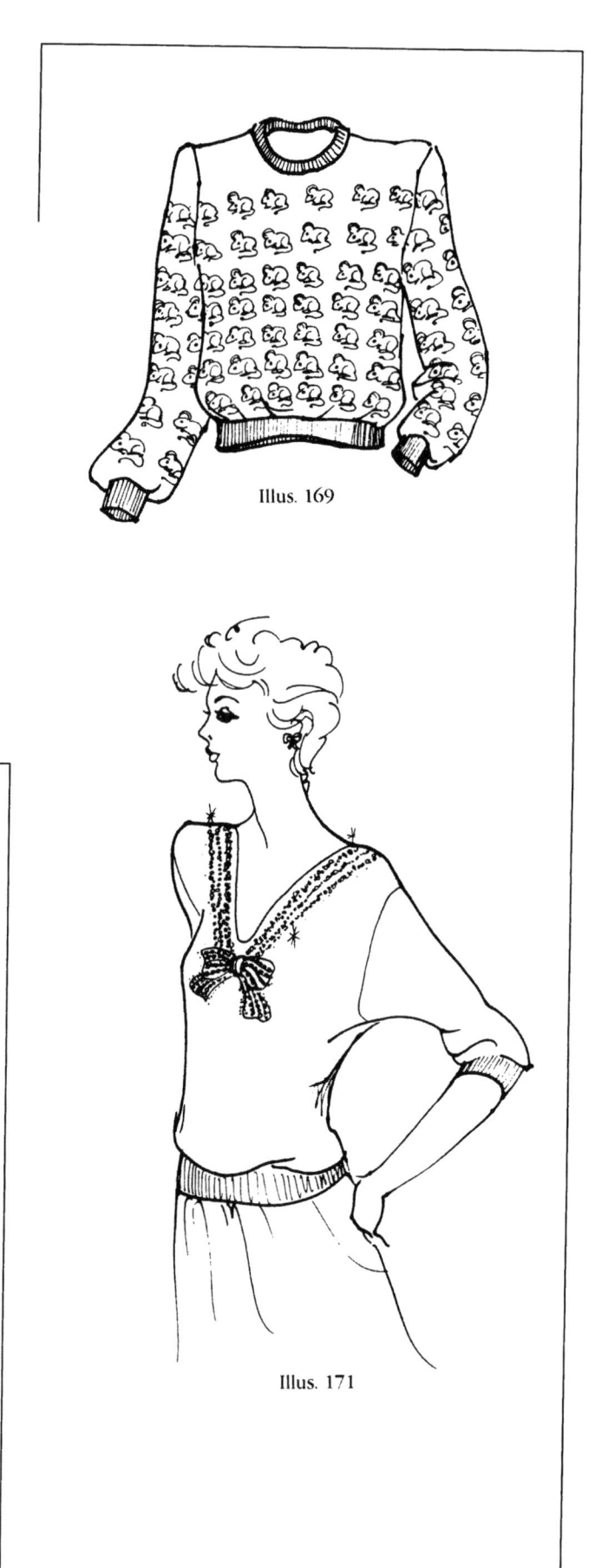

Illus. 169

Illus. 170

Illus. 171

- **Contrast** — Springs wear contrast, but it is a fresher, lighter, brighter contrast than the contrast of Winter. If the contrast is navy and white, with the Spring type it will be white collar or yoke treatment on navy with white cuffs perhaps or a little white print; or white with navy trim.

> **The overall look of Spring is one of tucks, scallops, pleats, gathers, and shirring, contrasted top stitching, pressed down pleats, fresh pert cute ideas, feminine tailoring and feminine knits.**

The Spring Man is people-oriented, popular, gregarious, physically active, and fun-loving. He likes adventure and to be on the move. Just as there is more variation in the likes and dislikes of the Spring woman style-wise, there is variety in the colors and styles of the Spring man. Some may favor colors associated with the blue and green shades of sky and water. Others, often considered more rugged types, may prefer colors from the browns and yellows. There are others who will gravitate to navy blue with white.

Like the Winter man, the Spring man also likes to dress well, but his look tends to be more casual. He likes his somewhat close fitting jackets to have pockets; they can be patch pockets with or without flaps or even multiple pockets. He likes the active look of polo and rugby shirts, Western detail, top-stitching, the Ivy League or nautical look, button-down collars, a bomber jacket, baseball jacket, Hawaiian or other flashy prints.

Just as the Spring woman is the golden girl or girl-next-door type, the Spring man also has that golden boy or boy-next-door appearance, partially due to his glowing skin with yellow undertones, but also because of his natural, youthful, out-going personality.

His neutrals, which he would use for his suit colors, might include: warm yellow-based ivory, beige, camels, taupes, and chocolate brown; or a clear bright navy or light to medium gray. He will probably like the more casual look of a plaid, twill, tweed, or herringbone jacket with gabardine or flannel slacks. His dress suit might be in a soft dove gray or a bright clear navy.

His basic colors are in the medium shades of a yellow-based red, a soft gold, clear blue, and a clear teal. A Spring man should look for these colors combined with neutrals in his suiting fabrics, e.g., a fine line of the orange red in a brown glen plaid.

Bright colors to be used for activewear, mixed in prints for his more casual looks, or as accents would include sky blue, violet, teal, periwinkle blue, coral, as well as the colors of fruit, such as cherry, lime, tangerine, orange and lemon.

His shirt colors would be taken from all of the pastels or lighter tones of the above mentioned bright colors of Spring, e.g., aqua, peach, cream, pale seafoam green, shell pink, light blue, light turquoise, light periwinkle. His pastels will not be quite so light as the icy pastels of the Winter type.

His ties will be the little Ivy League prints, e.g., multi-colored stripes, foulard, neats, or small dots in crisp fabrics; or solid knits, linen, etc. He will probably prefer yellow gold jewelry.

Some Famous Spring Women: June Allyson, Shirley Temple Black, Carol Channing, Doris Day, Zsa Zsa Gabor, Goldie Hawn, Judy Holliday, Angela Lansbury, Marilyn Monroe, Debbie Reynolds, Dinah Shore, Mary Martin, Helen Hayes, Shirley MacLean, Julie Andrews, Marsha Mason.

Some Famous Spring Men: Bob Hope, Robert Redford, Frank Sinatra.

Some Spring People that I Know: (add your own friends, relatives, clients, etc. that you believe to be Spring types.)

The following words have been attributed to the Spring Seasonal Color Harmony. (Using this list and the ones at the conclusion of each of the other seasons, **make a word portrait** of yourself by listing the words that relate to you in any way, such as your personality characteristics and/or physical attributes, your affinity for what the word describes, e.g., dancing. This word portrait may be an aid in discovering your percentages of each of the seasonal harmonies. Some words appear in more than one season.

active
adventuresome
airy
animated
athletic
beaming
blithesome
bold
boyish
bracing
bright
bubbly
buoyant
candid
casual
charming
cheerful
cheering
clean
clear
coquettish
coy
crisp
cute
dainty
dancing
daring
debonair
delectable
delicate

demure
devilish
dewy
easygoing
effervescent
elfin-like
enchanting
exuberant
fairy-like
feisty
feminine
festive
flirtatious
floral
frank
fresh
freshly-scrubbed
friendly
frivolous
frolicsome
fun
gamin-like
gay
glowing
golden
humorous
idyllic
impish
impudent
infectious

innocent
inspiriting
joyous
jubilant
jaunty
kicky
leaping
light
light-hearted
lilting
limpid
lively
lyrical
melodic
merry
mischievous
natural
naughty-but-nice
new
open
optimistic
outgoing
outspoken
perky
pert
piquant
pixie
playful
pretty
princess-like

provincial
quick
radiant
rapturous
refreshing
renewing
saucy
shining
simple
sincere
sparkling
spirited
spontaneous
sprightly
straightforward
sunny
twinkling
uncomplicated
unconcerned
unpremeditated
vital
vivacious
vivid
whimsical
winsome
youthful
zestful

Illus. 172

7
Summer

The hot summer sun beats down and brings a subtle change to the colors in my garden: they are softer, quieter, more muted and blended than those of spring. The perennial plants seem to blend together, both in color and in growth, often with many blooms to a stalk. Replacing the independent, distinct blooms of spring are the multi-floral Sweet William, candytuft, red coral bells, bleeding hearts, primroses, astilbe, phlox, and liatris. The lines of Summer are relaxed and undulating, the soft fluid movement of the S-curve corresponding to the lazy-in-the-shade softness and gentleness of the summer mood and the romance associated with an English perennial garden, as well as to the graceful lines of the long spikes of gladiola, hollyhock, columbine and delphinium. On the patio there are tubs of petunias, lobelia, and anemones; hanging baskets of fuchsias and begonias. Lush roses, the symbol of the Summer seasonal type, bloom exquisitely in abundance.

The Summer woman is similarly soft, quiet, muted and blended—both in coloring and personality. Her skin is a pink that usually doesn't tan (or shouldn't) or sometimes peach or light rose, all with lavender undertones, which subdues her coloring. (The undertones, in this case, lavender, can usually be seen around the eyes where the skin is thinnest.) She should avoid forced tanning, which usually produces mottled or freckled skin and often premature aging effects in the fragile Summer skin. Her hair is often a non-descript color, or combination of colors, not easily named, such as strawberry blonde, ash blonde, grayish

Illus. 173

Illus. 174

brown, light brown, or gray; her eyes are likewise often combinations of colors that are not easily described, such as misty-blue, gray-blue or powdery-blue; or sometimes gray-green, bottle green, brown, or what is often described as "hazel" for lack of a better term.

The Summer type is gentle and soft-spoken with relaxed mannerisms. Some words that help to conjure up a visual image of the Summer woman are: romantic, ladylike, sensitive, meticulous, ethereal, feminine, pretty, and graceful. She may seem iridescent and dreamy; her voice is usually soft and understated, almost musical in quality. Her mannerisms, her walk, and her way of speaking are all reminiscent of that lazy-in-the-shade summer day — much more leisurely, dreamy, and formal than her quick, light-bright Spring counterpart. She uses her long, tapering fingers and delicate, graceful hands in a similar manner.

She has a warm, loving nature. She usually has a well-cared-for look, which can probably be attributed to her meticulous attention to details in every aspect of her life. She tends to be careful, conscientious and fastidious. She is very sensitive, intuitive, and artistic and may seem just a little shy, but this may be accounted for by her typical ladylike reserve. These *gentle* words should not be construed to mean she is not strong, capable, and assertive; her ways of accomplishing things are just apt to be quiet and gentle.

Summer colors are similarly quiet and soft, appearing tinged with gray, blue or rose. The fresh new yellow-greens of spring turn blue-green in summer sun. The hot sun causes the clear or yellow-reds of spring to become blue-red; violet becomes soft lavender and mauve. As summer progresses, muted colors become even softer or more blended.

The Summer type's analogous colors are harmoniously worn together since they are blended one with the other all around the color wheel, with the exception of yellow. Yellows are rarely, if ever, included in a Summer's palette, as they usually cause her skin to appear yellow, sallow or jaundiced.

The Summer or gentle type wears cool-based colors that appear as though seen in the shade or, particularly in the case of her medium to dark colors, as though slightly faded from long exposure to the sun (or as cut roses look after they have been in a vase for a few days): blue-reds, purples,

Illus. 175

Illus. 176

blues, blue-greens, soft grayed greens, beiges and browns related to her skin tones, off white, and light to medium value grays. Her *best* colors are *medium to light value with medium to subdued intensities*. Her colors should not be so intense as to compete for attention and overpower her visual image and personality. If she wears colors which are too bright or intense, she is apt to appear washed-out, pale or ashen.

Design Lines: A Summer seasonal harmony type expresses herself best with the oval shape. She will wear finely tailored feminine designs in *soft and fine-grained* fabrics with undulating lines or S-curves (known as lines of grace), expressing softness, gentleness, romanticism, and elegance.

• The **outside silhouette** should provide an oval shape whenever possible with sloped shoulders rather than heavily padded square ones, full draping sleeves and other draped and or shirred effects. These lines of grace add the softness and feminine beauty and dignity necessary to create an image harmonious with the inner and outer qualities of the similarly soft, feminine and dignified Summer type woman.

124 The Color Connection

Illus. 177

Illus. 178

Illus. 179

- **Design Details:** The Summer type requires *fine tailoring* with draped, cascading, flowing or fluid lines, soft gathers or unpressed pleats. She wears soft ruffles, but her ruffles are wider and more relaxed than the crisp ones of Spring. Style details express fluidity: floating panels; capelets; handkerchief or other uneven hemlines; princess lines; short dressmaker jackets; circle or semi-circle skirts in soft, flowing fabrics; and butterfly, raglan or dolman sleeves. Styles adapted from other periods in history, such as Victorian or turn-of-the-century, are often romantic Summer looks.

Other details include cascading ruffles, trailing ribbons, soft bows, silk flowers, lace, soft wide brim picture hats, embroidery, and either covered or pearlized, small-to-medium buttons. Her ornamentation should convey movement through such design details as S-shapes, shell shapes or flowing ribbons.

Of all of the seasonal harmony types, it is especially important for the Summer woman to have continuity and consistency of design lines from head to toe, probably because she exudes a ladylike, well-cared-for, meticulous kind of image. The Summer woman will not only *appear* more centered and confident if she is harmoniously put together, she will feel more so, too. For this reason, she should pay special attention to consistency of details. Hairstyle and make-up should be soft and flattering. Handbags should have rounded corners or be oval in shape, perhaps with shirred effects that might be created by softly knotted, twisted or draped pieces of material. Details on shoes similarly should be oval in shape.

If she carries a datebook/organizer, she may prefer a romantic Edwardian diary or a blended floral print cloth covered book rather than a leather one. If she must carry a briefcase, she might consider a document bag of soft leather or a feminine tapestry fabric. This would be consistent with her overall look.

Illus. 180

Illus. 181

Illus. 182

- **Fabrics** should be both soft *and* fine-grained, drapable, smooth, pliable, or with a fluid quality, such as crepe de chine, georgette, batiste, chiffon, lawn, velvet, velveteen, soft wools, cashmere, angora, velour, delicate lace, cutwork, silk noil, soft broadcloth, silk tulle, challis, matte jersey, no-wale corduroy, or the new, very soft fine-wale corduroy, moiré, fine gauze, rayon-linen blends, fine linen or silk.

- **Surface Prints and Patterns:** Floral patterns in muted watercolors that are blended, misty, indistinct and vague are typical prints for the Summer type. Patterns should be delicate blends of color, tone on tone, quiet and watery-looking. Reproductions of the Summer flowers that are full and open, such as the rose or peonies, or ones that have undulating lines and/or trailing or cascading qualities, such as the gladiola, wisteria, columbine, or delphinium are especially appropriate for Summer prints.

- **Hair styles** may be short to medium length, softly oval styles, or a longer, more softly waved and romantic look to complement the oval, classic and often less well-defined coloring of the Summer type. Sometimes the face of the Summer woman has a molded, sculpted, or even chiseled and well-defined look, which will be softened by her choice of cascades of softly curled or wavy hair. She usually will not have quite the controlled look of the Winter woman nor will she have the casual wash-and-wear look of the Spring type. She may wear her hair softly up-swept with curling tendrils falling on the nape of her neck and about her ears, as in the Gibson Girl look.

- **Hats** should have soft, wide brims and undulating lines, as in the S-curve of a picture hat. The brims may be uneven from wide to narrow or oval in shape. They may be adorned with medium to large silky or velvet flowers, such as roses (which are the symbol of Summer), ostrich feathers, or with soft bows of lace, silk or velvet. Whatever the ornamentation, it should have some movement to it, as in the cascading flowers of Summer. The Summer type often enjoys flowers or bands of flowers in her hair.

- **Necklines** that drape softly are ideal, e.g., cowl, cascading, portrait necklines, stock ties, jabots, portrait collar treatments, or any that present an oval shape. For her business look, a Summer type may prefer a classic notched-collar blouse in a soft fabric, with some shirring off a yoke, at the sleeve cap, and at the cuffs of the sleeves. She may wear it with little or no ornamentation.
- **Sleeves:** The Summer type will usually favor a fuller sleeve in her blouses with some softness at both the shoulder and the cuff. She is not usually drawn to the exaggerated-shoulder look. If, however, she has a triangle or pear shape, she may wish to use some shoulder padding to balance her hips. The look of shoulder pads will often appear softer and therefore more pleasing to the Summer woman when they are used with a kimono or dolman sleeve rather than a set-in sleeve.

Instead of rolling the sleeves on her blouses and jackets, she may prefer a more buttoned-up look, since she stereotypically is more formal, refined and meticulous than her Spring sister. Note, however, that the Summer type who wishes to appear taller (and slimmer) may adopt the technique of pushing up her sleeves and lifting her collar, which will give the illusion of added inches to her height.

- **Buttons** of shell or pearlized materials, or very unobtrusive ones, such as buttons dyed-to-match fabric color or cloth covered buttons of medium scale, are preferable for the Summer type. Oval or shell shapes in buttons would also be excellent, as would a placket front to conceal the buttons. All other types of closures, e.g., zippers, should be concealed.

Illus. 183

Illus. 184

- Her **jewelry** metals are either silver, platinum or rose gold. Cameos, opals, amethysts, jade, turquoise, tourmaline, aquamarine, garnets, rose quartz, or combinations of iridescent gemstones are examples of summer jewelry. These should, of course, be set in one of her metals. S-curved or shell shapes in any of the above materials are an excellent choice for jewelry and/or belt ornamentation. Shells, as well as shell shapes, are also suggested for the Summer type. Pearls, especially in the longer opera lengths which will drape in an oval shape are excellent for Summer women. These may be worn in single or multiple strands or twisted to create the S-curves of Summer.

Her jewelry should be soft and romantic rather than cute or bold and chunky. The Summer type should not overdo ornamentation; her clothes and accessories should never overpower her own visual design. They should enhance with a look that is at once soft, feminine and elegant. For this reason, open work, filigree, braided or linked metals are preferable to heavy bangles or bands. Cloisonné in soft colors with floral designs are appropriate if romantic in feel.

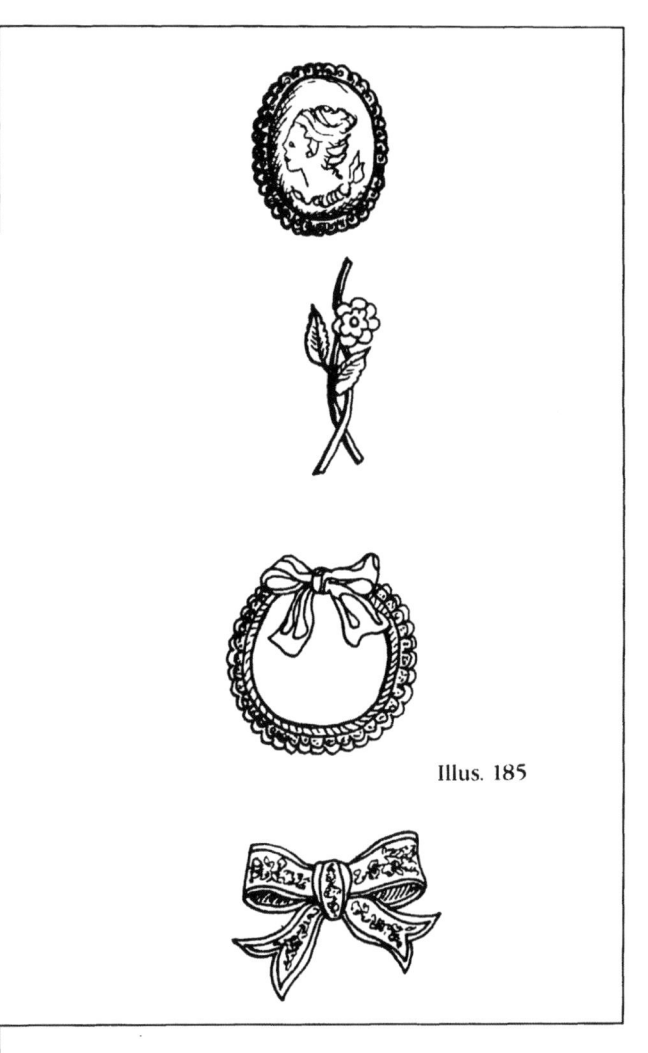

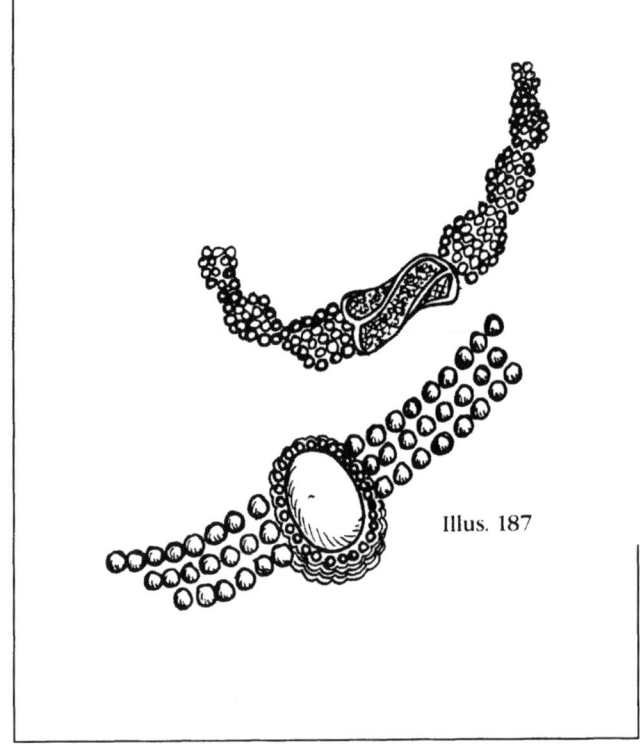

Illus. 185

Illus. 186

Illus. 187

130 The Color Connection

Illus. 188

Illus. 189

Illus. 190

Illus. 191

Illus. 192

Illus. 193

• **Skirts** may be gored, bias-cut circle or semi-circle ones, dirndls, wrap-around or other soft, flowing, draped designs. Handkerchief or other uneven hemlines are particularly appropriate for the Summer look. This is indeed fortunate since so many of the really drapable fabrics preferred by the Summer type, such as rayon, tend to *become* uneven at the hemline whether planned or not.

Whatever design she chooses, the fabric will need to be drapable to create a soft, flowy effect that will have movement and somewhat mold to the body.

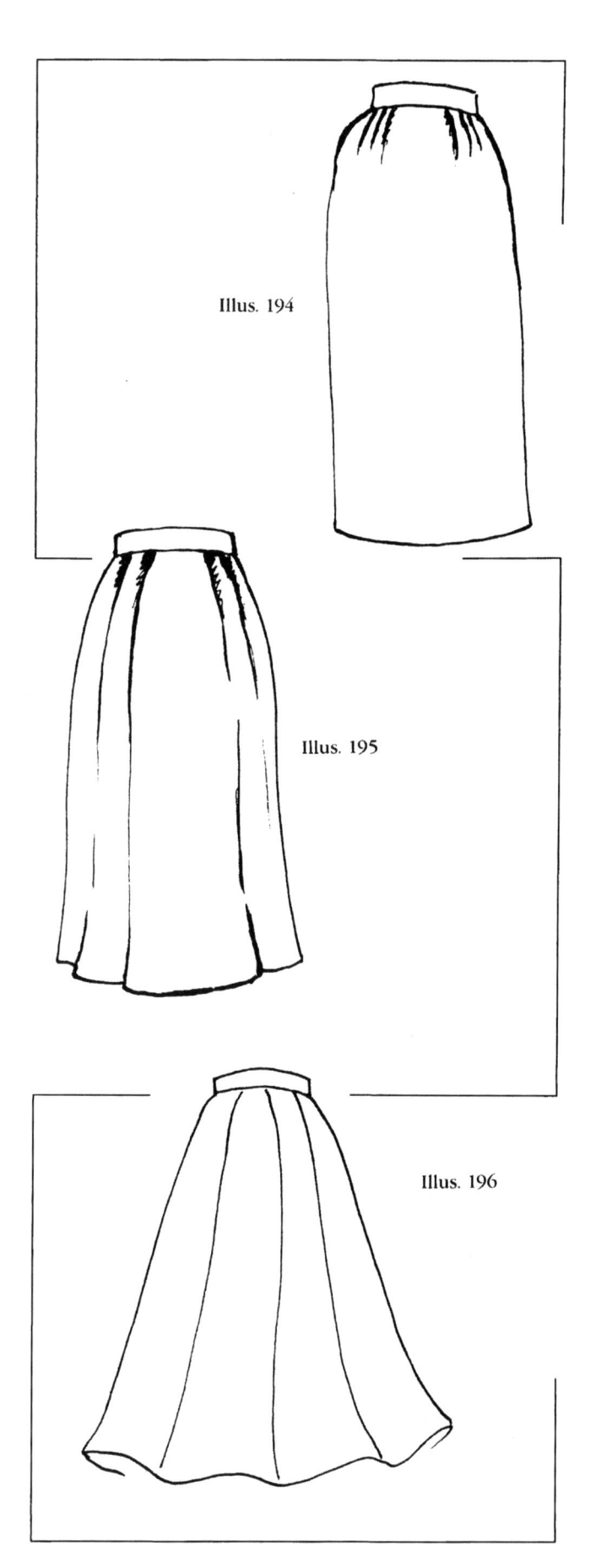

Illus. 194

Illus. 195

Illus. 196

132 The Color Connection

Illus. 197

Illus. 198

Summer

- **Dresses** for the summer woman should be refined, classically tailored, and soft and feminine in both line and fabric. Prints will be blended. Shirring, gathers, or feminine draping provide the requisite feminine lines. Surplice styling is appropriate, with a bit of shirring at the shoulders, but decolletage should remain ladylike to be accepted by most Summer women. The Summer type wears flowing and/or soft bows at the neckline. The wide portrait neckline styling for formal wear is enjoyed by the Summer woman who does not mind showing a little cleavage; most seem to prefer a more demure effect. Most Summer women seem to enjoy some waistline emphasis, although many will enjoy floats, particularly if in true Summer prints and colors.

The Summer woman must strive to appear neither too bland nor too exotic in her dress. To soften classic lines she will add lace, silk or chiffon scarves in water color prints or soft floral designs, or other romantic ornamentation. The recent *Amadeus* mood seems to have been designed for the Summer type.

Illus. 199

Illus. 200

Illus. 201

Illus. 202

Summer 135

- **Pants:** Trousers by definition are *worn by men* and are, therefore, considered by many to be masculine. It is only in our relatively recent past history that pants have been acceptable attire for women. Since *feminine* is the key word for the Summer seasonal type, any pants worn by the Summer woman should be soft and feminine.

The Summer type will look for pants that have a rounded yoke with perhaps a little shirring or soft pleats, either concealed side or quarter pockets, concealed zippers, no contrast stitching detail, and in fabrics that mold somewhat to the body. The more mature Summer woman usually doesn't like jeans but, if she does wear them, they will probably be in the soft styling of her other pants, with no top-stitching, appliques or other cute effects, and without the clutter of five pockets. She perhaps will prefer them in a stone-washed denim, which would be soft both in color and in fabric.

Illus. 203

Illus. 204

Illus. 205

The Color Connection

Illus. 206

Illus. 207

Illus. 208

- The **professional look** of the Summer woman will be classic, feminine tailored dresses, dressmaker or tailored suits, uncluttered, with a softness at the shoulder area and with minimal shoulder padding — certainly not square or exaggerated shoulder looks, unless it is necessary to balance a pear shaped figure. And even then, it should not be too extreme. I have noticed that she usually will prefer a shorter jacket with rounded lapels, even if she is quite tall. It is recommended that her skirt have some drapability and fullness, e.g., unpressed inverted front pleat or a soft dirndl skirt. She seems to prefer a longer length skirt.

Her interview suit will be in her best neutral (basic) color, which is most often the hair color. If this is a beige, it should be a rosy beige as opposed to a yellow beige; if gray it will have a blue cast.

A lace hanky in the pocket of the jacket or a cameo at the neckline of the blouse or a softly tied scarf will soften the look of a tailored suit that might otherwise seem too severe for the more yin Summer woman. Softly draped blouses in her colors, such as a cowl-draped blouse or one with a notched collar with soft gathers off the yoke in a soft rose, mauve or blue, might be worn with her neutrals to good effect. She should avoid too much contrast. For example, an ivory blouse with her dark colors might seem too severe, whereas the same blouse with her rosy beige would seem elegantly conservative.

Because color analysts continually stress "soft and somewhat muted colors", the Summer woman may lapse into not using *enough* color. If she wears her colors predominantly in the softer and grayer colors on her palette, neglecting her more vibrant tones, she can appear bland and unconvincing or non-authoritative. In selecting colors from her palette, she should consider how she wishes to be perceived.

Clothing influences not only our outward image and the way that we are perceived, but our own self-image as well. If a woman is wearing her more dynamic colors, she will not only be perceived as more dynamic, she in fact may well *feel* and *be* more dynamic and forceful. This is especially important for the professional Summer woman, who is often perceived as very soft and gentle — even shy.

If she is in an occupation which requires that

Illus. 209

Illus. 210

Illus. 211

Illus. 212

she be perceived as strong and authoritative, she may wish to use the more dynamic colors on her palette, at least as accents. She may wish to forego the old lace, cameos and roses, in favor of classic pearls. There may be other times when she will wish to appear very soft and feminine, and at those times the soft and grayed tones and extra ornamentation would be most appropriate. This image-influencing tactic is known as *mood dressing,* which, simply put, means that one manipulates the first impression of the observer.

Each of the seasonal types may need to control their professional image to some extent. The Winter type may need to guard against looking too striking and aloof, the Spring against looking too young and cute, and the Autumn too plain or too exotic and adorned. The Summer type must be careful not to appear too soft and feminine in her professional look. Each of the seasonal types should be sure to maintain a harmonious balance in her professional look, expressing outwardly her inner essence while at the same time developing a style which will portray confidence and competence.

• **Formal wear** for the Summer woman might be taken from some of the more romantic periods of history and art, such as Queen Anne, Flemish, Grecian, Roman, Empire, or American turn-of-the-century costumes. Draping or cascading effects augment the soft feminine look of the romantic Summer type, who so often wears her hair in waves or with soft tendrils for her more formal occasions. The more classic and conservative and very often slender Summer type may prefer a more conservative style in a chiffon, sheer lace, or perhaps velvet or panne velvet; the lines should, of course, be feminine.

Illus. 213

140 The Color Connection

Illus. 214

Illus. 215

Illus. 216

Illus. 217

Illus. 218

- **Shoes** should repeat the oval design lines and be consistent with the other design details of the seasonal harmony. Soft bows, shirred or draped effects, S-curves, swirls, oval toes and upper shapes, and classic styling in soft smooth leather are examples. The Summer woman often enjoys espadrilles or other shoes that lace up the ankle for wear with her flowy summer dresses. Her shoes should be light in feel: they should never appear heavy or burdensome.

- **Coats** should be in soft, refined fabrics and with feminine tailoring and without the clutter of patch pockets, heavy cuffs or little detail. Shirring off a curved yoke, soft gathers at the sleeve cap, or draped effects would be perfect for the Summer type. Again, she should not look bundled up and burdened by a heavy fabric but should look graceful and elegant. A soft wool will be her best choice for a winter coat; a rayon or rayon/linen blend would be a good choice for summer. She may also enjoy lacy shawls or those with silky fringe, especially if they are of watery-looking blended flowing fabrics.

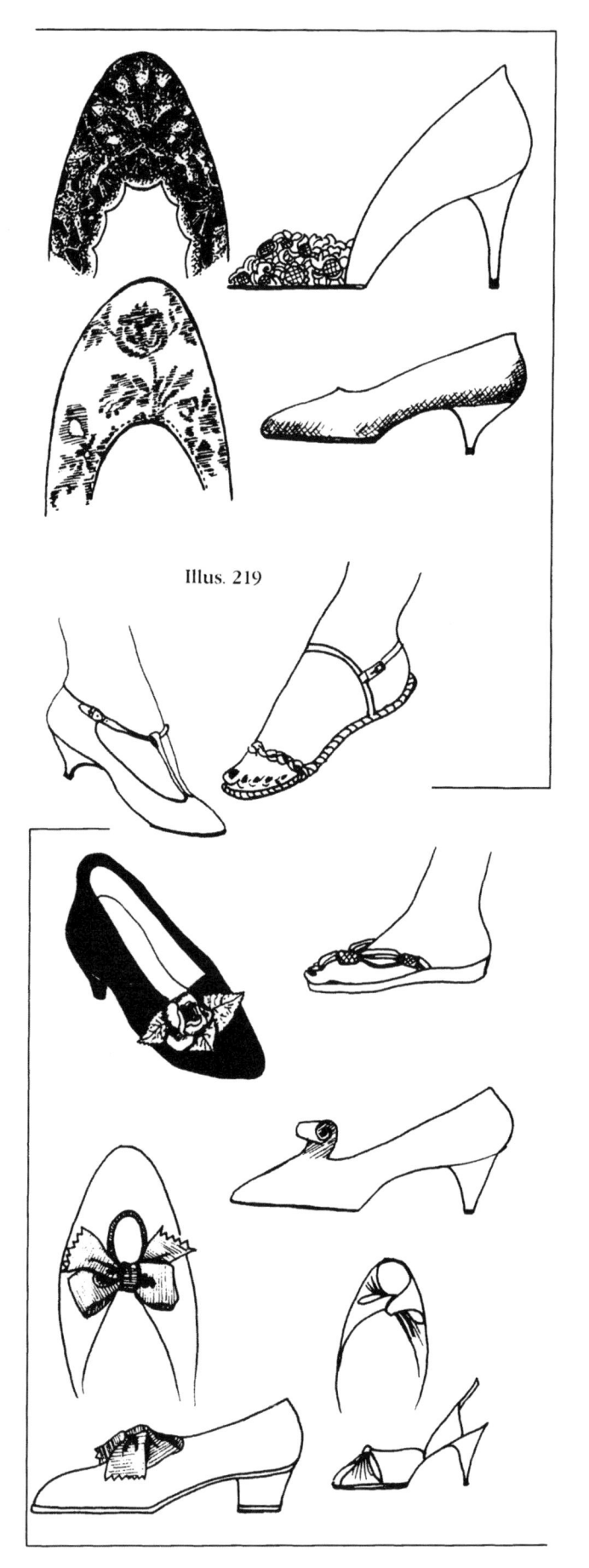

Illus. 219

142   The Color Connection

Illus. 220

Illus. 221

Illus. 222

- **Feminine knits** with open work, soft medium-scale intarsia in relatively low contrast, blended and muted colors, or fine cable detail done with small needles are good examples of Summer knits. Cowl necklines are excellent, as are some boat necks, rounded V-necks, blouson or draped surplice shapes.

> **Think soft, feminine, refined and fine-grained in blended prints and drapable fabrics for the Summer seasonal harmony type. Think formal, simple, conservative, and timeless.**

Illus. 224

Illus. 223

The Summer Man

Like the Summer woman, the Summer man is poised, outwardly calm, and gentle by nature, although his is a gentle masculinity. He tends to be friendly, interested in other people, content with his homelife and family. He has a great capacity for negotiation and makes a good businessman. Summer men are often introspective, interested in others, and tend to be the most intuitive and artistic of all men; many are poets, musicians, artists or composers; another popular field seems to be psychology. The Summer man shares all of the coloring of the Summer woman.

He can wear any simple, classic, dignified look, including finely tailored suits in fabric that is fine-grained with or without shaping. He may prefer the American cut with little or no shoulder padding. He probably will prefer solid fabrics or muted patterns, perhaps a subtle tone-on-tone plaid or stripe. He will not like heavy textures, nor will he like his clothing to have a sheen. He will wear traditional men's business shirts, but may also enjoy one with a rounded collar. His ties will be solid colors or quiet stripes, dots, paisley, or foulard prints.

His neutrals will be muted blues, such as slate blue, steel blue or a somewhat dusty navy; off-white; a light and medium rose beige or taupe, a darker rose-brown; a light blue gray and a silver gray. These will be used for suits and/or separates. He may particularly enjoy sweaters with slacks. I suspect that he would especially like the softness of cashmere sweaters were he to receive them as gifts.

He will enjoy accents of his basics most: the cranberries, burgundies, plums, often reserving his bright colors, such as medium bright blue, rose, mauve, grape, azalea, turquoise, sky blue, periwinkle and lavender for active sportswear. His light colors which would be used for shirts, sweaters, and sportswear are in what I would call the softly muted powder range of pink, seafoam green, powder blue, aqua, mauve, lilac and periwinkle blue. They will not be so light as the pastels of either Winter or Spring.

Some Famous Summer Women: Ursula Andress, Candice Bergen, Queen Elizabeth, Farrah Fawcett, Grace Kelly, Caroline Kennedy, Dina Merrill, Meryl Streep, Cheryl Tiegs, Loretta Young.

Some Famous Summer Men: Richard Chamberlain, Perry Como, Phil Donahue, Michael Fox, Merv Griffin, David Hartman, William Hurt, Paul Newman, Nick Nolte, Jimmy Stewart, Andy Williams.

Some Summer People I Know: (Add your own friends, relatives, clients, etc. that you believe to be Summers.)

Illus. 225

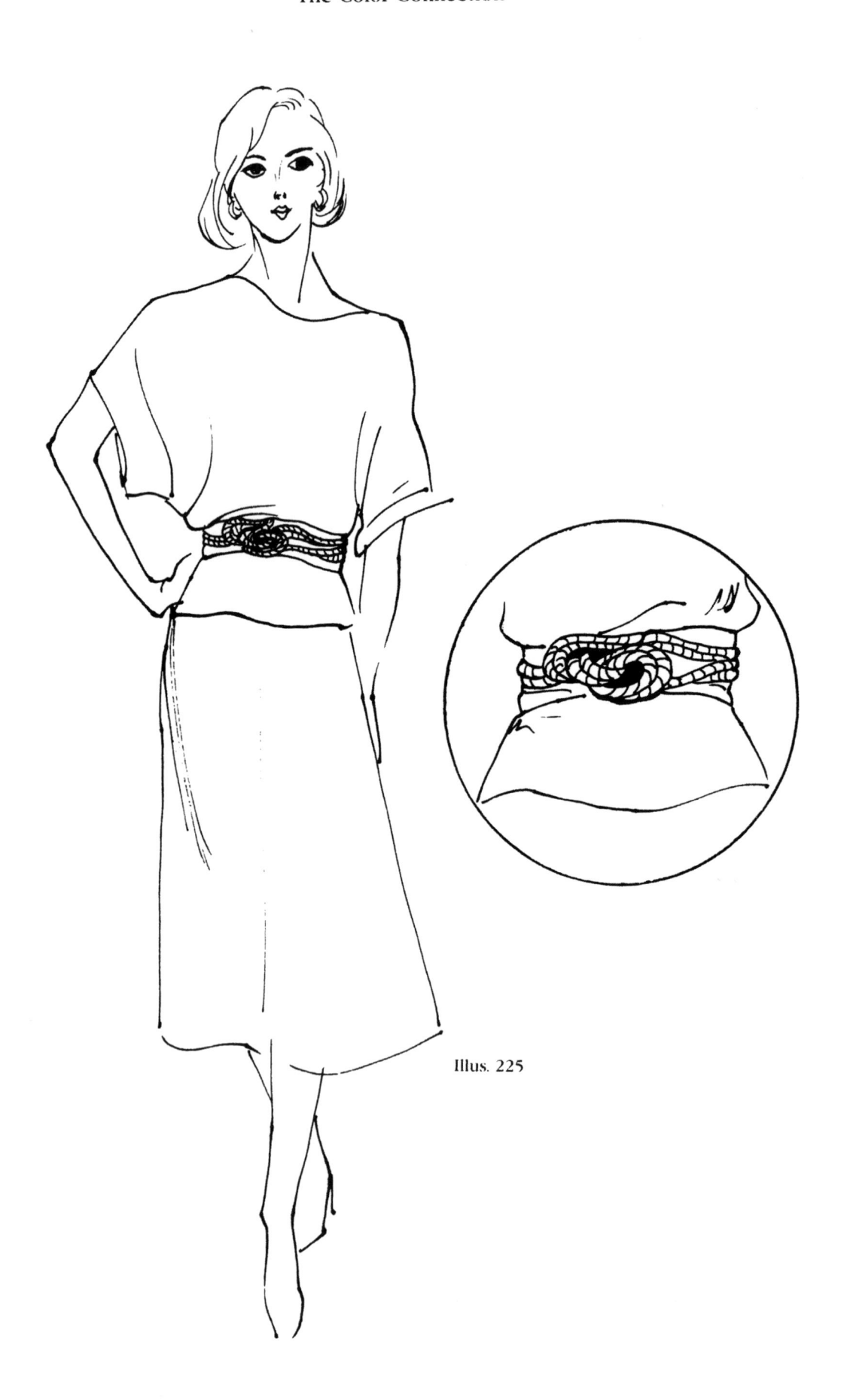

The following words have been attributed to the Summer Seasonal Color Harmony. (Using this list and the ones at the conclusion of each of the other seasons, make a *word portrait* of yourself by listing the words that relate to you in any way, such as your personality characteristics and/or physical attributes, your affinity for what the word describes, e.g., floral designs. This word portrait may be an aid in discovering your percentages of each of the seasonal harmonies. Some words appear in more than one season.

abundance	enchanting	light touch	renaissance
artistic	ethereal	loved	reserved
atmospheric quality	exquisite	lovely	restful
blended	fairylike	loving	restrained
calm	feminine	luscious	rhythmic
cameo quality	fine	luxurious	romantic
cared for	finesse	meticulous	rose-like
carefully groomed	floral	misty	sense of order
charming	fluidity	muted	sensitive
clouds	fragile	of another era	sentimental
comfortable	freeform	opalescent	shadowy
composed	gentility	organized	soft
coordinated	gentle	peaceful	soft-spoken
creative	gentleness	picturesque	spiritual
cultured	graceful	poised	sunsets
dainty	gracious	pretty	sweet
delicate	harmonized	quaint	tenderness
delightful	heavenly	queenly	tranquil
demure	idealistic	quiet	Victorian
dignified	inviting	refined	warm
dreamy	iridescent	regal	willowy
elegant	ladylike	relaxed	

148 The Color Connection

Illus. 226

8
Autumn

Autumn is a flashy time of the year. The leaves turn flamboyantly from soft greens to flaming orange and coral, deep brassy yellows, tawny reds, cinnamon, russet, umber and olive brown. My autumn garden will be full of chrysanthemums and tiger lilies; the liquidambar tree will quickly notify us that fall is here as it changes almost overnight after the first frost to brilliant red, russet and gold. The first big windstorm will litter the previously well-mown lawn with falling leaves, walnuts, and broken twigs in almost geometric designs.

When we think of autumn we think of the harvest of pumpkins, red apples, golden grains, deep purple, red and green grapes, walnuts, pecans, and almonds. The autumn season leaves us no doubt that it has arrived. Autumn is energetic, flamboyant and forceful. And so is the Autumn woman.

The Autumn personality words include accomplishing, adventurous, assertive, assured, bewitching, bold, bright, colorful, confident, dashing, decisive, direct, dramatic, dynamic, earthy, energetic, exotic, fiery, forceful, flamboyant, mellow, natural, spicy, and spirited. The Autumn woman tends to gets things done and often prefers to take charge and organize others rather than suffer the frustration of disorganization. While many women must learn to be assertive, it seems to come naturally to the Autumn woman. She tends to say what she means and mean what she says. She usually walks with a firm step — forceful and energetic.

The coloring of the Autumn type is as rich and intense as the season. The skin tones may range from cafe-au-lait to amber to yellowish brown. The skin may appear ruddy or brushed with copper or bronze. Or the skin may be ivory, cream or peach in tone. The eyes are usually very intense in color; they may be green, gray-green, yellow-green, topaz, hazel, olive, blue-green, or brown with flecks of rust. The Autumn type may have red hair, including dark auburn or copper brown, metallic blonde, brown with reddish or copper highlights. (Not all redheads are Autumns, however; many blue-eyed redheads are classified as Springs.)

Many Winters erroneously believe themselves to be Autumns because they like to wear brown, camel or beige. There are some fairly clear ways to distinguish between the two. The true Autumn type must be able to wear all the golds, orange, terra cotta, brick reds, and olive, mossy or forest greens. The skin of most Winters will appear yellow in these yellow-based colors. In addition, the eyebrows and eyelashes of the Autumn type are generally lighter and less prominent than those of the Winter. The undertones of the skin are yellow, and they rarely have as much natural color in their lips or cheeks as does the Winter. The hair of the Autumn type will usually have golden or reddish highlights.

The Autumn type usually has strong features, often with some angularity. While the Autumn woman may be very attractive, I tend to agree with Suzanne Caygill, who suggests that she "strive for smartness rather than prettiness." As a child, her look was not what you would call soft, feminine and pretty. One Autumn woman related that she always looked and felt somewhat out of place in ruffled pinafores and puffed sleeves, but always felt *terrific* in a favorite suede vest she wore with a corduroy skirt. Even as a child, she preferred the combinations of textures and the richness of styling preferred by most Autumn women.

The Autumn type, adult or child, can wear the rich colors of autumn: avocado, olive, moss, citron, lime, chartreuse, spruce, and pine greens, jade, emerald, peacock, teal, tourmaline, aquamarine, and rich Indian turquoise, copper, bronze, burnished gold, orange, corn yellow, saffron, mustard, curry, goldenrod, topaz, apricot, terra cotta, cinnamon, orange reds, rust, red poppy, green browns, red browns, and black-browns. She should avoid blue-based reds.

Her browns and beiges are determined by her skin and hair colors. As her hair turns more grayish than brown, the Autumn woman may elect to eliminate brown from her palette in favor of her best gray, which will have a greenish or pewter cast. She will wear off-white. A blond, brown-eyed Autumn who tans well may even wear a pure white. Depending on the lightness of her skin or the gray in her hair, the Autumn type may elect to wear black, but usually only if worn with her other colors in rich combinations. Black should not be the predominant color in Autumn prints.

There are no pure colors on the Autumn palette. Autumn colors are blended one with another or with earth browns, thus the term *earth tones*. They are best worn analogously or monochromatically with an accent of contrast.

Illus. 227

Illus. 228

152 The Color Connection

Illus. 229

Illus. 230

Illus. 231

- **Design Lines:**

The Autumn type expresses herself best with the rectangular form. Autumn design lines are based on straight lines, the rectangle or any part thereof. Examples in fashion would be any pointed detail, such as a V-neck, notched collars or lapels, squared shoulders, or squared patch pockets, epaulets, etc. Elizabethan effects are considered particularly apt for the Autumn type.

The Design Lines of Autumn are strong, sharply defined, natural, bold, oversized and angular, with vertical or diagonal lines. Design lines typical of Autumn are found in the safari look or in the gypsy-like exotic effects of ethnic styles. Design lines will often be similar to those of an electrical storm — jagged and with motion. These forceful, dynamic lines portraying electricity or impact lines are typical of Autumn. (Impact lines are lines that intersect in forceful ways, often in stitching detail, color blocking or intarsia knits.)

- **Design Details:** Leaf or feather shapes, rope, macrame, cork, bamboo, dried grasses, leaves and pods, animal skins, long fringe, patch pockets; leather patchwork, piping, or patches on sleeves; leather and wood buttons; brass and copper coins, Greek key, or V-shapes in flame stitch embroidery, knit or print patterns.

The Autumn type wears dynamic design lines in harmony with her own dynamic coloring, personality, and physical characteristics. She wears swift lines (lines that move or have motion), such as those in the maple leaf, the bird of paradise, an arrow, or a pheasant feather.

The Color Connection

Illus. 232

Illus. 233

Illus. 234

- The **silhouette** is rectangular in shape. **Wardrobe style** associated with Autumn includes suits, especially ones that are man-tailored with long jackets, shoulder pads, convertible collars, wide lapels, and/or asymmetrical closures; A-line or dirndl skirts, kick pleats, or split skirts, pleated walking skirts; knickers, trousers, jodhpurs; V-necklines, notched collars, tailored blouses usually without shirring or gathered effects unless very full as in a cossack shirt or a peasant blouse, trench coats, argyle sweaters and stockings; ties and scarves, but not usually bows. Simple man-tailoring and/or dynamic lines connote movement and action, adding yangness and forcefulness for the Autumn look.

- **Fabric choices** for the Autumn type must be firm, have substance and/or be textured, e.g., suede, ultrasuede, chamois; textured and/or tweedy wools, such as Harris or Donegal tweeds; gabardine, corduroy, faille, burlap, chenille, mohair, rough linen, oatmeal or butcher's linen, textured cotton, twill, heavy gauze, handwoven and homespun fabrics, monk's cloth, silk tussah, linen-wool blends, loden cloth, cavalry twills, Kente cloth, Indian cottons, tapestry, and oriental or gold metallic brocades. Other descriptive characteristics of the Autumn fabric choices might include nubby, primitive, heavy in body, loosely woven, raw or naturalistic.

The Autumn type may enjoy chiffon or heavy lace for her wedding gown or other very dressy occasions. But most often the Autumn woman will prefer the rich costume look of the brocades and tapestries that only she can do so well.

The Autumn woman typically has difficulty relating to Spring/Summer fashions, asking "What do I do in the Summertime? Everything is so pastel. The colors on my palette look so dark."

The colors of Autumn in linen, for example, do not look dark on a person with the rich coloring of the Autumn type. However, spring is typically a light, bright season and it is, therefore, unfortunately often very difficult for the Autumn shopper to find her colors in the stores. Designers of spring lines tend to be influenced by the season and drawn to the new fresh light/bright looks, often neglecting the needs of all the Winter and Autumn customers they might have if they would only provide them clothing in their colors.

The Autumn woman can wear natural raw silk,

156   The Color Connection

Illus. 235

Illus. 236

Illus. 237

coarse cotton or linen in all her neutrals or best colors: moss, brick, teal, gold, natural, etc. and look very chic. Typically, the spring selection for the Autumn woman is limited to the Banana Republic or safari look, some natural linen suiting and an occasional shirtwaist dress.

It takes special effort on the part of store buyers to fill this gap in their stores in order to meet the needs of the Autumn woman, who is rarely comfortable wearing white, pastels or light/bright colors or the dainty little prints or even the larger floral prints of Summer in the typically more feminine styling of the spring buying season. The retailer must search for more yang styling in autumn colors in a firm fabric, and admittedly this is not an easy task. Most Autumn women will grumble about their chronically sparse summer wardrobes. As a buyer I grumble and have often said, "Some manufacturer could make a fortune if they would only produce a summer line specifically for the sadly neglected Autumn woman."

The retail buyer should also be alert to the fact that designers and color forecasters traditionally turn to the colors that remind us of autumn and/or winter for clothing that will be shipped for that time period, just as they turn to the colors of spring and summer for delivery in the spring. The designs of the autumn delivery period also are frequently more dynamic and dramatic, just as spring and summer designs are apt to be soft and romantic in that delivery period.

Autumn and Winter colors and styles, although popular with designers for the autumn time period, cannot be successfully worn by probably more than half of the women shoppers. For this reason, just as the retailer must search for the Autumn colors and styles for spring delivery, it is equally important for the retail buyer to seek out designs and colors of the Spring and Summer types for their fall delivery period. I have noticed, however, that more designers are responding to this need, particularly for the Holiday/Cruise delivery.

The Color Connection

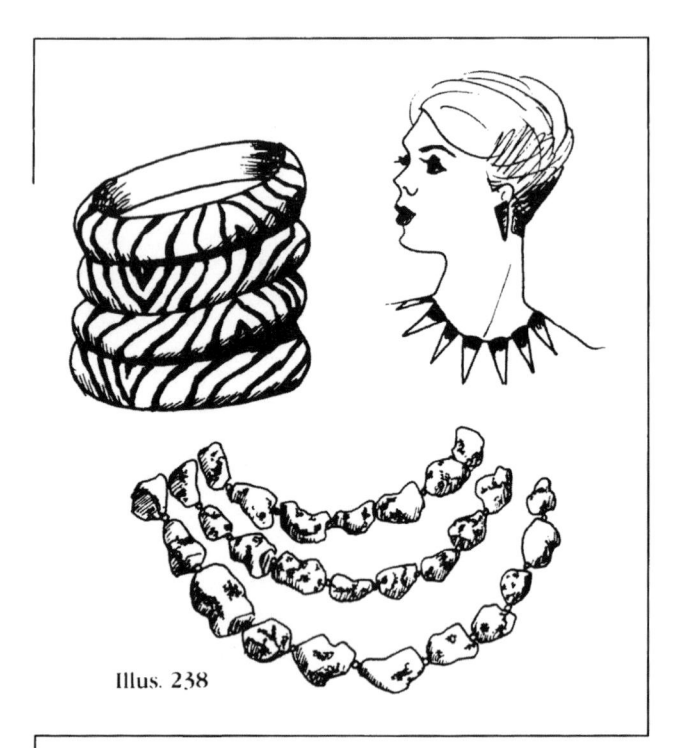

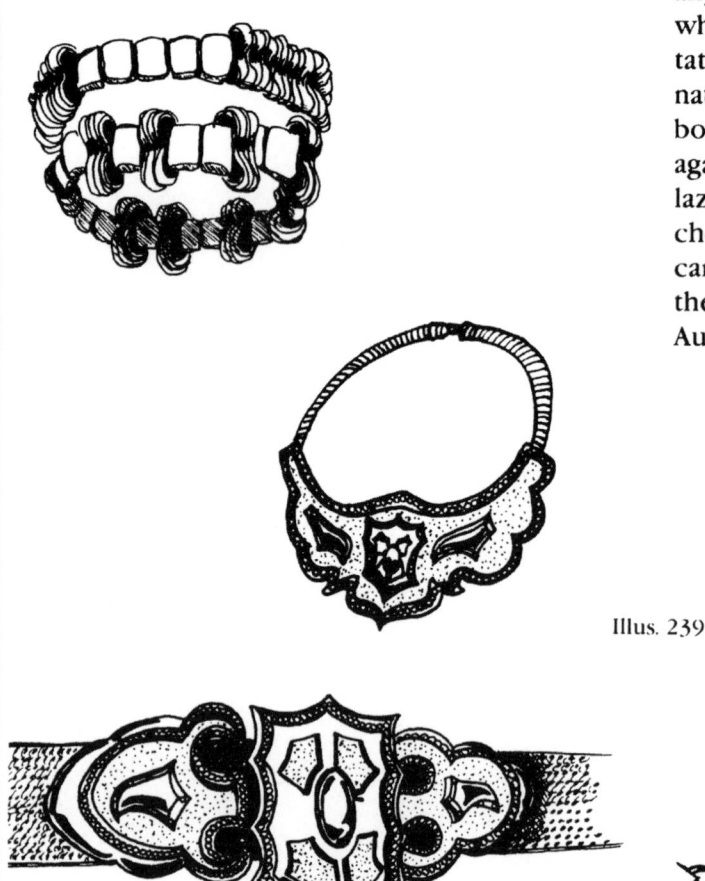

Illus. 238

- **Surface patterns** include leaf prints, overscaled plaids in warm, rich color combinations, asymmetrical designs, geometric or angular designs, herringbone, houndstooth, flamestitch, stripes, chevron, pyramid, paisley, oriental, reptile, ikat; exotic florals (although not those found in Hawaiian prints, which tend to be for Spring types), jungle or animal skin prints in blended Autumn colors. Paisley or ethnic fabrics shot with metallic threads are excellent for Autumn types. Prints that seem adapted from the paintings of the old masters (e.g. Van Gogh, Gaugin) are suitable for Autumns.

- **Jewelry:** The Autumn type typically wears jewelry lavishly — more is often better. (It should be noted, however, that a very natural or sporty Autumn type may prefer little or no jewelry.) What jewelry she does wear should be bold and solid-looking, never delicate. One little strand of anything is out of character for an Autumn type, while jangling bracelets are typical. Her ornamentation should be as unusual as possible, even naturalistic. Gold, brass, copper, baroque pearls, bone or ivory, tortoise shell, jade, topaz, tiger eye, agate, amber, carnelian, turquoise, coral, lapis lazuli, brass and copper coins are all good jewelry choices for the Autumn woman. Pods, inlaid or carved wood, leather thongs, or other materials of the earth are also in character for jewelry for the Autumn type.

Illus. 239

- **Hair styles** should be well shaped with contours depending largely on the face shape, the personality and life style of the individual. The Autumn woman may prefer to retain a very natural appearance even with some angularity in the shaping. Think of some of the Byzantine, Egyptian or Chinese hairstyles as examples of what some Autumn types may try. On the other hand, she may soften her look with waves or with curls, although this may tend to be a too-pretty look for many. The head of the Autumn woman is often on the large side in proportion to the rest of her body, and if this is so, she will not wish to emphasize that with a bouffant hair style. She should remember that whatever hair style she chooses, it should have movement, be in harmony with her personality and should serve to dramatize and enhance it. She should strive to look chic, rather than soft and feminine, and sometimes a rather angular natural-looking hair style is the most becoming to an Autumn woman.

- **Hats** might include a Robin Hood type with a pheasant feather, a fedora, or one with a geometric shape. Headwraps of all types are often just the touch of drama needed by the Autumn woman; she can usually carry them off very well in rich colors and fabrics, even braiding them with beads or other naturalistic effects. The hat of the Gaucho costume is also a fun look for the Autumn woman.

- Suggested **bags** are rectangular, firm and/or textured. They may be firm, crusty leather or textured leathers such as eelskin, snake, lizard, rhino, elephant, or ostrich. They might be of fabrics of animal fur prints, woven straw or banana leaf or other basketry bags, or ethnic handwoven bags, such as those from South American countries or Kenya. Autumn bags are often made of natural, earthy materials and can be unusual in shape and design.

Illus. 240

Illus. 241

For the Autumn woman's accessories, think interesting and exotic.

Illus. 242

- **Necklines** for the Autumn type are most typically V-necked or with notched collars. She likes wide lapels and asymmetrical closures. She will sometimes wear a boat neckline, but only if it is perfect in every other way and if she can't find the same look in a V-neck. She will often fill in the neckline with a turtleneck, although some Autumns may find the turtleneck too confining.

- **Buttons,** medium to large in scale, made of wood, leather, bone, horn or other natural materials in rectangular or tubular shapes are excellent. Wooden toggle buttons are an Autumn effect.

- **Skirts** should be designed for easy movement, as the Autumn type often moves with a loose-jointed and long, firm stride, her legs often being long in proportion to the rest of her somewhat angular body. She will like a pleated walking skirt, A-line, or straight skirt with side or back vents or kick pleats for easy movability — always in a firm fabric, often with texture.

Illus. 243

Illus. 244

Illus. 245

162   The Color Connection

Illus. 246

Illus. 247

Illus. 248

• **Sleeves** may be set-in or drop-shouldered, but whichever they are, they will be padded to give the effect of a rectangular appearance. The more man-tailored looking sleeve is usually preferred, with no gathers and softness. I have observed that the Autumn type does not typically push up her sleeves, although she may roll them. I suspect she finds fussing with push-up sleeves an annoyance.

• Her favorite **dresses** are very often trench coat in style or shirtwaist dresses in firm fabrics, although some heavy gauze gypsy-like dresses are favored by some Autumn types. Again, asymmetrical closures, perhaps with one large lapel buttoned back creating an impact line in the middle of the bodice, is a favorite Autumn look. Skirts should be adequate for easy movement. Sleeve treatment should provide some angularity.

Illus. 249

164 The Color Connection

Illus. 250

Illus. 251

Illus. 252

- Her **pants** are typically trousers — the Katharine Hepburn look — loose and comfortable. The safari look or that of Indiana Jones with patch pockets in khaki are more than acceptable, as are jumpsuits of all kinds. Knickers, gaucho pants or split skirts, jodhpurs, Bermuda shorts, and pants with zippers and snaps at the ankle or pleats down the sides with snap closures are all good Autumn styles. Autumns tend to be no-nonsense people and therefore like their clothes functional.

Illus. 253

Illus. 254

- The **professional look** of the Autumn woman is almost man-tailored. For interviews and more conservative places of business she will probably wear a suited look in her best neutrals. But usually she will prefer rich combinations of colors and textures, mixing and matching separates. She will even enjoy wearing trousers with her jackets if dress code permits. Her favorites will include tweeds, textured wools, handwoven and tapestry fabrics. Her jackets will be long, ample in size, and rectangular in shape. She will often enjoy asymmetrical details or closures. Her favorite jackets will have lapels as wide as current fashion will allow and, of course, shoulder pads.

The Autumn woman, who so often enjoys bangle bracelets, chunky jewelry, and almost the encrusted look, may need to restrain herself for her professional look. She will almost always enjoy a significant signature piece, however; a carved jade necklace, for example, that can be worn with all of her notched collar blouses. She should always remember that her bangle bracelets and favorite dangling earrings may present a distraction to her audience. The bracelets should always be removed before any presentation involving a microphone.

The Autumn woman will rarely wear bows, lacy or frilly looks, but will wear her scarves hacking style or in an ascot. She will follow the guidelines in terms of prints for her scarves and blouses, e.g., paisleys, leaf prints, animal print motifs.

Illus. 255

168 The Color Connection

Illus. 256

Illus. 257

Illus. 258

Illus. 259

Illus. 260

• For **formal wear** the Autumn woman should think of the opulence and luxury of tapestry, brocade, natural looking fibers, and of lace or chiffon in her more understated colors. An Autumn leaf print in a chiffon would be most appropriate, as would some very stylized floral prints in the colors of Autumn. Paisley shot with metallic threads would also be suitable for formal attire. The heavily encrusted, embroidered, beaded and ornamented styles, such as an Afghan or Bedouin dress or the one illustrated, are perfect. Autumn formal wear can be exotic and flamboyant.

Formal wear for the Autumn woman can be something of a problem if she thinks *traditional*. For example, an Autumn Mother of the Bride and/or Groom who must fit into a dusty rose or lavender color scheme of satin and lace will come into *Tarika* in abject despair, wondering how she will ever find anything suitable that she would care to be seen in. She is somewhat relieved to discover that with a dusty rose motif, she could probably go to one of her lighter but still rich shades of slightly browned berry, perhaps in a heavy lace, a brocade, or a chiffon. The more down-to-earth, natural or Town and Country Autumn may prefer a raw silk or firm gauze, perhaps in a shirtwaist. With the addition of jewelry this most casual Autumn type woman would feel appropriately dressed for such a wedding, yet comfortable in her own style.

An Elizabethan wedding gown in a brocade or other fabric encrusted with jewels would be an excellent choice for the Autumn bride. An Autumn bride or Mother of the Bride or Groom could wear a Grecian-type gown (see Illustration 38) of crystal pleating or of chiffon, pleated and controlled at the waist with a knot or belt.

The Autumn woman does not wear flowers very readily, often feeling that they are wearing her. Her choice of a corsage, if one is required, might be a green orchid, which has a definite design with a swiftness of line that is suited to the Autumn woman. Spider chrysanthemums would be a good choice for her bridal bouquet.

Illus. 261

Illus. 262

Illus. 263

Illus. 264

- **Coats** suitable for Autumn types might include Burberry or London Fog type trench coats, tweeds, safari looks, ponchos with Aztec designs. Large wrap coats or coats with an attached scarf that can be thrown over one shoulder, creating a long rectangular shape, are also good Autumn coat designs. Other design detail would include epaulets, big lapels, big buckles on belts, or patch pockets with big button detail. Some particularly good fabric choices for Autumn coats, in addition to the tweeds and textured wools, would be handwoven or tapestry fabrics, animal-print simulated fur, and leather or suede.

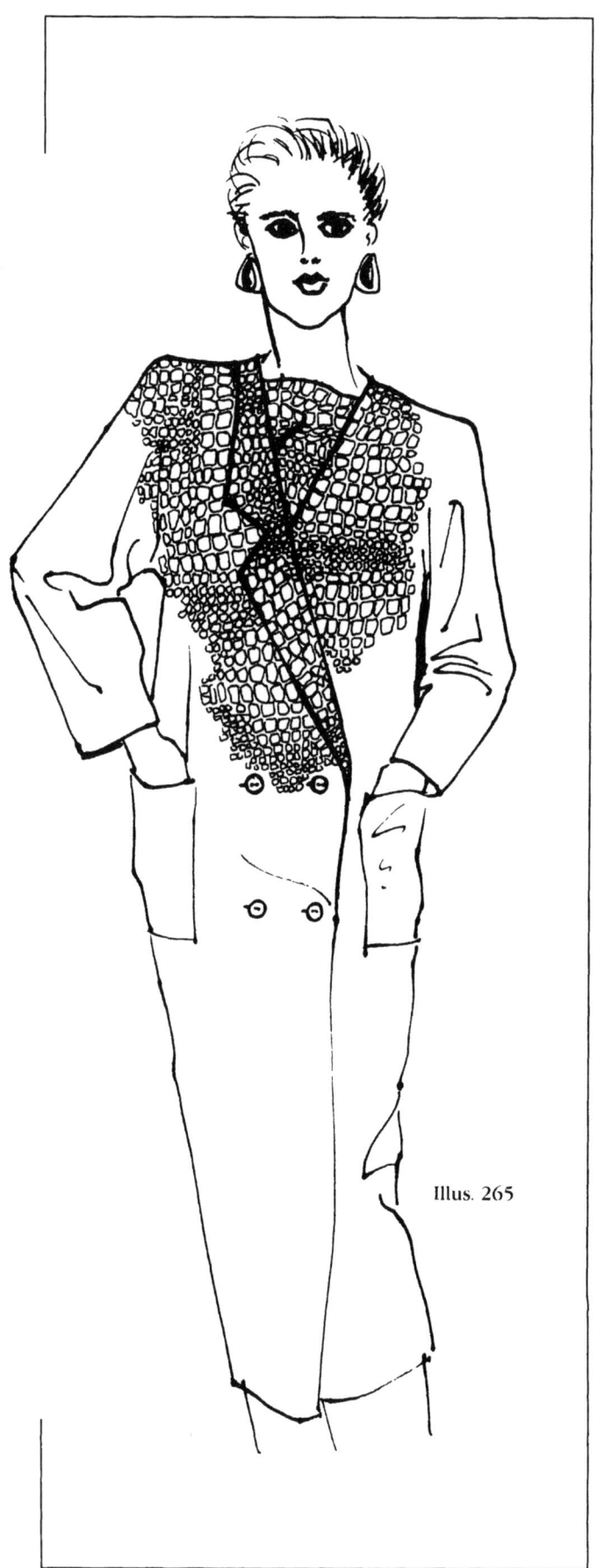

Illus. 265

172   The Color Connection

Illus. 266

Illus. 267

Illus. 268

• **Shoes** could include simple pumps, leather walking shoes with texture, such as loafers, brogues or moccasins in crusty leather or woven leathers, snake, lizard, perhaps with stacked leather or wooden heels. Simple boots or boots with bold details are appropriate for Autumn types. Shoes with rectangular or triangular details, as well as asymmetry and impact lines, are excellent examples of Autumn styling. Heavy-leather strapped sandals and canvas shoes with rope effects, especially in the luggage browns or other earth tones, are typical Autumn summer shoes.

Illus. 269

174 The Color Connection

Illus. 270

Illus. 271

Illus. 272

- **Knits** suitable for Autumn types are rich, nubby, textured and with padded shoulders, asymmetrical lines, or lines that create rectangular shapes. The rectangular shapes and impact lines created in argyles and color blocking are also excellent examples, especially in all of the rich color and textural combinations of Autumn. Bulky knits as well as leather trimmed sweaters, are excellent Autumn choices.

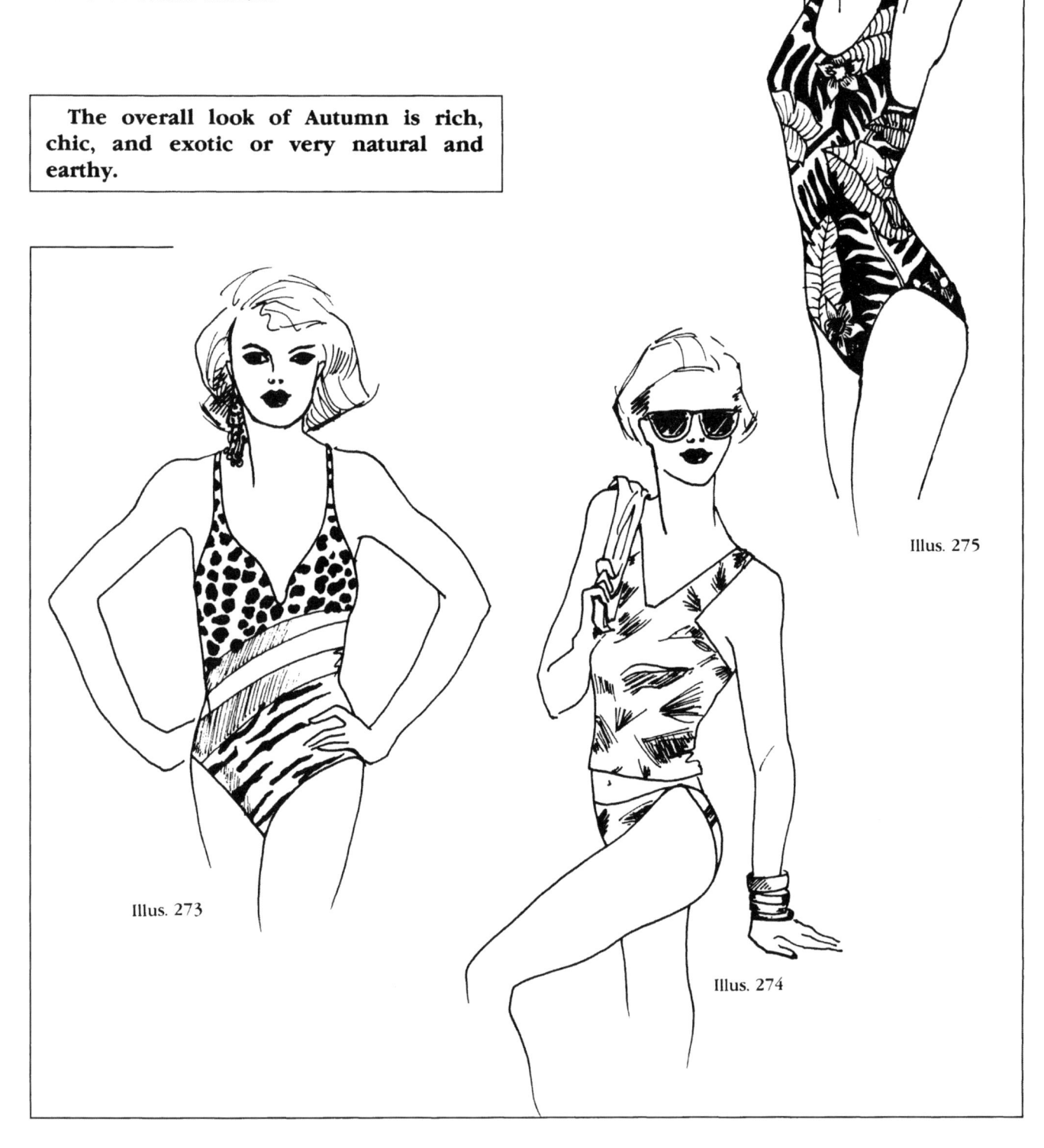

The overall look of Autumn is rich, chic, and exotic or very natural and earthy.

Illus. 273

Illus. 274

Illus. 275

The Autumn Man is a strong, forceful, and dramatic leader. I envision him in a wood-paneled room with a leather chair or in a rugged outdoor setting, perhaps with a hunting dog beside him. He is very natural, walks with a long free stride, and is somewhat windblown and casual. He is usually angular with irregular features.

Darker Autumn men have an almost bronze look to their skin, while the lighter ones are more of a cafe au lait color. The lighter-skinned Autumn type may very well freckle and sunburn. The darker ones tan more readily to a golden color. Their hair ranges from red to dark brown or almost black.

He likes his clothes functional. He will like patch pockets, even pleated ones that will hold more. Leather jackets, leather-bound buttons, leather patches on heavy cable knit sweaters or jackets, big lapels, shearling lined jackets, epaulets, the safari look, camel's hair coats, and sportswear are some of his favorite looks. He loves the texture and comfort of tweeds, corduroy, fatigues, and trench coats. He will enjoy argyle sweaters and socks. He rarely wears jewelry, but if he does it will be gold.

Comfort is very important to him. His suit jackets, for instance, will not have much contouring and will have a more than ample fit. He may not even like the feel of his jacket buttoned.

His ties will be of stripes, small paisley designs, some tone-on-tone plaids, or prints with dogs, horses, or geometric shapes.

The Autumn neutrals encompass everything between oyster white to dark chocolate brown. Warm beige, camel, coffee, cocoa, russet, and bronze, for example, may be his best suit colors.

His understated colors, or those that he would wear in combination with his neutrals in plaids, tweeds, etc., include olive and forest green, teal, gold and a rust red.

Colors that he would use in sportswear, in combination with his neutrals or as accents, include tangerine, brick red, terra cotta, orange, mustard, turquoise, teal, periwinkle blue, and moss, sage, avocado, or jade green. These would not be suitable for shirts for businesswear.

For both business and formal wear, as well as for sweaters, the Autumn man would choose his light colors, which are not quite so light as either Spring's or Winter's pastels. These light colors are medium peach, apricot, light sage, light turqouise or aqua, and a light periwinkle blue.

Some Famous Autumn Women: Lauren Bacall, Lucille Ball, Carol Burnett, Joan Crawford, Katharine Hepburn, Glenda Jackson, Sophia Loren, Vanessa Redgrave, Betty Thomas, Jane Wyman (Fall/Spring or Spring/Fall perhaps).

Some Famous Autumn Men: Humphrey Bogart, Howard Cosell, Clint Eastwood, Peter Falk, Harrison Ford, Rex Harrison, Charlton Heston, Walter Matthau, Spencer Tracy. While some say that Red Skelton and Danny Kaye are Autumns, I think their look so animated that I am casting my vote for Spring!

Some Autumn People I Know: (Add your own friends, relatives, clients, etc.)

The following words have been attributed to the Autumn Seasonal Color Harmony. (Using this list and the ones at the conclusion of each of the other seasons, make a *word portrait* of yourself by listing the words that relate to you in any way, such as your personality characteristics and/or physical attributes, your affinity for what the word describes, e.g., ornamentation. This word portrait may be an aid in discovering your percentages of each of the seasonal harmonies. Some words appear in more than one season.

ability to accomplish
adventurous
apache
assertive
assured
baroque-look
bewitching
bizarre
bold
bright
brilliant
colorful
confident
dangerous
daring
dark hues
dashing
decisive
deep expression
deepness
devastating
direct
dramatic
dynamic

earthy
energetic
exotic
feeling of dark earth
feeling of peacefulness
feeling of stability
fiery
firmness
flamboyant
forceful
freedom
glorious
glow
gypsy-like colors
having substance
high-spirited
intense
intensity
jangling bracelets
kinetic
latin-type look
leaves
look of health
looks very capable

lustre
magnetic
mature
maturity
mellow
natural
need to use their energy
nurturing
opulence
ornamentation
outdoor look
positive
power
profound
pungent
purposeful
put in charge of things
resplendent
rich
richness
robust
rusty browns
sense of abandon
showiness

smart
solidity
somberness
sophisticated
spicy
spirited
splendor
straightforward
strong
tambourines
tangy
tawny
tropical
unevenness
verve
vibrant
vigorous
vital
vivid
warm
warmth

178 The Color Connection

Illus. 276

9
Yin and Yang

It is said that the personality of men and women is a *dynamic phenomenon* caused by the interaction between the feminine and masculine elements of yin and yang. Fritjof Capra, author of *The Turning Point* (Bantam Books, 1983, pages 35-39), describes this ancient Chinese I Ching concept of yin and yang as "the dynamic interplay of these two archetypal poles, which are associated with many images of opposites taken from nature and from social life." He goes on to say that "nothing is only yin or only yang," but "...a continuous oscillation between the two poles, all transitions taking place gradually and in unbroken progression...", the natural order being one of dynamic balance between yin and yang.

Capra says that according to the Chinese philosophy neither yin nor yang is good in and of itself; it is the dynamic balance between the two that is good; "what is bad or harmful is imbalance."

Yin characteristics relate to Spring and Summer seasonal harmonies and are considered *feminine*, while yang characteristics are considered masculine and relate most closely to Autumn and Winter. It is important to again stress at this point that few, if any, are 100% any of the harmonies, any more than one has only yin or only yang characteristics.

I am reminded of a geode I received as a gift after a speaking engagement with this note: "We are all a little like the *geode;* more inside than meets the eye!" As you probably know, a geode appears to be a nobby, rather unattractive, not particularly interesting-looking large round stone. But when sliced in half it reveals a surprise — a cavity of often very beautiful colors, the center lined with crystals. Each is unique and you can never guess what's inside by looking at the exterior. A heartwarming analogy of the human spirit...often "more inside than meets the eye."

In her classes, Joan Songer relates this concept of uniqueness in another way: "Each of us is unique, in perfect harmony, — each with our own special kind of beauty."

One of the ways that we express what is inside is through our clothing statements or our style. Each of us has physical and personality characteristics that may be considered either yin or yang, and it is through a correlation of the two that people are categorized and advised as to their style.

Surely, without question, our proportion or balance of yin and yang personality characteristics must be at least somewhat environmental and constantly changing as our needs and our circumstances change: the "continuing oscillation between the two poles," that Capra talks about.

He associates yin not only with feminine but with "contractive, conservative, responsive, cooperative, intuitive, and synthesizing;" and yang with "masculine, expansive, demanding, aggressive, competitive, rational and analytic." He then goes on to remind us that our society has traditionally placed greater value on the characteristics associated with yang.

It is at least true that society has placed greater value on yang characteristics for men; until recently society certainly has advocated, if not demanded, yin characteristics for women. "She thinks like a man" was not always complimentary. Being aggressive is considered masculine and was not thought seemly for a woman, anymore than emotional displays or softness were thought appropriate for men.

With the popularization of the women's movement, more women are working outside the home and some are moving into positions of authority. Because of this shifting focus and perhaps a reappraisal of values by society, there seems to be a reapportionment of yin and yang qualities in women — more of a balance between the two. It is through balance that we achieve harmony.

And How Does That Relate to Fashion and Style?

As ancient Chinese wisdom associated personality characteristics with either yin or yang, there is an association for design line details as well:

> **Yin Effect is conservative, soft, feminine, demure, and light in feel.**

Yin Effect May Be Achieved By Use of the Following:

1. Lines that are conservative in feeling, conventional, symmetrical, small to medium scale motifs in conventional prints; unrelieved straight lines; horizontal lines; curves broken in order to produce small details; full circles; curved hemlines; handkerchief hemlines, circular skirts with or without ruffles.

2. Tailoring treatments that are conventional and symmetrical;

3. Contrast that is fresh and soft; medium to light colors; monochromatic and analogous color schemes; cool, blue-based hues that recede.

4. Horizontal lines that are small to medium in scale, with no distinct breaks.

5. Silhouettes that are modified by soft details, e.g., bouffant sleeves or skirts, short jackets, peplums;

6. Spaces that are broken into smaller areas, e.g., areas broken by gathers, tucks, shirring, pleats, pockets, seams, embroidery, applique, buttons.

7. Details that are small in scale, e.g., dainty trim details such as small buttons, rickrack, piping, bows, or lace; rounded or gathered yokes;

8. Prints that are small in scale and of conventional designs, e.g., flowers or polka dots that blend with the background color;

9. Textures that are soft, fine, matte finish, crisp, sheer, delicate, or napped, e.g., velvet, velveteen, velour, uncut corduroy.

These are for the most part repetitions of what is found in the Spring and/or Summer guidelines, and thus those seasonal harmony types are thought of as primarily yin. Yin effects may be used by a Winter or Autumn seasonal type, who is usually considered to have more yang qualities, but only by keeping the amount of yin effects in proportion to the amount of her yin qualities, in order to avoid looking too *cute* or frilly. An Autumn or Winter woman may wish to soften her look so as to appear less dynamic and dramatic, perhaps less intimidating or threatening, and if this is the case she can use some yin effects to accomplish this.

Yang Effect is liberal, bold, dramatic, and dynamic.

Yang Effect May be Achieved by Use of the Following:

1. Lines that are unconventional, liberal, asymmetrical, overscaled, with distinct breaks or space divisions between designs in prints that are strong, dynamic and flamboyant;

2. Tailoring treatments that are angular in shape, overscaled and/or asymmetrical; unrelieved unbroken areas; large bold lapel details;

3. Color contrast that is dramatic, from light to dark in value, with the use of rich, warm based and intensified colors;

4. Vertical or diagonal design lines that have sharp breaks;

5. Silhouettes that are rectangular with straight or modified straight lines; extreme shoulder and sleeve treatment; bouffant sleeves and/or skirts; chemise or tent dresses;

6. Garments and detail that are oversized or large in scale, e.g., large pockets, sleeves, collars, cuffs, and trimmings;

7. Fabric surface designs that are large to medium size, abstract stylized prints, exotic and/or ethnic in feel, with strong contrast in prints, plaids, or stripes;

8. Textures that are heavy, stiff, rough, uneven, drapable, lustrous, metallic, and which may be either voluminous or lightweight;

9. Colors that have light and dark variation providing dramatic contrast or ones that are dark, rich or warm; or that are strong in intensity.

Winter and Autumn seasonal harmony types, having stronger yang qualities, use many of these yang effects in their style. Yin types may use yang effects in moderation, being sure to *keep them in proportion to the yang qualities they possess*. Yin types who wish to project a stronger *Dress for Success* image may wish to add additional touches of yang effects beyond their actual inner essence, but if this is overdone they will not necessarily be perceived as *stronger*, but may appear almost as a child does when dressed in adult clothing. Yang effects may also be used by the more yin types to good advantage as an illusionary camouflage for certain figure challenges.

A comparison chart of the harmonies (see p. 274-275) shows, at a glance, a comparison of the harmonies in terms of overall effect; skin, eye, and hair color; colors to wear; qualities being expressed; textures, prints, lines and preferred jewelry. (For example: Texture — The *Autumn* type is most highly yang and needs textures that are coarsely woven and uneven or with surface interest; the *Winter* type uses fabric that is smoother, more refined, drapable and less bulky; the *Spring* type uses crisp, dainty fabrics with buoyant feeling; the *Summer* type is the most yin and uses fabrics that are soft and fine-grained, pliable, and very drapable.)

While not every color analyst may be using the actual yin/yang theory per se, there does seem to be a consistency of style information that relates to the above guidelines. Often a client is invited to circle her various characteristics (see pages 182-183) totaling her yin and yang features in order to discover her own unique profile and gain more insight into the types of clothing and accessories that will most accurately reflect those characteristics.

YOUR YIN AND YANG PROFILE

(Circle those features that apply to you. Write in totals for the section and write in spaces at right. Total at end to determine your percentages of each.)

	Yin	Yang

Physique

Yin: Petite, small boned body, well proportioned, delicately formed, dainty, fragile, feminine, small or rounded features.

Yang: Tall, large boned body, well proportioned, erect posture, strong, stately, forceful, vital, dynamic energy, angular.

Medium Build and Height are equally yin and yang — well balanced.

Attitudes

Yin: Intuitive, desire to follow, receptive, submissive, yielding, angelic, fragile, tactful, desire to please, gentle, sensitive to your own needs, sensitive to the needs of others, unaffected, simple, frank, idealistic, shy, friendly, happy, coy, active, spiritual.

Yang: Objective, ambitious, compelling, aggressive, assertive, formal, desire to lead, strong willed, independent, mischievous, poised, quiet, desire to protect, dignified, dominating, decisive, dramatic, dynamic, realistic, sophisticated.

Demeanor

Yin: Light, airy, flighty, clumsy, graceful, quick.

Yang: Firm, purposeful, decisive, vigorous. Stride is heavy, controlled, deliberate, slow.

Voice

Yin: Soft, mellow, rapid, distinct, mumble, lilting, musical, calm.

Yang: Loud, strong, deep, clear, slow.

Maturity (This is not chronological age, but how you act and think)

Yin: Youthful, young, very young.

Yang: Mature, older, very old.

Complexion (Coloring)

Yin: Subdued, slight contrast, weak or soft, light golden, peach, pink, cool, delicate, blue undertones, does not tan.

Yang: Vivid, strong contrast, strong or rich coloring, dark golden, yellow beige, ruddy, olive undertones, tans readily.

Yin-Yang Questionnaire

Complexion (Skin quality and texture)

Yin: Sensitive, delicate, smooth, fresh, translucent, sometimes coarse, lightly freckled. _____

Yang: Rich, smooth, tending to be heavy texture, sometimes coarse, darker freckles, character lines. _____

Hair

Yin: Ash blonde, golden, brown with gold highlights, strawberry blonde, grayed. _____

Yang: Warm brown, black, red, frosted, bleached, sunbleached, dark auburn. _____

Eyes (Color)

Yin: Blue, purple blue, icy green, hazel, gray-blue, blue-green, green-blue, or blends of colors. _____

Yang: Brown, yellow-green, yellow, icy blue gray, rust, ebony, jewel green, jewel blue, gray-green, pale green, light blue green, topaz. _____

Eyes (Shape)

Yin: Rounded, wide open, almond, slanting downward, protruding, drooping eyelids, overhanging eyelids, large lids. _____

Yang: Oval, large, long, almond, slanting upward, narrower, deep set, close set. _____

Nose

Yin: Short, turned, up, round, delicate. _____

Yang: Long, large, straight, hooked, aquiline, flared nostrils. _____

Mouth

Yin: Small, thin line, heart shaped, delicate. _____

Yang: Large, well defined, cupid bow. _____

Profile

Yin: Small chin, receding, slanting profile, flat cheekbones, round. _____

Yang: Strong chin, strong jawline, high cheekbones, straight profile, angular. _____

Facial Shape

Yin: Oblong, rounded cheeks, heart shaped, round. _____

Yang: Long, oval, triangular, pear shaped, square, diamond, widows peak. _____

Total _____ _____

184

The Color Connection

Formalwear for All Seasons

Autumn
Illus. 277

Summer
Illus. 278

Winter
Illus. 279

Spring
Illus. 280

Key to Arrangement of Winter's Colors

Illus. 281

All Winters, but because of visual design each is on a different position on the continuum (see pages 34-39).

Exotic Winter   Target Winter   Romantic Winter

Illus. 282

One's personality position may vary not only at different times of her life, but even in the space of a day.

Winter

Illus. 283

188   The Color Connection

Illus. 284

Key to Arrangement of Spring's Colors

Illus. 285

190 The Color Connection

Illus. 286

Spring

Illus. 287

192   The Color Connection

Winter

Spring

Winter   Spring

Mothers and Daughters

Autumn   Winter

Spring

Illus. 288

Key to Arrangement of Summer's Colors

Illus. 289

Summer

Illus. 290

Illus. 291

There are many more interesting looks for the Autumn woman than a navy blue suit.

"Style is natural, never contrived. It's that special something that makes things look so easy. It's a positive, confident attitude toward life and self-expression. It's the freedom of being at peace with yourself and the way you appear to others..."
— Henry Grethel.

Winter/Spring

Illus. 292

Key to Arrangement of Autumn's Colors

Illus. 293

198 The Color Connection

Illus. 294

199

Autumn

Illus. 295

About the Author

Twelve years ago Joan Callaway opened her first store, *Centering,* an art gallery/gift store, which evolved into a gift/jewelry store with a strong emphasis on earrings. Five years later, after much urging by many of her customers, who hoped that what she had done for gifts and jewelry in their small town she would do for women's clothing, she opened *Tarika*. The two stores later were combined to form one eclectic specialty store.

She had had no prior experience in working in a clothing store, much less in buying for one — nor had she even had a great interest in fashion. Opening a clothing store had not been a long awaited dream. She was not one of those women who makes a tour of all the shops regularly or who knows all the latest trends and where to find them. She read a couple of fashion magazines a year. She had a comfortable style of her own and she did know something about the principles of art and design. She had taken tailoring classes and had sewn for herself, her three daughters and two sons.

She approached the opening of Tarika strictly as a business — not an emotionally satisfying experience. Although she reports that it has been. She decided that a consistency of taste and an interest in her customers and their needs were probably the most important things for her to remember in this new venture. Caring about customers as people was what had made the first store a success.

This sounded easy enough. But, of course, the market is full of representatives of manufacturers (reps), would-be-manufacturers, importers, and would-be-importers with a plethora of samples of merchandise to be ordered. As in any marketplace, there are varying levels of quality. This she had expected. Zeroing in on the level of merchandise that she wanted to carry in her new store was not difficult. Narrowing the selection down to her budget, however, was a major problem.

The next couple of years were a significant learning experience for Joan. Also, needless to say, she made some mistakes.

She barely had the doors open when she began to learn about COLOR...and what she has come to call *"The Color Connection."*

10
People Are a Lot Like Pasta
— or How to Use the Basic Recipe

People are a lot like pasta. And pasta? It's a lot like people. Of course, people and pasta are obviously made up of vastly different components and without any similarity in degree of complexity of composition. But, each classification is made up of its same basic *ingredients*. And those same basic ingredients come in a variety of shapes, sizes and configurations

All pasta is made up of flour and eggs. The varieties of pasta take up an entire section in the supermarket. The basic pasta — uncooked, undressed, *unaccessorized* — is a little bland, but each has its own unique character. There are endless recipes for sauces — you might think of sauce as clothing for the pasta. The possibilities seem almost inexhaustible.

When I think of fettucini — I think of Fettucini Alfredo, which I occasionally order at restaurants. I'm always amazed at how much variation there can be, even though the basic ingredients are the same. It makes a difference if the parmesan and nutmeg are freshly ground and if the chef uses real butter and cream.

When I think of linguine, I think of clam sauce. Again, the same basic ingredients can come out so differently. And the same holds true for spaghetti and lasagna. Each chef takes a basic recipe, adds his own touches to create his own unique creation — an unexpected herb, spice, mushrooms, or maybe ripe olives. A whole pantry full of possibilities!

That goes for people, too. They are all made up of the same basic ingredients, looking pretty much the same until they begin to choose from the endless possibilities to create their own unique look. The Seasonal Color Harmony system provides the basic recipe.

Just as someone with a discriminating eye and palate can recognize spaghetti, linguine, fettucini, noodles or macaroni and distinguish the differences between them, color analysts can usually identify the dominant seasonal harmony of an individual. But just as the chef adds to the original recipe a little of this and a little of that to come up with her own unique creation, each person must, in effect, be *the chef* in creating her own unique style.

Most people would probably agree that they would no doubt get bored if they ate even their most favorite pasta dish every night for dinner. But by varying the forms of pasta, the sauces, the color and the texture and by adding new and different garnishes, it is possible to enjoy pasta on a frequent basis.

The same is true of clothing. By varying a basic wardrobe in her/his colors and textures, and by adding new and different accessories to infuse one's own uniqueness, it is possible for a basic wardrobe to be enjoyed on a regular and frequent basis and simultaneously create an individual style.

The preceding chapters on the four seasons gave some basic recipes — the colors, design lines, and textures appropriate for each season. If the recipes are followed just as they are written, the wardrobe results should be good. The wearer would be well dressed in her own colors and in harmonious design lines. No one would go wrong by following the basic guidelines.

However, just as each of us has our own unique coloring and our own unique personality, each has her own natural *outer style* preferences. It is by altering the basic fashion guidelines, adding our own little zest, our own little softness, our own little zing that we express that individuality known as *style*.

The guidelines in the preceding chapters are just that — guidelines. I have come to believe that the rules of the color consultants are not arbitrary rules. They seem based on *truth*. They seem based on colors, design lines, accessories, etc. to which most people within a seasonal type intuitively will be attracted. These guidelines have evolved through observations such as mine.

It is predictable which seasonal type will buy a specific garment. It is further true that not every person within that season will be attracted to the same garment. It is also true that some garments will be purchased by more than one seasonal type. In many instances, color will be the deciding factor. For example, clothing that we call *classic* is often selected and worn by more than one seasonal type.

Just as there are different types of basic pasta (e.g., fettucini, linguine), there are different types of clothing personalities, even within a seasonal harmony, e.g., chic, elegant, sophisticated, sporty, romantic, classic, and even zany. Just as a chef adds oregano, basil, or some other herb or spice to his pasta sauces, a color-wise person can add yin and yang effects to her basic clothing to express her personality more accurately.

* * *

You may wonder about the advantages of designing or buying for a specific seasonal type. Especially when it seems that nearly everyone is a combination of seasons — when nearly everyone is altering that *ideal* in some way, adding a little of this and a little of that to make the style uniquely theirs. That's a very good question.

A garment designed and manufactured as closely as possible to the specifications for a *target* seasonal harmony — in design, color and fabrication — should assure acceptability to the greatest number of people. Each consumer would then be able to add to that ideal *target* basic style those elements that would make it more perfectly hers.

For example, the perfect *target* Spring dress conceivably might be purchased by not only the classic Spring type, but also by a Spring type with secondaries of other seasons, e.g., Golden Spring (Spring/Autumn), Floral Spring (Spring/Summer), or Vital Spring (Spring/Winter).

The more yang type Spring (tailored, classic, preppy) may buy a target Spring dress for her more romantic, frivolous occasions; the yin type will wear it for every occasion. Very likely the Summer type with a Spring secondary will enjoy it also providing the fabric is not too crisp. Clearly, the broader the appeal of a design, the more probability of sales without markdown.

With the original *recipes* clearly in mind, a designer or buyer could evaluate which yin or yang effects could be added to a specific design.

They could decide how much yin or yang could be added and still have the design palatable to an acceptable number of shoppers. And once the consumer knows the guidelines for style, the rules of yin and yang, and the laws of color, she will also know when and how she can break those rules and still appear harmoniously put together.

Unfortunately, this isn't something one can learn by poring over the fashion magazines. Trying to find perfect examples of *seasonally correct* outfits with accessories in even the best of magazines is like trying to find the proverbial needle in the haystack. Many a magazine illustration will feature an outfit containing design elements from all four seasons! It is good training and a great exercise for the eye, however, to critique and annotate such illustrations, using the guidelines in this book.

Whether you are a designer, a buyer, a sales associate or a consumer, it is useful to train your eye to recognize *good design*—design that is consistent with the guidelines. From this new perspective, practice as you peruse the fashion magazines, watch fashion shows, etc. Annotate the photographs. Decide which styles would be worn by which seasonal type and which are *design errors*—designs that are inconsistent with the guidelines. Just as you have trained your eye to recognize what formerly was thought to be good design, you must now learn new criteria and become even more discerning, incorporating design line, detail and color. For designers and buyers this will become increasingly important as the consumer becomes more season-wise.

You will learn the guidelines best and most quickly if, as you look at each item of clothing, each accessory or piece of jewelry, shoe, etc., you ask yourself the following questions:

- Who can wear this? Which seasonal color type?
- What is her clothing personality type? Would she be considered natural, dramatic, romantic, classic, ingenue? (And, if you are a retailer: Does she shop in my store? If not, is this a clientele I would like to cultivate?)
- What are the wearers saying about themselves? How do they seem to wish to be perceived?
- Are the color, pattern and design consistent with the seasonal harmony of the person who will wear it? Is the fabric texture and weight appropriate for the seasonal type? Is the style in harmony with the hair style of the model? With her accessories?
- Is there unity of design lines e.g., rounded silhouette with rounded design details?
- Does the garment express yin or yang predominantly?
- If the garment is one neutral color, where will the wearer be able to add color? (See p. 250 for guidelines for wearing neutral colors.)

This system is effective in buying. It is effective in training staff. It should be effective for designers. And, in terms of the retail clothing store, it would be effective even if customer are not carrying color swatches, matching their colors, comparing design lines, etc., because one does not have to be aware *intellectually* of these rules or guidelines to respond *emotionally* to clothing that adheres to them. These guidelines were not arbitrarily determined by someone to be *The Color Law!* They came about because many women in these categories actually have been observed to have these preferences. The guidelines have evolved because of the observations of many—a kind of informal research!

Choose Your Own Ending

Author's Note: It has been an interesting experience to try to focus this book. The book started as a training manual for my sales staff. It then evolved into a book for the retailer — buyers and sales associates. I quickly realized, however, that it all begins with the designer, that without their involvement and cooperation it could well become an exercise in futility for the buyer. And furthermore the retailer's buying task could be so much easier and more rewarding if the guidelines being taught to consumers across the nation were incorporated by more designers into their designs.

And just as I was becoming fairly comfortable with that concept, many of my customers began to look forward to this new book — one with explicit guidelines that heretofore had been quite ephemeral, one with concrete examples in the form of illustrations.

How to write to all potential readers became the challenge. My answer is a book in which you, the reader, **choose your own ending:**

It all begins with the *designer,* so if you are a designer, turn to page 205).

If you are a *retailer/buyer,* turn to page 221.

If you are a *sales associate,* turn to Chapter 13 and 14, beginning on p. 239.

If you are a *consumer,* turn to Chapter 14 and 15, beginning on p. 249.

And, if you are interested in the multi-faceted symbiotic relationship that exists between all segments of the retail clothing business, the consumer, and this relatively new theory, just read on!

11

"What If..." — For Designers and Would-Be-Designers

If you have read this far, you already know the Seasonal Color Harmony theory asserts that people with similar coloring and personalities have a natural preference for similar design details, silhouettes, and fabrics, as well as color. And, moreover, there is a correlation between them. Just as we each have our own natural *inner style,* we each have our own natural *outer style* preferences which are related to our coloring and personality.

This natural inclination to fancy one style and/or color over another seems present in a person even when they have not had their colors analyzed. Color analysis almost always *verifies* this natural preference.

Color analysis often provides the reason why a person has been attracted to particular styles and/or colors. It provides the explanation of why some styles and/or colors never seem quite right. It provides guidelines or principles which usually are consistent with the individual's already existing clothing preferences.

The Seasonal Color Harmony Guidelines evolved over time much as the natural laws of the physical world were developed. It was noted that people who had similar coloring, physical characteristics, and often very similar personality traits seemingly instinctively or intuitively selected similar colors for their clothing. It was from these generalizations that the four natural color groupings corresponding to the four seasons were derived.

There also seemed to be a consistency of design lines and design details which were preferred by the four seasonal types. From these generalizations, it became predictable which seasonal type would prefer which design lines in which colors.

This has an obvious application for the retailer/buyer and the designer:

• If it is predictable which seasonal type will buy a specific silhouette, a retailer can rule out all of those colors, prints and/or fabrics which are inconsistent with the guidelines for that seasonal harmony. And so can a designer.

For example, S. F. designer Eloise Strickland's *Etidorpha* soft, drapable jacket and bias-cut circle skirt in a rayon/linen blend cricket cloth is ideal for the Summer seasonal type. It also will be worn by some Winters, who tend to like it in natural and black; and by some Spring's, who will buy natural, occasionally black, and their very best colors, which are in the light/bright range. Most Springs ultimately will find the fabric not quite crisp enough; most Winters will wish it didn't wrinkle so. Rarely will an Autumn try it even if it is in her best colors, because the fabric is not firm enough and the style seems a bit too fluid for her tastes.

It would seem logical, therefore, for retail buyers to avoid buying *Etidorpha* styles in Autumn earthtones. The soft colors of Summer would be optimal it would appear, and the best of all worlds would be to select colors which could be worn by not only Summers, but by Winters and Springs, as well.

The Summer customer returns season after season, asking to see the latest *Etidorpha* fashions. She looks forward to the arrival of the new colors and styles confident they will be *her* style. Why does she know this? Because the *Etidorpha* designer consistently adheres to the Summer seasonal guidelines (whether she knows it or not) in shape, fabric, and fit.

Only once in the years I have been buying the line, did I notice the designer succumb to dictates of fashion, e.g., a more constructed blazer with no shirring, no fullness. I suspect those designs did not work for the traditional and loyal *Etidorpha* customer. And, while the tried and true *Etidorpha* jacket is still going strong, year after year, season after season, the blazer was never repeated; Ms. Strickland returned once again to the successful soft Summer styling. However, the Summer customer has been disappointed some seasons when *Etidorpha* has included no Summer colors in her color options.

The word *Etidorpha* is almost *Aphrodite* spelled backward. Aphrodite, the Goddess of love and beauty, embodies the qualities so often found in the Summer woman — gentleness and romanticism. I would propose Ms. Strickland, *Etidorpha's* designer-owner, had found her *target market* even as she selected the name of her company. And for the most part, she has been true to that image, much as *Jessica McClintock, J. G. Hook, Banana Republic* and *Esprit* have been true to theirs.

She does, however, sometimes produce the line in colors which are not consistent with the guidelines. I have been ordering the line for years (and editing the color selection). That, of course, is always the prerogative of the buyer — to *weed out* any ill-considered colors. But I have always wanted to tell *Etidorpha* that I would buy much more, if only she would offer more Summer colors.

By definition a designer creates or invents new things, which in this case are items of clothing, accessories or perhaps jewelry. Some would suggest the seasonal color harmony guidelines would suppress, repress, stifle or otherwise impede and preclude the creative process. While I would agree the market demands freshness and newness, I would argue that the guidelines need not restrict or interfere in any way with the creativity of a designer, who can approach a new season from any of three perspectives: color, fabric or silhouette.

- **Color.** It is predictable which seasonal type will be attracted to a specific color. Thus, it would seem a designer, wishing to adhere to the current color trends, could design with the *target* seasonal type — the one that would wear that particular color — in mind.

Who would wear that color? (The designer should keep in mind that most seasonal types can wear almost every color; it is the value, intensity or clarity, and whether it is blue- or yellow-based that determines the seasonal type who will wear a specific color.) It should also be noted that some shades of a given color can be worn by more than one seasonal type. Once the designer has zeroed in on the hue, the value, and the intensity, as well as the seasonal type who will be inclined to wear it:

Which silhouettes would be best for that seasonal type?

What kind of design detail would be appropriate for her?

What would be her fabric choice?

- **Fabric.** It is predictable which seasonal type will buy a specific fabric, e.g., because of its textural qualities, pattern, or drapability. Thus, it seems reasonable to suggest that designers would do well to select colorations and prints in harmony with the guidelines, asking:

Who is going to be most attracted to this fabric?

What are its qualities? Is it crisp (Spring)? Is it firm (Autumn)? Does it have a sheen? Will it drape (Winter)? Is it soft and drapable (Summer)?

If it is a print, which seasonal type will have a particular affinity for it?

Answers to these questions could lead the designer to determine an appropriate silhouette and design detail, and invariably those preferred by the seasonal types will be consistent with good design practices.

A good example of this might be the aforementioned cricket cloth, an ideal fabric for the Summer type. Some designers have put patch pockets on their cricket cloth jackets; they tend to droop. Summer types really don't like patch pockets. Another example might be that of Autumn's firm fabrics, which do not lend themselves to shirring and draping. The Autumn woman doesn't appreciate those design details anyway. A happy coincidence?

- **Silhouette.** A designer could have an inspiration for an innovative silhouette. It is predictable which seasonal type will have a preference for a specific silhouette, so it would seem advisable to determine which seasonal type might wear this new design. It would seem both practical and profitable for a designer to consider not only fabrics into which that silhouette could be translated, but which colors would then be consistent with the *target* market for the design lines and the fabric.

It seems to me this allows plenty of room for creative expression. And once those decisions have been made, there is design detail to consider.

- **Design Detail.** It is further predictable which seasonal type will be partial to specific design details, e.g., collars, pockets, buttons, trim.

Many of the sketches in this book are *re-*

designed styles from photographs and/or drawings found in magazines. We have changed buttons, necklines, pockets, etc. to try to make each illustration more consistent with the appropriate seasonal harmony.

It has not been uncommon for me to say: "Jo Ann, we need to redesign this a bit. Make the cuff a little narrower for the Spring. And I think the Spring would like the fit to be a bit closer to the body." Or "That belt would *cascade* for the Summer type if the fabric were softer. It should be soft at the ends, not squared. And I doubt she would like that much cleavage showing. Let's make the neckline just a tad more discrete." Or "The lapels can be a little wider for the Autumn. And she'd like it to be a bit more ample in fit."

More than once Jo Ann said, "Thank heavens for Pink Pearl!" And I bemoaned the fact that unfortunately, we don't have erasers to correct *design errors* so easily once the garments have reached the floor in the store (although I have been known to remove belts, change buttons, add pleating to camp shirt sleeves, etc.).

In our magazine survey we found some designs perfect. Others were perfect in everything but color. In some instances, the designer had chosen colors that were deemed *the fashion colors* for the season. We also noted, however, in many cases the fabric and/or silhouette were not the right ones for the seasonal type who would wear the illustrated fashion color in its particular value or intensity.

An example which immediately comes to mind is a handwoven tweed vest with exaggerated shoulder detail in soft, blue-based colors. The fabric and style were perfect for the Autumn woman; the color, however, was that of the Summer type. Beautiful fabric and beautiful colors — indeed, ones which would no doubt be highly successful in some designs.

But in this instance, the design lines led us to predict the person who would be attracted by that color and/or fabric would not fancy the style — either because she has been taught by a color analyst or because of her natural style preferences. And the Autumn person who might be attracted to the style and willing to compromise on the color would ultimately discover these colors would not coordinate well with anything else in her closet — thus a closet mistake!

The woman who has had her colors analyzed

will discover this is one of the primary causes of her past *closet mistakes*. She has been tempted too often to buy something because she *loved the style* or because it was such a bargain, only to later discover the colors were *just not right* for her. This usually means: 1) she did not look well in the colors; or 2) the colors did not coordinate with others in her existing wardrobe, e.g., the new color is bright or intense, while those in her closet are dusty, muted or subdued; or the new color is yellow-based, while *her best colors* are blue-based.

While the fabric and the style of the vest in question would be perfect for an Autumn, the colors are too soft in value, and, in this instance, blue-based. The Autumn colors are rich and yellow-based, meaning that if the Autumn type purchased the vest, she would probably have to buy new basics and new accessories to make this non-Autumn color work for her. And the usefulness of these yet-to-be-purchased basics would be limited, inasmuch as the bulk of her wardrobe would not coordinate with the new basics and accessories. Thus, she would have a whole group of closet mistakes.

It's not a Summer item either. While the color is perfect for the Summer type, most would feel overwhelmed by the exaggerated shoulder detail, the texture and the volume of the garment. (The Summer type who is *on the cusp* near Autumn might enjoy a handwoven kimono style (but without the exaggerated shoulder detail) in a lighter weight and more drapable fabric.) And, of course, the Summer would not have to buy a new wardrobe and accessories to go with the soft, blue-based vest, so it would work better for her than it ever would for the Autumn.

The designer might argue, "But it sold!" And, yes, it no doubt did. There may even have been re-orders. But how many more could perhaps have been sold if it had been in the rich yellow-based colors of Autumn. And of those that did sell, how many were hugely successful for the retailer and the consumer? How many hang virtually unworn in the closet of the consumer awaiting the purchase of something that will make it work for her?

Designers of prints might also consider the seasonal types for whom they design. All too often we see lovely silk scarves, for example, offered in a variety of colors; perhaps a small, distinct, scattered, floral print offered in four colors, i.e., buttercup yellow, mauve, olive green, and electric blue.

Clearly, the scarf designer had the four seasonal types in mind. But a little knowledge can be a dangerous thing! The Spring type will love the light/bright print — and the buttercup yellow. The Summer type will be attracted to the mauve, but wish the print were a bit larger, not quite so distinct, more blended and soft in feel. The olive green is perfect for the Autumn type, but she will react negatively to the little almost animated flowers, wishing for geometric or leaf shapes — or even an animal print motif. The electric blue is an obvious choice for the Winter type, but again "Not little flowers!" She'd rather have a striking abstract design, uneven stripes or perhaps a snowflake motif.

Just as the design of a garment or accessory dictates which material should be used, or as the fabric (shell, gemstone, leather, metal, etc.) will suggest a possible style to a designer, the style *and* fabric dictate the best colors for the item — colors in which that style and fabric will be most successful at retail.

Not every design *should* be translated into a color suitable for each of the four seasons nor should every design be translated into all of the *fashion colors* deemed by the color forecasters to be *in*. If the style, fabric and color are in harmony with one of the seasonal types, the item is sure to be more successful at retail — and certainly more successful for the consumer. And ultimately more successful for the designer: a customer truly satisfied with an outfit will seek out that name brand again and again.

The theory is also applicable to the design of jewelry, shoes, hats, bags and even to some extent interior design, although I have not gone into that in this book. (See chapters relating to each season).

In *jewelry,* for example:

For *Winter,* think about icy looks, jewels which sparkle, oval shapes, sculpted or abstract designs; silver, white gold or platinum settings; clear intense colors, etc. For *Spring,* consider trendy, whimsical or cute ideas, round shapes, flowers, hearts, teddy bears, etc. all on a small scale. *Summer* types will prefer their jewelry to create oval shapes, as in the drape of longer length pearls, S-shapes as in twisted pearls; oval shapes in pins, earrings, etc.; shell shapes, roses or other medium scale flowers, iridescent jewels in jewel tones, e.g., amethyst, rose quartz, etc. For *Autumn* remember the rectangle or any part thereof, (e.g., triangular shapes), leaf shapes, rich colors, texture, copper, gold, wood, leather, leather thongs, pods or other naturalistic effects.

Designers should think of the *mood* of the jewelry, accessory, shoe, print, etc. Is it animated, pert and perky (Spring)? soft and romantic (Summer)? earthy and exotic (Autumn)? or striking, sophisticated, and regal (Winter)?

The above described scarf was definitely pert and perky with almost animated little flowers scattered over the solid background. This retailer purchased the scarf only in the buttercup yellow. Had the scarf also been offered in colors like shrimp, periwinkle blue, and cherry red, for example, I would have purchased all four colors, knowing my Spring customers would love them all.

Fashion coordinators for fashion shows and magazines would also do well to consider the mood of the clothing to be modeled and the seasonal harmony of the model they are outfitting. We always get a chuckle out of some of the accessory magazines for the trade that find their way into our store: the model often looks much as she probably did as a little girl when she played dress-up, overladen with all of the jewelry she could find in her mother's drawers. Hardly an example for a retailer or a consumer to emulate, unless, of course, she is an Autumn. Remember, retailers and consumers look to you for fashion direction. Don't lead them to excess — or astray!

* * *

"Why Is It So Hard to Find My Colors?"

Retailers hear that question a lot. They hear it from Autumns and sometimes Winters in the spring and summer months; they hear it from Springs and Summers during the fall of the year.

"What do I wear in the summer months, Joan? Everything is so pastel. The colors on my palette look so dark," from an Autumn type. The answer, of course, is that if she can find her medium to dark colors in linen, linen blends, raw silk, a coarse cotton, etc., the darker colors will look just right on her — neither dark nor hot.

The Autumn woman can wear natural, beige, khaki, moss greens, terra cotta, gold, mustard, teal, lime green, avocado, jade, etc., *if she can find them*. Now therein lies the rub! Typically, the spring selection for the Autumn type is restricted to the Banana Republic or safari look, some natural linen suiting and an occasional shirtwaist dress.

I am reminded of a sportswear designer who produced a great Autumn style in the Spring of 1985. I noticed that much of the collection, unfortunately, ended up on the sales rack in both the Sacramento and San Francisco Bay areas. The designer had turned to the traditionally lighter colors for Spring, although not pastels. The exaggerated shoulder padded look of the twill Eisenhower jacket with its military styling, complete with epaulettes and wonderful big pleated patch pockets, could have been perfect for the Autumn woman. The pants were also suited to her — an easy pleated trouser with a front zipper, cropped at the ankle.

The entire collection was in Autumn styling. Not one piece was in an Autumn color. The jacket and trousers were offered in soft cadet blue or a dusty fuchsia — both Summer colors. One shirt for the group was in a little woven print of dusty fucshia within a soft gray stripe on white; the other was a white ground with stripes of the soft fuchsia and the dusty blue. Both were oversized and shoulder-padded camp shirts in wonderful fabric. Rarely will an Autumn wear stark white; and the other colors were also much too soft and Summer-like. Yet, rarely would a Summer type wear such a bold, masculine look. A great group *gone wrong* because of a *design error* in color selection.

Spring is traditionally a light, bright season. Designers of spring lines tend to be influenced by the season and drawn to the fresh, new spring flowers and light/bright Spring colors or the soft colors of Summer, often neglecting the needs of Autumn and Winter shoppers. (It often seems easier for the Winter type. She can always wear red, black or white!) Even so, many Winters also complain that it is much more difficult to feel *put together* during the Summer months.

It takes special effort on the part of store buyers to fill this gap in their stores in order to meet the needs of the Autumn woman, who is rarely comfortable wearing white, pastels, or light/bright colors, and certainly not the dainty little prints or even the large floral prints of Summer in the typically more feminine styling associated with the spring buying season. The retailer must search for Autumn colors in more yang styling and in firmer fabrics, and this is not an easy task. Most Autumn women will grumble about their sparse summer wardrobes. As a buyer I grumble and have often said, "Some manufacturer could make a fortune if he would only produce a summer line specifically for the sadly neglected Autumn woman."

It is likewise true that the color forecasters and designers seem to turn to the colors of the autumn and winter season for their colors for that delivery period. The designs of the autumn and winter season are also apt to be more dramatic and dynamic, more yang in feel. And, of course, that makes buying for the Spring and Summer types more difficult. Happily, this trend seems to be changing.

There seem to be more *pretty* colors available during this time period than in the past. But traditionally people have gravitated to darker colors for their heavier clothing during the much colder and wetter fall/winter season.

In the olden days, before clothes dryers and dry cleaning, winter clothes always had to be hung to dry in the basement or by the kitchen stove. They took forever to dry. Dark clothes were no doubt worn because they scarcely showed the dirt and didn't have to be laundered so often. Surely we can abandon that outmoded tradition now.

Autumn and Winter colors and styles, although popular with the designers for the *autumn time period,* cannot be successfully worn by over half the buying population. Spring and Summer colors and styles, likewise popular with the designers for the *spring delivery period* are similarly inadequate. Just as I have urged the retailers to search for Autumn colors and styles for spring delivery, etc., I now urge designers to respond to this need and to the needs of the other seasonal types, as well.

I look at the designer-retailer-consumer relationship as a symbiotic one — mutually advantageous. It is so clear to me that I would find buying much easier and that I could sell more merchandise if the designers were influenced by the seasonal harmony principles.

My customers have become more discriminating and *color* sophisticated. For the most part, they are satisfied customers. They like the quality. They like the service. They like the fact that they can count on us to help them discover their style. Obviously, I have to stock garments that are as true to the seasonal *target* principles as possible.

I can hear it now if I should bring in merchandise that is not within the guidelines: "Joan, who's going to buy this? It has a Spring collar and buttons, the drape of a Summer skirt, and a print of Winter." (And I will grant that there may be a very limited market for that design—a Winter with a Spring/Summer secondary perhaps. A Spring with a Winter/Summer secondary would probably find the print too large, but might be willing to compromise if it were in her colors or some might on impulse buy it if it were a hot new fad; the Winter print would undoubtedly be too overpowering for the Summer type, even if she did have a Spring/Winter secondary.) This type of garment is definitely *at-risk* for a markdown.

As greater numbers of shoppers learn about the seasonal color harmony and become more discriminating, I suspect fewer of those mixed-message styles will be purchased—even at markdown prices. I certainly urge my customers to buy off the sale rack only if they would have paid full retail for it, i.e., the item is perfect for them.

I hear increasingly often, "Well, I guess I'll have to have it made," as another frustrated shopper turns to her seamstress or tailor to create her best styles with her distinctive design details in her best colors. This shopper could be a *customer.* She'd rather buy a ready-to-wear garment that she can try on, one that she knows is right, since there's always risk the first time a pattern is used. She doesn't really have the time for fittings, much less time to traipse around to fabric stores, etc. But if she can't find her colors in her style in the stores, what else can she do?

So What's a Designer to Do?

Designers and manufacturers are no doubt as interested in greater customer satisfaction, fewer markdowns, and increased profitability as retailers. At least, from my perspective, consumer dissatisfaction and/or excessive markdowns related to a given manufacturer will negatively impact my re-orders and, I suspect, ultimately the profitability picture of that vendor if enough retailers have similar reactions. Surely that will sooner or later ripple to affect the designer and everyone in that organization.

Planning tends to be my answer to almost everything, and I'm sure that every designer has to do a lot of that, too. A part of my planning process always includes a bit of fantasy, a bit of "What if...?"

My Fantasy

This is how I imagine it could be — in simplified and abbreviated form, of course:

The designer sits in his/her studio, looking over the style numbers of the past season and how they have been received by the consumer. Now is the time to think about how the *hot* numbers of the current or past seasons can be improved upon, whether they should be refabricated in the new fashion colors, prints, novelties, etc.

Once the color trends are announced, fabric companies begin to call and send information, giving designers fashion direction. The designer begins to review available fabrics, which stimulate his/her imagination. Sketches of possible design directions are made; sample yardage is ordered. Some proven bodies from previous seasons may be refabricated.

It's cost effective to re-use as many of these bestseller patterns as possible since size grading and patternmaking have already been done and the manufacturer knows they are successful at retail. But newness and freshness are needed, so new designs will be created and new patterns will be made.

Draping, sketching and patternmaking follow. The story boards are exciting. The styles have been costed out, some styles have been eliminated, others added — that *weeding out* process that always occurs. Everyone is hopeful for a successful new season. But everybody makes mistakes!

What if in this *weeding out* process there was an evaluation by a seasonal-color-harmony-experienced eye?

What if there was a critique even before the samples are cut? The designer might wish to make modifications, but it would be early-on in the design process. The repercussions at this point would be fewer by far than is currently the case if a collection is not accepted by retailers at market, i.e., if the needed orders are not forthcoming. This critique could occur long before a rep has taken the collection to market, long before a great investment has been made in time or money.

Sometimes suggested changes might be major ones, but often even subtle changes could make a big difference. Changes, such as softly rounding the edge of a notched collar, adding a bit more shirring at the sleeve cap, using buttons made of a different material or in a different shape, or narrowing a cuff or a ruffle could mean greatly increased sales.

Or in the case of the Autumn sportswear group produced in Summer colors, the consultant probably would have said, "This is a great collection, but it is really an Autumn look. I think it would do far better at retail if you cut it in this same twill, but darken that cadet blue to a rich teal or a jade green and the soft fucshia could be replaced by a terra cotta. I wouldn't change another thing. It's great!"

The objective trained eye of a consultant could quickly spot the discordant details or *design errors* — she would perform much like my editor and proofreader.

Which leads me to a little philosophical aside: There is an old adage, which goes something like "only those who are doing things make mistakes", implying that those who don't make any mistakes are perhaps playing it too safe. I don't think there's anything wrong with not being perfect — with making a grammatical error or a *design error*. In fact, the drive to be perfect can be absolutely stultifying and crippling.

I admire so much the parents and teachers of my nine-year-old granddaughter, who is a talented and prolific writer. Much of her spelling is phonetic. In another era that would have been criticized to such an extent that she might have confined her writing only to words that she could spell, which, of course, would have been very limiting. As it is, once she has her ideas on paper, she can go back with the help of a *consultant,* who points out her errors. She can correct them. The end result is a much more interesting letter or composition than would have been possible had she not been willing to make a mistake.

As I write this chapter, which is the last to be written, I am aware that it needs to be thoroughly proofread. I've read and re-read the book — and yet, each time I read it I make corrections. I find grammatical errors. I find typographical errors. And I find ideas I want to add and things I want to change. I suspect that even as it goes to press that will be true.

When I have done my best, when I can no longer be objective, when I cannot see my own errors, I send it off to a *consultant,* an editor, who will look at it with a fresh, new objective eye. That is what I am suggesting — an editor or a proofreader.

Only instead of being concerned with punctuation and spelling, the designer's editor or proofreader would be a consultant who would critique the line in terms of the seasonal color harmony principles. And just as the author has the right to disagree with an editor whether to change a clause or use a dash, semicolon or period, the designer, of course, would have veto power. But, of course, just as an author is interested in making his book as easily understood and accepted by readers as possible, the designer would hopefully want to make the corrections necessary to make the design consistent with the guidelines for the specific *target* seasonal type, and thus make it desirable to more retailers and consumers.

At this point, samples would be made. The finished collection, of course, would already have been coordinated to mix and match and/or display well together.

What if the collection were annotated as to the appropriate seasonal harmony for each style number? (What if they used symbols similar to those used by *Garanimals* for children's clothing. But instead of lions and tigers to indicate groups that coordinate, maybe a daffodil could be used for Spring, a rose for Summer, a snowflake for Winter, and an autumn leaf for Autumn.

What if, to carry this one step further, there were also included on the line sheets (or as a part of the style number) an indication as to which items were intended to be used with others? This could certainly prevent a buyer from inadvertently selecting the wrong skirt or blouse, ones designed to go with a jacket other than the one she ordered. This would be a great convenience for the buyer, who would immediately know that each design was within the boundaries of a seasonal harmony, as well as how the designer envisioned the coordination of the group.

What if there was a standardization of sizes so that a buyer would know in advance which sizes to order? What if a size 4 was always a size 4? Not sometimes equivalent to a size 6. Obviously, the *fit* would still vary from line to line, but there would not be such a drastic variance between the same labeled sizes from the different vendors.

What if the rep became more knowledgeable about the seasonal color harmony system and how his line relates to it? He would be on the *cutting edge*. The rep might find this a great sales aid. A truly color-knowledgeable rep could be of great service to retailers. And as more and more retailers become concerned about meeting the needs of their color-savvy customers, this could give a color-wise rep a decided advantage. Of course, this will only work if the designer of his line has opted to buy-in to the concept.

To carry on with my fantasy:

The line is shown in showrooms and markets across the country to delighted retailers who buy in larger than ever quantities. But we all know that in retail the consumer always has the last word. Even so, in my fantasy they all live happily ever after with color-sophisticated customers flocking to the stores in greater than ever numbers, clearing the racks like locusts and filling their closets with clothes that coordinate as never before — ones that express perfectly their inner essence.

* * *

The symbiotic designer/retailer/consumer relationship is ever present. The retailer must buy merchandise for his store to meet the needs of his customers. Currently the market is replete with designs inconsistent with the seasonal harmony theory — an idea whose time has come.

Clearly, if the retailers reject *design errors*, designers will ultimately get the message. It is my fantasy that a more positive approach could make the transition smoother and shorter — and lead to greater acceptance, satisfaction, and profitability for all.

220   The Color Connection

A Coat for All Seasons

Winter

Illus. 296

Spring   Illus. 297

Summer

Illus. 298

Autumn   Illus. 299

12

Rags to Riches or Markdown Madness — A Retailer's Choice

It may all begin with the designer, but it is the retailer who can make or break a line. Today's ready-to-wear retailer as never before must offer more and better service, always honing his skills — of buying, merchandising, and selling.

Skill and service must, of necessity, begin with the *buying* — the *editing* of the lines at market, the *weeding out* of all the lines and price points that are inappropriate for his customers. Equally, if not more important, is the elimination of styles in certain colors and fabrics that are inappropriate for the target or near-target seasonal harmony types, as well as colors that are inappropriate in certain fabrics and styles, etc. By *target,* of course, I mean the true, pure 100% seasonal type — the original recipe!

What I am suggesting, of course, is a substitution of skill and service in place of markdowns, having at most two clearance sales a year. And being sure that during those clearance sales there is plenty of exciting new merchandise on hand that may be sold at full retail in addition to sale items. Creative merchandising, alert staff and suggestive selling of related merchandise of non-sale items can *water down* the disastrous effect of excessive markdowns during a clearance sale.

Markdowns are the easy way out. Not only do they cut into your profits, but continuous markdowns with the inevitable accompanying cramped and cluttered look have a detrimental effect on the atmosphere and the image of a specialty store. "But everybody seems to be doing it!" you might add. Retailers seem to feel that if they are to be competitive with the proliferating discount stores they must discount, too.

Many stores find themselves competing solely on the basis of price, worrying constantly about what the major department stores and the discounters are doing. A small boutique or specialty store cannot expect to compete with a major department store in terms of buying power, or even in getting markdown money from the manufacturers.

What the specialty store retailer must realize, of course, is that the discounter has made special purchases — bought off-price goods — and is dealing with large volume purchases and high traffic. The high volume, heavy traffic store is able to show a profit, even though maintaining a lower mark-up. In contrast to the full specialty store, it relies not only on high volume but also on holding down expenses percentage-wise through such devices as low rent, low sales clerk to customer ratio with cashiers instead of helpful clerks, fewer amenities, community dressing rooms, etc.

Why all the big fuss about markdowns? Markdowns can be defined in retail as any reduction in the retail price. If you have ever wondered at the end of a great month why your bottom line figure — your net profit — showed a loss or only a very small profit, *markdowns* are no doubt the guilty factor.

Markdowns — Or Where Did All the Money Go?

Obviously, a profitable retailer sells more at full retail than at markdown prices, but many retailers markdown rather haphazardly. And this is how it usually works. A sportswear group is purchased; most of them sell at full retail. But there are a few odds and ends left on the racks — not really enough to put together for a customer. So you, the retailer, mark them down. How do you know whether your profit goal on this group will be met? Let's assume your goal was 15% profit...and work backward.

Let's also assume that you *keystone* or markup 50% retail.

Retail Price	100%
Less Cost of Goods	− 50%
Equals Gross Profit	50%
Less Expenses	− 35%
Equals Net Profit	15%

This assumes that you are able to sell all the merchandise at full retail. Let's take a look at what happens if you reduce only one of the group by 20%. Assume that six jackets were purchased at $75 each (keystone price equals $150) and that:

5 sold at full retail	$750
1 sold at 20% off	120
Total net sales =	$870

The Gross Profit = Net Sales ($870) minus Cost of Goods ($450) = $420.

• Your *maintained markup* on this jacket is the *percentage the gross profit is of the initial retail price for all six pieces.* (maintained markup (x%) = gross profit divided by full retail price)

$$\frac{\text{Gross Profit } (\$420)}{\text{Full Retail } (\$900)} = 46.6\%$$

Your maintained markup was 46.6%. To determine your net profit, subtract your operating expenses of 35%. Your net profit is 11.6%, or 3.4% less than your projected profit figure of 15%.

Were you to sell only four of the jackets at full retail ($600), one at 20% off ($120) and one at one-third off ($100), you would reduce your maintained markup to 41% and your net profit to 6%. If you sell four of the jackets at full retail, one at one-third off and one at 50% off, your maintained markup will plummet to 36% and your profit to 1%. AND THAT'S WHERE THE MONEY GOES!

As you can clearly see, it behooves the retailer to find ways to reduce markdowns. And that's where the Color Connection comes in: offering improved buying, better merchandising, improved sales techniques, etc.

Substitute Service for Markdowns

It is a well known fact that retailers lose millions of dollars each year in markdowns. Sales have become a habit! I hear customers say of the major department stores, "Why pay full retail when I can wait two weeks for it to go on sale?" New browsers at Tarika sometimes ask me when the price on an item will be reduced. My response is always, "When I can't sell it at full retail: perhaps when the sizes are so broken it is no longer possible to put an outfit together, or if I can't put it with another group for a terrific look!"

My regular customers *value* what *Tarika* has to offer. Most don't seem all that concerned with price — they do want fashion and they like service. They like the merchandise we have selected — and the way we help them put it together. They appreciate that we understand their style and are willing to buy for them. For the most part, they do not want the struggle of shopping even at department stores, much less discount stores.

Each season, my staff and I have *edited* the market, selecting what we consider the best merchandise in the correct colors, design lines, etc. for each of the seasonal types. We offer service — wardrobe consulting by knowledgeable personnel, skill in helping our customers put themselves together, alterations and personal shopping for our clients. We even make *house calls,* doing what we have come to call *Closet Consultations.* We present Personal Image classes in which we overview The Color Connection. We sponsor Dominant Harmony Seminars, which are attended only by people who share that one particular seasonal type.

These Dominant Harmony seminars are always enlightening. As we were showing some scarf samples to a group during a Winter Dominant Harmony seminar, one Winter woman said that she hated bows and therefore never used scarves. We said that was not surprising as many Winter women feel the same way, that they often prefer their scarves tied loosely in an ascot, etc. The women, all Winters, were surprised that they were all so compatible in their thinking about many aspects of their wardrobes. It was not surprising to those of us who have been studying the subject.

If your customers are not yet *color sophisticated,* this is your chance to bring in a color consultant for a seminar or make-over. This will be good training for staff, too. Or when you feel comfortable with the concept, demonstrate similarly how knowledgeable you and your staff have become. Or if you wish to be more subtle about it, practice showing shoppers seasonally correct on-target dresses, accessories or complete outfits. They will think you ever so clever to choose the perfect thing when you don't even know them.

Honing Buying Skills Is Another Way to Reduce Markdowns

Try to ascertain at the time you write your purchase order whether the manufacturer sells to off-price retailers. If he does, you might want to reconsider your order, knowing that the items you order may very well appear in a nearby discount store at a price with which you cannot compete. I believe that the only way to discourage this practice is to make it known that you will not buy from companies that sell to off-price retailers. Why should you show your confidence in a line by committing your money months ahead with your signed purchase order, pay full dollars for the privilege, when that same merchandise is either being currently discounted to stores with more buying clout or being dumped as overstock in mid-season to anyone who will take it — meaning almost certain markdowns for you if those stores happen to be nearby?

Think about making this a part of your purchase order agreement. A written, contractual agreement will provide recourse to go back to the manufacturer for markdown money if you should discover current season merchandise that you've just gotten onto the selling floor on sale at greatly reduced prices at nearby discount stores.

Incidentally, the manufacturers and their reps can't be expected to know your problems unless you tell them! On more than one occasion, I have gone back to a rep with a complaint about finding current merchandise off-price in a nearby discount store, as well as an occasional incidence of the cut or fit of a garment being unsatisfactory, and graciously been given markdown money.

The Weeding Out Process

• *Train your eye.* Go through fashion magazines, *Women's Wear Daily,* etc., critiquing the fashions in terms of consistency of design line and detail, color and style. Which seasonal type will wear the garment? Think of specific customers — which of them will wear which styles? Is the color correct for the design lines? Is the color, print pattern and/or fabric correct for the seasonal type who will wear the style?

When going through fashion magazines, etc. be aware that it is not always possible to ascertain accurately the *season* of the models, since for photo sessions they usually wear heavy make-up and sometimes colored contacts, and occasionally bleached or dyed hair. In addition, models wear colors and styles they are given to wear, not necessarily what is *right* for them; additional make-up compensates for *mistakes*. And sometimes they look as though the outfits were put together by the three blind mice. The models may be wearing a jacket suitable for one season, the hat and bag of another, and jewelry from yet another—none looking particularly appropriate for her visual design and hair style. This would be a fashion coordination error.

Look for design errors within a specific garment, as well as fashion coordination errors, e.g., blouse collar inconsistent with the design lines of the jacket, wrong belt, etc. Look, too, for designs which seem inconsistent with visual image of model, such as a soft, feminine style on a very angular, natural Autumn seasonal harmony type.

● *Look for unity of design.* Design lines should be consistent throughout an outfit in terms of art principles, but also in terms of the Seasonal Color Harmony. For example:

a) If a jacket has an asymmetrical closure, there should be no center front detail on skirt. With a tailored sleeve, this will be the preference of the Autumn seasonal type and will therefore probably sell better in rich earthtone coloration and with other design details based on the rectangle and/or natural effects (e.g., horn or wooden buttons). In addition, the Autumn types will like texture and body in their fabrics and they tend to like things a bit oversized — never skimpy.

b) Rounded lapels mean rounded or concealed pocket detail and softer sleeve treatment. This style will probably appeal to Spring, Summer and perhaps Winter types, depending on fabric, length of jacket, and details. Spring types will like the fabric to be crisp; Summers will like fabrics soft and fine-grained with feminine tailoring and simple lines. This might also be suitable for a Winter, if done in Winter colors, but she would prefer a longer jacket, with uncluttered lines. She might appreciate more sophisticated or even somewhat exaggerated high fashion styling or uncluttered simplicity in smooth fabrics. (See Comparative Chart, page 274.)

c) Raglan sleeves should have a French dart rather than a straight bust dart for unity of design.

● *Design lines can create shapes.* Design lines can create oval, rounded, triangular, and rectangular shapes; they can create shell, heart, petal or leaf shapes also. They can create these shapes and others that remind one of shapes that relate to a specific seasonal type.

Watch those inner design line shapes in conjunction with outer silhouette, colors and fabrics for consistency in terms of their suitability for the various seasonal harmony types.

a) Be aware that shapes are created by *stitching lines, braids, ribbons, quilting, rickrack,* etc.

b) *Shapes created by yokes* may be rounded, v-shaped, or ovals. Gathers on yokes create softness, as do ruffles.

c) Observe *shapes created by gores,* e.g., tulip, a-shape, tent.

d) Watch *shapes created by sleeves,* e.g., rectangle, square, oval, petal, shell.

e) Think about *belt shapes, buckles, buttons,* etc. in terms of seasonal harmony types. Belts and buckles come in many shapes and materials: and can be round, heart shaped, teddy bears, and other animated and whimsical ideas (Spring (Sp)), shells, knots or ovals in fabric or in silver metals (Summer (SU)), ovals or abstract designs in silver (Winter (W)), square, rectangular or leaf shapes in brass, gold, copper, wood, bone (Autumn (A)). Some examples that might be considered design errors would be rectangular shapes in silver, ovals in gold, etc. If an animal print fabric is being used, the belt buckle would be best in Autumn's gold, brass, copper, wood or bone, since she is most apt to be the one to wear it. We currently have a belt in the shape and color of a slice of watermelon, complete with black beads for the seeds. I feel fairly confident that a Spring type will love it!

All design detail should relate to the seasonal design rules. Think about the target seasonal type when you look at belts, for example: a self-tie belt, one with double D-rings, obi tie belts, tassled sashes, chain link, elasticized, Guatemalan handwoven sashes, floral or tapestry prints, webbing, contour or shaped contour belts or ones with trapunto stitching, multi-ribbon effects, knots, beads, macrame.

Don't let an imperfect belt deter you from buying the garment if all else is perfect. Often belts can be removed, priced and sold as separate items. Usually you will have a better belt in stock, which will provide an add-on sale. I recall once having a khaki pant that came with a yellow-red web belt. It was displayed with a narrow striped khaki/red Reminiscence boatneck ¾ sleeve T-shirt. It sold very well until we ran out of the T-shirt. When there was no longer the perfectly matched shirt, there was no longer any interest in this very basic pant. When the red belt was removed (and put in a basket marked "free belt with purchase of khaki pants"), the pant sold out immediately at the full retail price.

I have had similar experience in removing bows from blouses, especially if the bow happens to be in an off-beat color that doesn't relate to other merchandise in stock. The blouse may be perfect otherwise, but if the bow is in the wrong color or if the shopper isn't a *bow person,* sometimes it can be a real obstacle. She may not wish to buy the perfect blouse because she doesn't want the tie!

f) Think about *collar shapes* in terms of seasonal harmony: basic ring, shawl, portrait, v-neck, square, jabot, mandarin, straight band, Peter Pan, Pilgrim, turtle, cowl, etc.

g) Think about *skirt shapes,* but more for different figure types than for seasonal color harmonies, although there is some correlation. Examples: Autumn and Winter types often are more angular and can often wear slimmer straight skirts, while Spring and Summer types are often more rounded, requiring more fullness. Autumn types frequently have a brisker stride and prefer kick pleats, etc. Summer types prefer the softness of inverted soft pleats.

h) *Look at pockets.* While almost every woman enjoys pockets in skirts, dresses and jackets, remember that Summer and Winter seasonal types prefer an uncluttered look. Because patch pockets visually add bulk, larger sizes will not want pockets over hip areas or bust, depending on their particular figure challenges. Pockets emphasize and draw the eye of the observer to the area of placement. Therefore, it is probably better to buy those garments with patch pockets over the chest or in the hip area only in smaller sizes even in the colors of Spring and Autumn.

A pant pocket lining peeking through is most unattractive and distracting, so be sure concealed pockets are really *concealed.* This same warning also applies to the ubiquitous shoulder pad. Shoulder pads should not be seen! Many sheeting fabrics and drapable blends are too sheer or clingy for either pocket treatment or shoulder pads. Examine fabric for see-through qualities. If you intend to purchase an item in white (and while this phenomenon is particularly true for white, it can also be a problem with other light colors), and the garment is sampled only in colored fabric, be sure to check the white fabric swatch for opacity. Pockets or shoulder pads may not show through in a colored fabric, but often will be very obvious in white or lighter fabrics which are less dense.

• *Look for button placement.* Your bosomy customer will be forever grateful if you help her to discover the trick to avoid *gaposis*. Encourage her to buy only blouses that are perfect for her bustline — with buttons placed parallel to the apex of her bust, as well as at the neck, waist and hipline. Sometimes a correctly fitting bra, of course, will make a big difference in location of *apex* of bustline. It continues to amaze me how few women know how to determine their correct bra size for a proper fit. My customers appreciate a reminder now and then, either posted in dressing rooms or in my newsletter. (See p. 261.)

• Remember to watch for *design-on-design*. This is a particularly important consideration when selecting blouses to wear with suit jackets. Lines should repeat — not oppose. Notches need to be same general shape even if they don't match perfectly. With a shawl collar, for example, you would not want to use the opposing design lines of a notched collar, but with a notched lapel you would use a smaller notched collar that was similarly shaped and was generally aligned.

• *A balanced mix of merchandise will increase sales. Add one more category to your Open-to-Buy.* As retailers, you no doubt currently plan your purchases in terms of financial limitations, cash flow projections, projected sales, and need for various types of clothing for your clientele (loosely defined as Open To Buy (OTB). This last item is what this book is all about. In addition to the right mix by classification and price point, timed deliveries so that you can pay for them, etc., add a *balanced mix — a proportional representation of the seasonal harmonies in relation to your clientele.*

Just as some stores cater to petites, others confining their merchandise to tall and big, etc., I suppose it would be possible to specialize in just one season. In fact, I know of a store that without knowing it, was a *Winter* specialty store, because the buyer was a Winter and bought primarily for herself. It was a paradise for the Winter shopper!

Dismal for every other seasonal type.

The very trendy store with a mix of upbeat, light and bright, fun clothing is naturally going to have more appeal for Spring types, as well as the very young. Ethnic clothing boutiques and stores that specialize in hand-woven garments or *Banana Republic* looks are likewise a dream come true for some Autumn types.

For broader appeal, you may want to *achieve a more balanced mix of merchandise according to the seasonal harmony theory*. Do a bit of market research before your next market. Enlist the aid of your clientele. Develop a short questionnaire, asking whether customer has had a color analysis, and, if so, her season; if not, her favorite colors, her favorite designers, etc. Even if she doesn't know her seasonal harmony type, a listing of her *favorite colors* will usually be a good indication of her season, interestingly enough. You might entice a good response by the use of a *Help us Update Our Mailing List* or a *Join Our Birthday Club* card.

Once again, be aware that you may already have influenced the mix of your clientele with *your buying* just as the previously mentioned Winter store. (Incidentally, I doubt the store owner was aware that she had created a Winter store — it was not advertised as such.) If you currently don't buy with a good mix of designs for the seasonal harmony types, you too, could have an imbalance in your clientele mix. For example, I was unable to find many good Autumn styles and colors at the last spring market, so Autumn types are finding Tarika *slim pickin's* this spring much to my and their chagrin and consternation! Unfortunately, because of this lack of balance in merchandise many Autumn types who walk through my store this Spring may never come back — they may decide Tarika is just not their style!

You need to take this balance of merchandise into consideration when you are setting your goals and objectives. *Do you want to broaden your appeal to include all seasons and perhaps thereby increase your clientele and increase your profits?* How many women walk through your store, browse, and walk out — perhaps never to come back, because you are *just not their style?* It's something to ponder!

How to Remember What You've Seen

Do not be discouraged if it seems overwhelming at the beginning. And remember, you may not get it perfectly first try. It takes time to learn the theory and be able to apply it. I hired a color analyst to work for me part time for awhile. It helped her; it helped me. She learned more about the industry and more about fashion in general, which helped her business. She went to market with me one season and helped me critique the lines.

You will make mistakes. But you are making mistakes now, too. Much more importantly, you will do more things right. You'll improve your buying in other ways. I have found that I have become even more discerning of all details, e.g., pocket placement, fit, etc., since applying the theory to my buying practices. Even subtle improvements count.

I can almost hear you muttering, "How on earth do you remember everything, especially over a long buying season." Obviously, it would help if you had a photographic memory and a computer-like mind. But I don't. And if I can do it, *you can do it!*

- *Train your eye* to quickly recognize design errors, etc.
- Take good notes. (See reviewing a line, p. 232.)
- *Make sketches or take snapshots.* (I always try to have at least one person on my staff who is fairly skilled in making quick sketches.) I also carry a small camera and take photos of the groups that I'm thinking about. My photo shop gives 4-hour service on color, so I can quickly attach the photos to my notes. Some people use polaroid cameras.
- Ask for swatches. Some vendors are able to make them available to you, but unfortunately many are not.
- *Develop a code to rate the lines* as you review them, e.g., three stars for *must buy,* two stars for *think about,* and one star for *check out next market.* (You may be using a star system for each style number, too, which may seem confusing. It really isn't, since one set of stars appears by the name of the manufacturer and the other by the style number.)

Reviewing a Line

- *Establish whether the vendor meets your criteria.* Ask the manufacturer's representative:
- *Does the vendor already have an account in my area?* There is no point in wasting your time and that of the rep if they already sell to your nearby competitor. Rarely is there any merchandise worth duplicating. It is much more exciting and profitable to bring something new to your area — something that your competition has not yet discovered.
- *Do they sell to off-price retailers?* If you buy from vendors who sell to off-price competitors, you will later surely find yourself faced with unprofitable markdowns.
- *What are their minimums per order? per style?* If yours is a small store, maybe the minimum requirements of some manufacturers will be excessive.
- *Rate the styles* as you're taking notes. Develop a code to make it easy. (I use a three star system: three stars for a must buy; two stars for *think about*; and one star is *good* and certainly worth consideration if I need to fill in later and it is still available, maybe even at off-price.) Keep your notes until later in the season for handy reference when you talk to your rep about availability of fill-in merchandise.
- *Identify seasonal harmony of each style you plan to order.* Develop a code to tell you the seasonal harmony style, e.g., SP (Spring), SU (Summer), A (Autumn), W (Winter), noting beside each style number the seasonal code and the preferred color for each. You may later wish to balance your orders according to the proportion of the seasonal harmonies of your clientele. This coding will facilitate this balancing act!
- *Evaluate items as you go.* Make a *scarecrow* on the rep's rack of the items that you like most so that:

   a) You can *visualize* how they might look together on a rack in your store;

   b) You can *take a photograph* to refresh your memory later as you go over your notes and sketches. It sometimes helps to *block the order* on vendor's purchase order, making size choices for each style number, noting appropriate seasonal harmony, etc.

   c) *Sketch the styles* that you like and make notations referring to style numbers, colors in which it is available, sizes, etc.

d) Be sure to note *completion dates, terms, size range, style numbers* that you like, *name of representative, address,* etc. A small kit containing a mini-stapler and paper clips, as well as a measuring tape are often helpful if not essential to the task.

• *Compare colors with a color chart.* I have accumulated little swatches of approximately 1500 colors, which have each been assigned a number. Once I have decided on a style (given it a three star rating), particularly if it is a suit that will need to be matched to blouses or a dress that will need to be accessorized, I will match the color of the garment to a color on my color chart, assigning it the closest number or indicating that it is between two color numbers. Later, when I find blouses, sweaters and accessories to complement or match the suits, etc., I am able to verify my impressions by comparing their colors to the notated color number rather than having to rely on my color memory, which the experts say is about *15 inches long* for most of us!

A shopper appreciates having a variety of lines that work together displayed on one rack. She can find a variety of blouses and sweaters to go with her basics, not just the one that was designed for them, and obviously more multiple sales will be generated by such an approach. But more importantly from the customer's point of view, because there is variety she is much more apt to be able to create a distinctive look rather than one just like the ad in the magazine or the one the designer had in mind. She can, in effect, become her own designer.

• *What sizes are best in each style?* It is not always essential, or even advisable, to get a full size range in every style. Determine which sizes are best suited for the style and make a notation beside the style number. Develop a code to tell you if it is O.K. in all sizes or *BEST* in particular sizes, or maybe even every other size (4-8-12-16) if the style is *forgiving* size-wise. For example, (OK4-10) could mean O.K. in all sizes, but if you have to cut back, eliminate sizes over size 10; or (OK8-16) would mean all sizes O.K., but exceptionally good for the larger sizes; (4-10) would mean that it would not be advisable to order larger than a size 10; (8-14) would mean not smaller than size 8 nor larger than size 14. This is the coding system that I use, but I think it is sometimes easier to develop your own codes than it is to try to memorize someone else's.

You may be able to purchase some styles in every other size and mark them in as S/M/L rather than sized. (I have even been convinced occasionally that some sized merchandise, as well as some marked S/M/L, has little or no variation in size when it comes in. Vendors clearly want to sell greater numbers of each item; more sizes from which to choose assures this. They like to sell full size ranges, but it isn't always necessary to buy all sizes offered in order to accommodate your full range of customers (unless, of course, merchandise is pre-packed). It is obviously much better to meet the vendor's minimums in your most saleable sizes. It is also wise to ascertain whether the stated sizes conform to standard sizing — or do manufacturers, wishing to flatter their customers, size down, i.e., is their size 4 really a standard size 6?

● *Write your orders based on the total market picture.* While reps prefer that you leave orders at market — and urge you to do so with all kinds of dire predictions of what will happen if the order isn't turned in *today,* I don't recommend it.

If you overview the market before placing your orders, you can analyze what you have selected and compare the dollars spent, as well as the number of units per classification per seasonal harmony per completion date, in the calm and unemotional setting of your office.

More than once something that was exciting and fresh at the beginning of a market has looked trite and tired three days later after we've seen variations on the same theme in endless showrooms.

While you want fashion items, you may not want something that is flooding the market. At the very least this prominence in the marketplace will encourage you to bring it in early before the fad has peaked, and everyone who would want trendy items would already have found them elsewhere.

If it doesn't retain interest and excitement for you and your staff during the space of a market week, you can be fairly sure that it is not such a *hot* look for you after all. You may revise your opinion of some three-star items — you may even find things you like better! You may find better prices and better terms for similar items that may prove to be a consideration. And you may discover that you have an imbalance of colors and styles for the seasonal harmonies. (Rarely have I lost out on something that I wanted because I did not leave orders at market.)

Your business mind can then take over back in your office, leaving your emotions and the influence of eager reps, along with the hype and the hullabaloo, behind at the mart. You can write your final orders based on the total picture.

If you do *leave paper* be sure to make a notation on the order that *Confirmation will follow*. To prevent possible double shipments, be sure to mark confirmation order, *Confirmation Only—Duplicate Order*, preferably in red.

- *How does this line relate to others you've seen?* Sometimes your decision about whether to buy can be based on how the various lines relate to one another. Make a chart by *completion date* of the proposed orders, attaching photographs or swatches. Draw colored lines between on-order merchandise from one vendor that will be complemented by that from another, perhaps at a different completion date. If you need to adjust orders due to budget problems, this will help to establish priorities. Those items that do not relate to other merchandise would obviously be the first to be cut should you have to make adjustments downward to adhere to your OTB.

This chart can subsequently be used in meetings to inform staff of what is *on order*. You can use this same chart for pre-selling with clients. At a glance, you can determine approximately when shipments are due and in what colors, etc.

This chart can also be an aid in wardrobe planning with your clients. Besides being helpful in letting them know that you will have things coming in especially for them, they like being included in the *inside* stuff. It gives them an idea of how much goes into getting just the right assortment of merchandise on the racks...and they appreciate it even more.

Emotions

Don't let the personal relationship that you have with a *rep* influence your decisions regarding his/her line. You are responsible for your business, not his *numbers!* Don't be influenced by what's *hot* in New York...what's really *checking!* You've probably had more than one of these *hot items* fall flat. Is it right for your customer? Is it too traditional? Too trendy? In addition to being seasonally correct *design-wise*, is it seasonally correct for your location climate-wise?

Do your homework before a market. Read

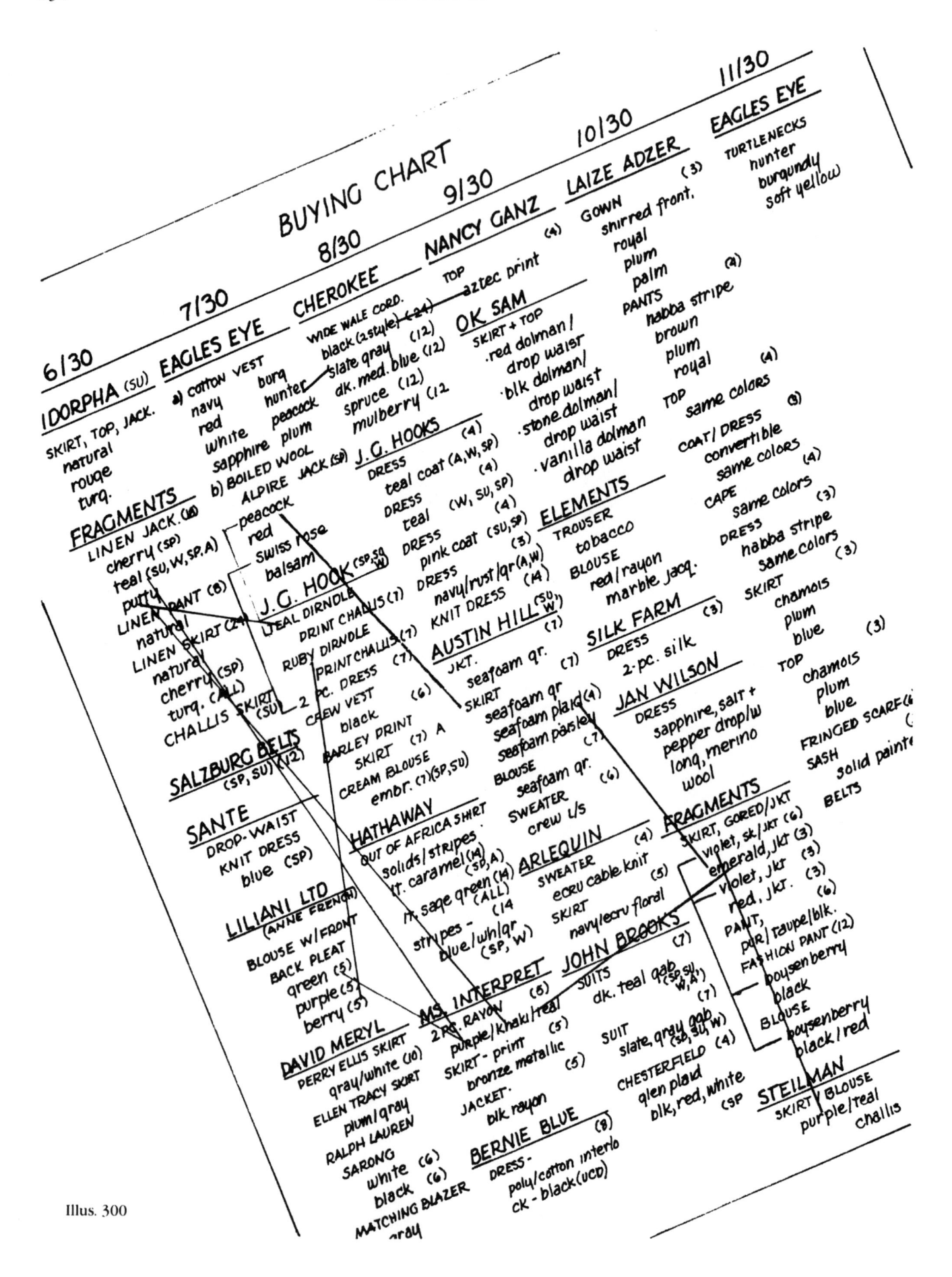

The Color Connection

BUYING CHART

6/30 — IDORPHA (SU)
SKIRT, TOP, JACK.
natural
rouge
turq.

FRAGMENTS
LINEN JACK. (10)
cherry (SP)
teal (SU,W,SP,A)
putty
LINEN PANT (8)
natural
LINEN SKIRT (24)
natural
cherry (SP)
turq. (ALL)
CHALLIS SKIRT (SU)

SALZBURG BELTS
(SP, SU) (12)

SANTE
DROP-WAIST
KNIT DRESS
blue (SP)

LILIANI LTD
(ANNE FRENCH)
BLOUSE W/FRONT
BACK PLEAT
green (5)
purple (5)
berry (5)

DAVID MERYL
PERRY ELLIS SKIRT
gray/white (10)
ELLEN TRACY SKIRT
plum/gray
RALPH LAUREN
SARONG
white (6)
black (6)
MATCHING BLAZER
gray

7/30 — EAGLES EYE
a) COTTON VEST
navy   burg
red   hunter
white   peacock
sapphire   plum
b) BOILED WOOL
ALPIRE JACK (SP)
peacock
red
Swiss rose
balsam

J.G. HOOK (SP, SU)
TEAL DIRNDLE
PRINT CHALLIS (7)
RUBY DIRNDLE
PRINT CHALLIS (7)
2 PC. DRESS (6)
CREW VEST
black
BARLEY PRINT
SKIRT (7) A
CREAM BLOUSE
embr. (7)(SP, SU)

HATHAWAY
OUT OF AFRICA SHIRT
solids/stripes
lt. caramel (4) (SP, A)
lt. sage green (4)
(ALL)
stripes — (14)
blue/wh/qr
(SP, W)

MS. INTERPRET
2 PC. RAYON (5)
purple/khaki/teal
SKIRT - PRINT
bronze metallic
JACKET
blk rayon

BERNIE BLUE (8)
DRESS -
poly/cotton interlo
ck - black (UCD)

8/30 — CHEROKEE
WIDE WALE CORD.
black (2 style) (24)
slate gray (12)
dk. med. blue (12)
spruce (12)
mulberry (12)

J.G. HOOKS (4)
DRESS
teal coat (A, W, SP)
DRESS (4)
teal (W, SU, SP)
DRESS (4)
pink coat (SU, SP) (3)
DRESS
navy/rust/gr (A, W)
KNIT DRESS (4)

AUSTIN HILL (SU, W)
JKT. (7)
seafoam gr. (7)
SKIRT
seafoam gr
seafoam plaid (4)
seafoam parsley
BLOUSE (7)
seafoam gr. (6)
SWEATER
crew L/S

ARLEQUIN (4)
SWEATER
ecru cable knit (5)
SKIRT
navy/ecru floral

JOHN BROOKS (7)
SUITS
dk. teal gab (SP, SU, W, A)
SUIT (7)
slate, gray gab (SP, SU, W) (4)
CHESTERFIELD
glen plaid
blk, red, white (SP)

9/30 — NANCY GANZ (4)
TOP
aztec print

OK SAM
SKIRT + TOP
· red dolman/
  drop waist
· blk dolman/
  drop waist
· stone dolman/
  drop waist
· vanilla dolman
  drop waist

ELEMENTS
TROUSER
tobacco
BLOUSE
red/rayon
marble jacq.

SILK FARM (3)
DRESS
2-pc. silk

JAN WILSON
DRESS
sapphire, salt +
pepper drop/w
long, merino
wool

10/30 — LAIZE ADZER (3)
GOWN
shirred front,
royal
plum
palm (2)
PANTS
habba stripe
brown
plum
royal (4)
TOP
same colors (3)
COAT/DRESS
convertible
same colors (4)
CAPE
same colors (3)
DRESS
habba stripe
same colors (3)
SKIRT
chamois
plum
blue (3)
TOP
chamois
plum
blue
FRINGED SCARF (6)
SASH
solid painted

11/30 — EAGLES EYE
TURTLENECKS
hunter
burgundy
soft yellow

FRAGMENTS
SKIRT, GORED/JKT
violet, sk/JKT (6)
emerald, JKT (3)
violet, JKT (3)
red, JKT (6)
PANT,
pur/taupe/blk
FASHION PANT (12)
boysenberry
black
BLOUSE
boysenberry
black/red

STEILMAN
SKIRT/BLOUSE
purple/teal
challis

Illus. 300

Women's Wear Daily, the fashion magazines, and other regional apparel news magazines. Watch for trends. Be aware of current fad or fashion peaks and when they seem to be on the downhill side of the curve.

Try to get an overview of what's out there. Listen to your customers and your staff as to their needs and desires. If you have reservations about a line, follow those instincts. On the other hand, if you are drawn to a new line or fashion forward style within a line, buy a small quantity and test it out in your store.

Whose Style — Yours or That of Your Customers?

• For a *balanced store with broad appeal* be sure to consider your customers, their life style and that of your locale.

It is a real temptation to let your own personal seasonal harmony and your own personal style preferences unduly influence your buying. I remember one season when my *Winter* manager and I attended a holiday market. We were both drawn to all of the holiday looks, and consequently purchased far too much black and far too much holiday wear, for small-town Davis, where *dressing* for the holidays is far different from New York, L.A., or San Francisco!

You can't always sell what you would wear, nor wear what you will sell. Buy for your customers; not for yourself.

Consistency of taste is important, of course. Never buy something that you don't personally find attractive — at least for someone else. You'll surely place it badly in your store...and it will never sell.

And Once You've Done the Buying and the Merchandise Arrives — What Then?

First of all, be sure the sales associates know just what you had in mind when you ordered the merchandise, e.g., how the styles are currently being worn, and the relationship you envisioned between the various lines. The previously mentioned chart (page 236) is a great aid in this.

If you are buying according to the Seasonal Color Harmony theory, your staff should be trained in its use. There are *Color Connection*

Study Guides for both buyers and sales associates, as well as videotapes, to assist in that training. The excitement and rewards are great for sales associates who have learned the technique in order to help their clients to better express themselves through their clothing, sometimes even as they watch the metamorphosis of a lovely Summer woman who has been masquerading as an Autumn. No longer will the *"just a sales clerk"* apply.

Salaries are probably your single biggest expense, so be sure you're getting the most for your money. Your staff should be well trained and motivated to be of real service to your clientele. Staff that are just standing around chatting with each other are not a good value. Staff that lose interest the minute someone says they are "just browsing" or only make half-hearted attempts to help a customer leave you with what might as well be a self-service store. These people never become really important to you or your clientele. And they usually feel like they are "just a sales clerk." They may be even more detrimental than you think, since they may actually be turning people away from your store with very negative feelings.

• *Valuable staff members* stop whatever they are doing, greet, and help customers the minute they come in. They consider a browser a challenge — a potential customer, a potential friend. They are not judgmental about customers. They respect their privacy. They do not gossip about them with their co-workers or anyone else.

They use imagination and energy to make their job satisfying — they are a real part of the team and are of great value. They are able to introduce related add-on items, as well as find substitutes for requested items that are unavailable whenever appropriate. They keep in touch with their customers by phone or postcard, letting them know whenever they come across something especially for them. They follow-through on inquiries, special orders, returns, etc. Their customers know they can depend on them. Their customers ask for them whenever they come in. Their efforts are acknowledged and rewarded. They feel satisfaction in a job well done. They know they are much more than "just a sales clerk."

13
Want to Be More Than "Just a Sales Clerk"?

It is wondrous strange to be able to tell so much about someone's personality, so accurately, just by looking at her visual image. And moreover, to be able to tell so accurately what clothing style is apt to feel right to her based on her visual image and personality traits.

Generalities? Certainly. But generalities which apply more often than not. There are obviously exceptions to the *Rules of Personality and Style,* but there is such a remarkable conformity to the personality characteristics it is uncanny, similar to that of the astrological signs, I imagine. It is eerie to have someone say to you, "Oh, you must be an Aquarius...right?" Sometimes people who have studied astrology are able to chat with someone, get to know her thought processes a bit, and almost magically *guess*—determine—her sign! Amazing!

The Seasonal Color Harmony *technique* is a similarly remarkable tool for anyone who wishes to be more than *just a clerk*. You can amaze, confound and impress a shopper with your competency, when, much like a magician pulling a rabbit out of a hat, you can pull from the racks a dressing room full of clothes, all of which are really perfect for her and her style.

One of the services customers say they wish for the most is an honest answer to "Does it look good?" Perhaps if a shopper has to ask the question there is something intuitively nagging her that says: "This isn't quite right for me.

I don't believe most sales clerks are deliberately dishonest (although certainly commissions and the desire to move merchandise perhaps make that a temptation). Whether an outfit looks good on the customer may not be relevant. It may look great, but not be appropriate for her seasonal type — may not be her style.

By learning the *technique* you may be able to solve the riddle: "The color is pretty. The fit is great. Although it's a really good style for her figure, she doesn't like the dress. Why?" The Color Connection may reveal the answer. Perhaps the color isn't *her* color. Maybe the style isn't *her* style.

There are several *schools of thought* about color and style. Probably those color analysts using yin and yang or giving secondary harmonies or sub-groupings such as early Spring, golden Spring, floral Spring, or vital Spring, are closer to the Color Connection, which views the seasonal types as on a continuum (see page 34-9).

Betty Nethery in her book *Uniquely You* (Tyndale House Publishers, Inc. Wheaton, Ill., 1984) invites us to "discover the 12-month season color system," in which she has three categories for each season, *bright, classic, or gentle.*

Gerrie Pinckney and Marge Swenson, in their very useful *New Image for Women,* also refer to sub-groupings which relate to personality types: yin personality types being *classic, romantic, or ingenue;* yang types *dramatic, natural and gamin.* According to their theory, conceivably any of the seasonal color types may be any of these personality types. In fact, they consider the six personality types on a continuum, with one's personality position varying not only at different times of her life but even altering in the space of a day.

One example they give is of a 180 pound, statuesque Natural-Classic-Summer-Ingenue woman who downplayed her femininity while capably managing a large corporation during the day. At home she allowed herself to appear more vulnerable and encouraged help with household tasks from her husband, who perceived her to be incapable of managing alone. After a full day at the office, she may have elected to appear demure, dependent, weak, and indeed, needful of help.

Her husband's perceptions of her seemed quite different from that of the calm, gracious, independent and always capable executive seen at her place of work. She may have used her feminine wiles to prevent double-shifting, the all too-typical plight of many working wives. Another strategy, of course, could have been a more straight-forward involvement of her husband in the division of household chores. The latter behavior would have been more consistent with her assertive professional mode.

Even though Pinckney and Swenson describe their six personality types as having no relationship to the seasonal types, they do, in their description of the seasonal types, include for each season *Your Inner Season* descriptions very similar to the generalities of personality traits found elsewhere in the color literature. Generalities? Of course. But I often wonder why the generalities are so often apt.

Which came first, the chicken or the egg? Did the dimpled, blue eyed gamin-like Spring child become effervescent, mischievous, perky, pert, and very animated because she was so cute she could get away with anything? Did the Summer somewhat fragile-looking daughter, appearing to be more soft and ethereal, invite being cared for and caring for others in return through her soft, muted coloring? Did the flamboyant, richly colored Autumn with more angular, sturdy, strong looks become more assertive and self-assured because of her looks? Was she assumed able to take care of herself and others, and to have the ability to accomplish? A self-fulfilling prophecy perhaps? Did the striking Winter type, often thought of as aloof, controlled and serene, looking dramatic and somewhat intimidating even as a young child, perhaps need the protection of aloofness and control?

Genetic influences? Of course. Environmental influences. Probably. A dynamic phenomenon? Perhaps. I wonder just how much environment influences our *inner season*.

In any event, the *technique* is a remarkable tool to use to better serve your client. Have you ever had someone come into your store and tell you she needs a dress for a special occasion? When you showed her some beautiful dresses, ones you thought particularly appropriate for the type of occasion she described, she looked at them very disinterestedly and away from you as though almost embarrassed or irritated. Chances are you didn't understand her — or her style. Often that person when confronted by a selection which is inappropriate for *her style,* will leave the store quickly, not even able to express her frustration and often her feelings of inadequacy. What the salesperson deems appropriate for the described occasion, the customer knows instinctively she could never wear comfortably.

She may even suspect she is a *misfit*. She isn't a misfit. The salesperson is probably trying to fit a round peg into a square hole, e.g., trying to put a Spring style dress on an Autumn type woman, or to put it another way, a romantic style on a classic or natural Town and Country type. It may be something as simple as too much fullness at the top of the sleeve and a round jewel neckline in a soft, shimmery silk fabric, which is too yin, too soft and feminine, for most Autumn seasonal types. The same woman may be able to wear the same silk fabric, although she might prefer a matte finish, in a more tailored dress with a V-neck or notched collar and a less puffed sleeve, adorned with some substantial jewelry — equally appropriate for any occasion. Or she might prefer to wear a flamboyant handwoven nubby gauze dress with fringe detail, laden with jewelry — also suitable. She may not know what she wants, but she certainly knows what she doesn't want.

Using the Seasonal Harmony technique, you would do a quick survey of the prospective customer's coloring, her visual design, the way she walks, and the way she talks. There are many non-verbal ways of giving and getting information about personality, style and design.

It's a rare person who doesn't respond favorably to someone taking an interest in her, particularly in larger cities, where there is such a feeling of anonymity in what can feel like a very impersonal world. It is, of course, important to be attuned to the vibrations from the customer, adapting your style to hers. For example, if she clearly wishes to be left alone, don't persist with more questions, just let her know you are available if she needs you. If she is exuberant, you can be more so; if she is subdued, suppress your exuberance, etc.

There are many better things to ask a customer than "May I help you?" Many sales technique books will tell you to ask open ended questions, ones without *yes or no* answers, but they rarely give concrete examples of open ended questions which might be useful.

While I'm not going to give you a canned sales pitch, I am including some specific topics which I have found helpful in my experience. Questions which get a good response are ones which are somewhat personal in nature, such as a sincere comment about her appearance, "I really like your haircut. Who does it for you?" or "That's a great color for you. I'll bet you've had your colors done, haven't you?" and then, if she responds positively, "Do you have them with you?"

As you are chatting with the customer, you may be able to glean valuable information without appearing obvious or conducting the *Great Inquisition*. After she leaves the store, make notes on a client card or a sheet in a notebook.

All questions should be asked in conversational tone of course — casually and with sincere interest in the person. Listen for unsaid things in the shopper's voice. You might ask yourself or the customer as you chat:

- What seasonal harmony type are you? (It's O.K. to ask if you're uncertain. Just ask if she's had her colors done. The customer will usually volunteer more information at that point about her style and with a bit of luck will produce color samples.)
- What kind of clothing do you like most? (Classic, tailored, natural, sporty casual, elegant, off-beat and trendy, preppy, conservative, sexy, pert and perky, expensive, sophisticated, romantic, youthful, mature, daring, etc. Does she seem content with her style? Does she seem interested in making a change?)

Personal style is the very best indicator of which items to show a customer. For instance, a customer has indicated she needs a dress for a wedding which she is to attend as a guest. If she's a romantic, soft-spoken Summer, for instance, it's a waste of time to try to get her into a dress with exaggerated shoulders, epaulettes, big patch pockets, web belt, etc.; whereas you will probably have great success if you have one with shirring off a yoke and fullness in the sleeve in a soft drapable fabric.

- How does the customer view herself? I recently had a long-standing, loyal customer (Summer type with platinum blonde hair, very pale ivory skin, very light aqua eyes) tell me, as I was steering her away from a bright and very bold pair of Laurel Burch toucan earrings to much quieter, soft ones, "Joan, you see me as a parakeet, but I'm really a toucan!" There was some truth to what she said for she is bolder and more flamboyant in her personality than she is in her appearance. Yet she knew I was right, too. I pointed out to her that the bright toucans would *outshout* her subtle coloring and the observer would only remember *TOUCANS!* and not her. She needs more subtle ways to express her *toucan qualities!* because of her very quiet visual design.

- What are her shopping habits?
- Does she like to be a fashion leader or wait until a trend is firmly entrenched before making a purchase? Does she avoid fashion because it goes out of style too quickly?
- Does she spend a lot of money on her clothing and accessories?
- Does she sew? If so, you might then steer her to items which she would not be apt to make herself, ones which would enhance and enrich her own creations.
- Does she spend a lot of time shopping? Does she enjoy it? Or does she want to come in and do it very quickly?
- Does she shop only when she needs something?
- Consider the event for which she is shopping. Ask some questions about where it will take place. How formal? Climate? Etc.
- Consider her lifestyle. She will thank you if you steer her to something appropriate which she can use for not only this occasion, but again and again.
- Is she happy with her lifestyle? Sometimes limited wardrobes actually restrict lifestyle, e.g., she never seems to have the appropriate thing to wear for certain occasions, so refuses invitations, etc.
- How does she want to be perceived for the occasion for which she is shopping? Does she want to show another side of herself? Does she want to depart from her usual style?

In addition to gaining much useful information for this potential sale, you will have made a friend. Remember shopping for clothing is not a pleasurable experience for all women. Your concern and your efforts to assure a comfortable and confident purchase will be deeply appreciated by most. Remember also that a shopper often seeks more than the product she asks for...and it is those intangible extras (friendship, ego massage, etc.) which may cause her to return to you and your shop again and again.

- Be sure to *record customer's name, address and phone number* so that you can let her know if and when something which might be of interest to her comes in. Set up a file or *client book* and review it once a week or so — and *make your calls!*

As you make your calls, log them on a sheet detailing date, whom you called, which item you have invited her to come in to try, etc. Then, if you are not there when she comes, others in the store will be able to assist her in finding the item. There are few things more frustrating than to have traveled across town through traffic to try on what is promised to be the *perfect* dress, only to discover no one in the store has a clue as to what the call was about! So if you don't have a telephone log system at your store, perhaps you can institute one.

If you anticipate delivery of an especially appropriate item for a specific customer, alert the stockroom to let you know when it comes in. At Tarika, we *note on the purchase order* the customer's name, address and phone number, clerk's name, as well as the size, color and style number of the item which is to be saved for the customer. When the order comes in, the merchandise is held and the customer is notified. She typically feels very special and cared for.

Some other things which you may want to note on your client's record might include:

- Does she seem to be feeling any pressure to change her clothing image — and why, e.g., friends, family, job, curiosity, man, age, figure challenges, weight loss or gain, change of life style, etc?
- What kind of image does she want to project? Does she wish to look older, younger, more authoritative, less threatening, etc.? For social events, how does she like to look?
- What is her lifestyle? Is she at home with or without children full time? Is she contemplating entering the job market? Or retiring? Is she a student? Is she employed? Does she work? Full or part time? What kind of work does she do? What are the dress requirements at her place of employment, whether written or unwritten.
- What does she like best about her body? These are things she will want to emphasize. You can help her do that with accessories, etc.
- Any figure challenges? Is she over her desired weight? Underweight? Note her approximate height and weight. Note sizes which worked for her as she was trying things on, as well as any design lines or manufacturers which were particular favorites.

- Is she well proportioned? Pear shaped (one or more sizes larger on the bottom than on the top?) Is her hip high on the sides? Or low? Does she have an hourglass figure, i.e., large bust, small waist, large hips? Is she top heavy? Does she have a straight up and down boyish figure? Midriff bulge? Protruding tummy? Large derrière? Heavy upper arms? Upper thighs? Thin arms? Long thin neck? Thick short neck?
- Is she big boned, small or average frame?
- Does she have a large bust or small? Does either seem to be a concern to her?
- Wide shoulders? Narrow shoulders? Sloping shoulders? Average?

• **Your customer may wish to look younger.**

You might advise her to try some unusual quality accessory items to update her look. And one of the easiest and quickest ways to enhance the look of a woman who is maybe feeling the impact of a few wrinkles or additional chins is a new, current hair style.

Another suggestion for this woman would be to review and update her make-up. Advise her to stay current and to use *Lip-Fix* and lip liner to keep lipstick from running into the lines which have suddenly appeared around her mouth.

And probably the soundest advice which you can give her is to wear more color. When the hair has grayed and the eyes and skin have softened, one often can effectively wear brighter colors than before. Sometimes having a personal color analysis is just the lift a woman needs at this time of her life when she tends to be overly concerned about wrinkles, sagging, etc. When she wears her very best colors, mixing and matching fabrics and colors in interesting ways, she will appear even more attractive. This and softer styling will give the older woman a more contemporary look.

• **When your customer shows concern about the expense of clothing** urge her to think not so much about the cost of an individual item of clothing, but of the *cost per wearing* which she can anticipate. A not-quite-perfect-but-it-will-do-for-the-occasion $100 dress bought on sale for $50, which one wears only twice, costs $25 per wearing. A $150 dress which one loves, wears twice a month for two years, costs $3.10 per wearing. Which dress is the more expensive?

Help her to see the value in buying the best she can afford. A medium to better price bracket for basics is often the best value, because as a rule this better priced garment will hold its shape and last longer.

She will appreciate your honest sincere input. Let her know you want her to buy only those items which suit her and that you will never tell her something looks terrific unless it really does. You may lose a sale now and then, but in the long run she will appreciate your honest feedback. If you think she can do better stylewise or colorwise, tell her so, even if she seems to like the item. Your credibility can only be enhanced by this approach. It will reflect badly on you and your store if she wears something she purchased from you which is not flattering.

This, of course, can be done gently and graciously with a "Let's try something else; I think we can do better." Guide her into trying new-for-her looks which you think will suit her.

I have one very natural Autumn type who is really only truly comfortable in pants, sweaters and jackets. She is a professional woman, however, who often needs a suited look and suffers to wear one when she must. She also is required to attend some dressier occasions such as receptions, etc., which always create a wardrobe crisis for her.

I have been looking the past three markets for the perfect dress to fill the gap in her wardrobe. Every once in awhile, she'll ask if I've found anything for her yet. Recently I introduced her to what I thought might be the perfect answer: a loosely woven, textured, natural linen dress, with natural/russet finely striped sleeves, a similarly striped band at the dropped waist which tied asymmetrically over the hips. The neckline, unhappily, was a jewel neckline, but that could be covered with interesting jewelry; the sleeves as it turned out were a bit *fluttery*.

Although I talked her into trying it on, she bounced back out of the dressing room saying it was too big. I urged her to put it back on, knowing full well she hadn't bothered to button up the back or tied the belted effect, or even gotten used to the idea of having a dress on! When we got her back into the dress, I suggested she come out to the accessory area, where we could add some jewelry and gain some time for her to get used to the idea — and the dress. After a few minutes of wearing the dress, it seemed to grow on her and she commented, "It's not bad."

That was a breakthrough. She didn't buy the dress that day, but she did ask us to hold it so that she could think about it. She is unaccustomed to seeing herself in a dress. She needs to get used to the idea. Whether she purchased the dress is not important; we did make inroads by giving her the experience.

- ○ **Try the soft-sell approach.** Recently a woman came into Tarika, exclaiming, "I've been masquerading twenty years as an Autumn. I've just found out I'm really a Summer." She had been wearing camels, khakis, and rust for years but had just discovered her best colors were those of the Summer seasonal harmony. She agreed she did look much better in the Summer colors. Yet she wasn't quite comfortable with the idea of *soft and romantic* in her clothing, although her hair style was soft with tendrils.

  I took her figuratively by the hand and said, "Let's do some research. I'm going to pick out some styles from your new-found season. I'd like you to try them on. We'll accessorize, play dress-up as if for a fashion show. You can get the feel of these new styles — see how you like them. I'm not expecting you to buy anything. O.K.?"

  We had a wonderful time. She did, in fact, buy several things. But the most important thing was that she learned she did enjoy many of the Summer styles we selected. And her parting comments that day were, "Joan, I really appreciate what you did for me today. I usually shop sales and discount stores where you don't get any help. The soft sell approach meant a lot to me. I'll be back."

- **Train your eye to notice figure challenges.** Just as being a good listener is an invaluable asset in retailing, being observant is equally important. Train your eye to notice camouflage techniques the customer is currently using — and think of additional ones which might benefit her. Learn some of the *tricks of the trade* — tricks of camouflage and illusion. (See Chapter 15).

14
Color — and How to Use It a Review of Some Basic Art Principles

There Are Three Elements of Color

Hue — the name of the color.
Value — How light or how dark it is, with white the highest value and black the lowest value.
Intensity — How bright or how dull.
  Bright refers to pure or fully saturated colors.
  Soft, dull or muted refers to colors which are mixed with their complement or with gray, rose or brown.

• The *primary colors, yellow, red and blue, are the colors which are mixed to create all other colors.*
• The *secondary colors* are mixtures of any two of the primary colors, i.e., orange is a combination of yellow and red; green comes from yellow and blue; violet is the result of mixing red and blue.
• *Tertiary colors* are mixtures of one primary and one secondary color, e.g., red and orange combined make red-orange, while yellow mixed with orange makes a yellow-orange, etc.

Color Has Energy

Some colors have more energy than others.
• **Neutrals** have the least amount of energy. They are the very quietest statement and are the backdrop for other colors and for an individual's coloring. They are excellent for conservative business or basic items not worn near the face, e.g., skirts, slacks, jackets, coats, handbags, shoes, belts, hosiery. White or off-white and black are usually the only neutrals considered really appropriate for party wear.

Neutrals are so quiet, so conservative, refined

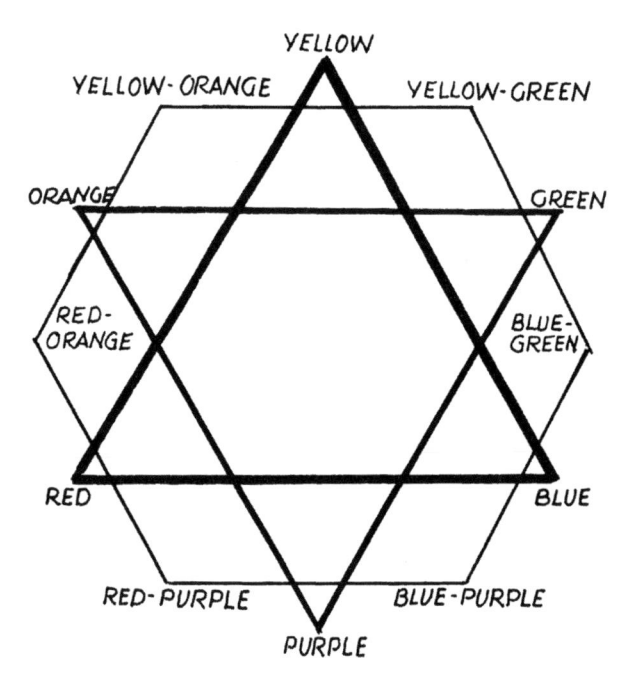

Illus. 301

and, in fact, subtle that without the addition of some contrast they appear rather uninteresting. They should not be required to stand alone. It is recommended, therefore, that one neutral never be worn alone without the addition of color in the form of a scarf, jewelry, blouse, etc. Sometimes one's own visual image can provide the needed contrast. For example, for an all-white outfit, dark hair will provide contrast which is not presented by a blond, wearing the same outfit, unless she is very tan.

When someone is wearing *two neutrals* (with no added color) it is recommended that, to avoid monotony, two of the following principles be observed:

o Use value contrast. Tone-on-tone neutrals or monochromatic combinations have value contrast, as do two *different* neutrals: one light and one dark.

o Use textural interest (weave, lustre, etc.).

o Use a print or woven surface pattern interest (stripe, floral print, plaid).

o Use an unusual, dramatic or interesting line.

There are no similar restrictions for other colors. They may be worn in large amounts and without contrast, texture, pattern, etc.

• **White.** Contrasts of white with colors are most appropriate for Spring and Winter seasonal harmonies. Winters can wear pure or chalk white; Springs will wear ivory best and Summer a soft off-white. Autumn types will wear the natural whites found in raw fabrics or oyster white. In no case should a person wear a white which is much whiter than her teeth, as it may make the teeth appear yellow.

White or off-white blouses are good for *authority* suit looks. The more contrast between the blouse and the suit, the more authoritative the appearance. In fact, a navy or black suit with a white blouse can be perceived as so authoritative on some women as to be harsh and inconsistent with their total look.

• **Black** is best worn by Winter seasonal types with hair which is black, charcoal gray, salt and pepper, or dark brown. Blonds and redheads who have dark eyebrows may also enjoy black feminine prints. Many Spring types will wear black but will want to maintain a light/bright feel. Black is, of course, a very useful basic which is easily worn by women with black and nearly black hair. Many women who should not wear large amounts of black near their face will elect to limit its use to skirts and pants and will wear them with color.

The woman who cannot wear black near her face should use caution when purchasing a plaid or print skirt containing black and just one other color; the second color may be popular during the season it is purchased, but be unavailable forever after, making purchasing additional coordinated tops impossible. She should buy several coordinating tops while the color is available.

• **Grays** are very impersonal and conservative. They are considered excellent for business. Gray is generally worn where other colors can set the mood. The Winter seasonal type with high contrast in her own personal coloring can wear the many gradations of gray from black to white without adding color. The other seasonal types should wear color with their grays. The Summer grays will be blue-based; the Spring gray will be either a light or dark dove gray or will have a yellowish cast. The Autumn will usually prefer brown as her best neutral, at least until her hair begins to gray, at which time she may wish to change to a gray with a pewter or greenish cast.

• **Beige.** There are endless varieties of beige from the almond, buff, pecan, camel, light walnut, caramel, butterscotch, honey beige, and natural raw silk or linen worn by Spring seasonal types to the warm beige or brassier wheat, amber, pigskin, chamois of Autumn. Rose beige, taupe, and fawn are for Summer. Most Winters will prefer a grayed taupe as their best beige.

• **Navy Blue** comes in many shades. Springs will wear a bright royal navy; Summers will wear a dark grayed French navy; Winters will prefer a clear navy blue.

While navy could probably be worn by some Autumn types, the brown haired Autumn, at least, will probably prefer all of her rich browns over navy as her best neutral. Navy and brown are not usually worn together, as our eye currently does not view this combination as harmonious or fashionable, although this could change. A more workable wardrobe is created by eliminating navy for the Autumn woman, in favor of what for most would be considered a requisite rich earth tone. Navy is not considered a sabotage color for the Autumn type and could be included, but it would necessitate accessories in the two different color families and for most Autumns would simply not be worth it.

- **Brown** is a color best worn by those with brown hair. It is especially good for the Autumn type when worn with her teal or russet tones in rich combination. Some Summers will have a rich chocolate brown on their palette, as will some brown haired Winters. The Spring brown will be a medium warm brown or a cinnamon brown. The Autumn type usually has a wide range of browns on her palette.
- Certain **reds, greens and blues** may also be considered neutrals when handled with subtlety and are excellent for basics because they add color to the face and can stand alone. Another term sometimes used for this category of almost neutrals is *understated,* which would include for Winter such colors as dark to medium shades of true or blue based reds, royal blues, pine greens or teal; Spring would use the clear medium values of yellow reds, blues, yellow-greens and golds; Summers would wear muted medium to dark shades of their blue based red, gray-blues, and blue-greens; Autumns will wear their medium to dark dusty muted olive, forest and teal greens, as well as their rusty reds.
- The most becoming neutral will usually be the color of the hair with the exception of Blacks and Orientals. Even though the hair of a non-Caucasian may be black, I have not always found black to be her best neutral. While most color analysts seem to categorize all **Orientals and Blacks** as Winters, I do not believe this to be true. My impressions are that her skin tone is the determining factor. Suzanne Caygill suggests the following guidelines:

   peach cast to the skin (Spring),
   rose cast (Summer),
   apricot cast (Autumn),
   violet cast (Winter),

(*Color, The Essence of You,* page 138). I have found this to work very well in determining the most becoming colors of both Orientals and Blacks.
- The **skintone** is an excellent color for lingerie, as it is the least apt to show through fabrics. It is also especially flattering in a dinner dress, as it has a very soft and feminine effect.

Color Creates a Mood

- The **Eye Color** is considered calm and pacifying, non-threatening, a quiet statement. Most people's eyes have varying shades of the same color at the very least; some may have as many as 15 to 20 different colors in their eyes. The eye color selected for the palette is the composite color — that seen from your best personal distance of two to three feet.

The eye always seeks to repeat color, so if one is wearing her eye color, the eye of the observer will automatically be drawn to the eyes. Because eye contact is considered an essential element of sincerity, the eye color is often called one's *sincere color.* The eye color is therefore an excellent color to wear when meeting people in a non-assertive situation.

- **Reds** are considered the most sensuous, romantic and feminine color — a high energy color. Colors ranging from coral to deep rust and from pink to burgundy are all considered reds, some blue-based and others yellow-based, some with great clarity, others with less, each distinctive in value and intensity. All are excellent for parties, sports activities, or loungewear.

Reds in the lighter and brighter shades are typically used only in small amounts for business. A women wearing a pink suit, for example, which is considered quite feminine, might not be taken seriously, especially by her male colleagues or clients. However, darker reds, (e.g., burgundy or berry) are considered understated or almost neutral in statement and are appropriate.

Related reds are the ones which will be most in harmony with your own personal coloring and probably the most flattering for nail polish, blush, etc.

One good way for an individual to determine her very best related red, especially when she is standing at the cosmetic counter trying to select a lipstick, is to check the reds in the palm of the hand for the lighter tones; squeeze a finger to bring the blood to the surface to determine best darker red. Verify this sometime at the fabric store: take several samples of various reds to a mirror in natural light. See if you've picked the right ones with the *hand test.*

- **Dramatic or complementary** colors are often called *star colors* or the *high shade.* Complementary colors are opposite each other on the color wheel. These colors are said to complement and heighten each other. For most people, their greens, blues, and/or blue-greens are their dramatic or high shade because they are opposite their reddish or red-orange skin tones.

These are high visibility colors in which you can *lead the parade*. They are attention getting, charismatic, and are therefore excellent for speeches, presentations, and parties. A politician, for example, who wishes to be noticed will want to have a collection of clothing in her dramatic colors. Some color analysts call this the *high shade* because it heightens the color of the wearer — and she *will be seen!* For this reason, one usually needs to feel good about herself in order to feel comfortable in this color; it is not usually a color to wear when one is tired, inasmuch as the *heightening* of color will unfortunately extend to dark circles under the eyes, too.

- **Elegant** colors refer to those which are more refined and regal than the dramatic colors. Sophisticated, quiet, or soft-sell are other words which might be used to describe elegant colors. They are used for social functions, theatre, or business where you do not wish to be the center of attention. Elegant colors are appropriate for any occasion, so when in doubt they are always a good choice.
- **Understated** colors are quieter than elegant but offer more color than a neutral.
- **Carefree** colors have high energy and appear casual, active and happy. They are used primarily for sportswear, sundresses, beachwear, blouses, scarves, or casual accessories.

Colors Can Be Combined in Different Ways

- **Monochromatic combinations** use shades of the same hue, varying the value and intensity, e.g., pink, rose and burgundy or off-white and beige. There are varying degrees of contrast in monochromatic combinations. If wearing two neutrals in a monochromatic combination without another color, one should follow the rules for wearing neutrals (see page 249) and use one of the following to prevent a monotonous look: interesting texture or print, an interesting or unusual line in the garment, etc.
- **Analogous colors** are the two colors to the left and the two colors to the right of each of the colors on the color wheel, e.g., colors analogous to red would be red-orange and orange on one side and red-violet and violet on the other.

When color analysts say, "Wear your colors in analogous combinations," they do not mean to wear red, for instance, with all of its analogous colors. This would tend to create a look similar to that of the circus clown. They mean for you to add no more than two analogous colors to the main color you have selected, e.g., to red, you might add red-orange and violet or red-violet and violet and have a pleasing effect. In the case of these very vivid colors, you would probably not use them in equal amounts on any one outfit, but would use one as an accent. Subtle colors, such as pink, lavender and coral, could be used in equal amounts.

Autumn and Summer types wear their colors in analogous combinations. For example, an Autumn might wear a russet suit with a gold blouse and an accent of yellow; a Summer type might wear a lavender dress with lavender-blue and aqua accessories.

- **Complementary Colors:** Colors on opposite sides of the color wheel are called complementary because they intensify each other. It is best, therefore, to accent an outfit with a complementary color rather than use equal amounts, e.g., accessorize a red dress with green, as opposed to wearing a red blouse with a green skirt.
- **Split Complementary Colors** are the colors on either side of the complementary colors. If you accessorize the red dress with split complementary colors, e.g., yellow-green and green-blue, it will have an even more interesting look.
- **Triad colors** are those colors which make up a triangle on the color wheel. Spring types often wear their colors in triad combinations.
- **Sabotage Colors** are those colors which not only do not enhance personal coloring, but unfavorably drain color from or darken the skin, turn it yellow or greenish, wash it out, etc. These colors near the face may appear to cast a dark shadow on the face, deaden eye color, exaggerate wrinkles, dark circles, and make blemishes or other undesirable facial discoloration more obvious. Certain yellows, yellow greens, greens and oranges are often called *sabotage colors* for Winter and Summer types. Hot pink and blue-based reds often do the same for Autumn types.
- **Prints.** Not all colors in a print need be on one's color palette for it to be acceptable. When selecting a print, it is the *dominant* color which is most important. Stand three to four feet away from a mirror, squint your eyes, and observe

which color has the most impact. Is that color one of *your* colors? Does it enhance your skin coloring? Your eyes?

Although men have been combining prints in one outfit for a long time, it is a relatively new phenomenon for women, who are now using the men's wear patterns, including pin dot, paisleys or foulard prints, herringbone, pinstripes, neats, and glen plaids, as well as their own feminized floral prints, in interesting ways. They have found they can mix them and tie them together with color, e.g., the same or closely related colors, but in a variety of print patterns; or by using the same prints, but in two or more different colors.

Illusion

Summer
Illus. 304

Winter
Illus. 303

Autumn
Illus. 302

Spring
Illus. 305

15
Illusion Is a Woman's Best Friend

Illusion is a mild form of deception. The intention of illusion is to alter the perception of proportions. In the case of clothing, illusion is used to cause proportions to appear as close to *ideal* as possible.

It is surprising the number of women who are insecure about some part of their body. Very often there seem to be no faults of any great significance that a fairly observant eye can see, but to the insecure woman even a slight imperfection can seem a very real problem.

What is beautiful? This is, of course, very subjective. It is cultural, geographic — and, unfortunately, constantly evolving. Fashions change seasonally, often because of television, the movies, or our changing role models. Remember Lara in *Dr. Zhivago,* Grace Kelly, *Annie Hall,* Twiggy, Madonna, Jacqueline Kennedy, Lady Di, and most recently the *Out of Africa* look of Meryl Streep. Our ideas of beauty change. The body which was terrific yesterday may be passé today!

Think of the ages of fashion — the beautiful women portrayed by the great masters throughout the ages: the bustles which enlarged the hip area, the corsets which cinched in the waist and pushed the bosom unnaturally upward to create an hourglass figure — that was considered beautiful. Recall the pin-up girls — Betty Grable, Jane Russell, Lana Turner, Marilyn Monroe...? Remember the 50's and the latex panty girdle which made women look as though they had one rounded, firmly packed derrière? Remember when every teenager wished to look like Twiggy?

Women are in a no-win situation. While we can send yesterday's outdated fashions off to Goodwill or have a garage sale — or even put them away in a cedar chest *hoping* they'll come around again, we can't trade in our bodies each year. There is no way any one person can conform to the dictates of fashion beauty every year. But she can use illusion.

Color creates illusion

- *Light or bright colors* tend to increase apparent size as do *warm* hues. *Warm hues* on the spectrum (red, yellow, orange, and any combination thereof) are *advancing* colors and carry the illusion of weight. Simply put, this means the *eye of the observer will go first to warm hues.* If someone is too thin in an area, they could create the illusion of being larger by spotlighting that area with light, bright or warm colors: red, orange, reddish purple, yellow, reddish brown, yellow brown, reddish beige. Simultaneously, they would be drawing the eye of the observer *away* from the larger area.
- *Dark or middle value colors* seem to diminish apparent size. The *cool hues* on the spectrum (blue, blue green, blue violet, bluish brown, greenish brown, bluish gray, green, bluish green, etc.) are *receding* colors and tend to minimize size. If someone is heavy in an area, she can create the illusion of being smaller by wearing dark or middle values of cool hues.
- The eye will go to *color change* or to wherever light and dark shades meet, e.g., in the case of a white sweater with a black skirt, the eye will go to where the sweater ends and the skirt begins. So if the waist is small and hips large, the wearer will want a short sweater that ends near the waist rather than at her hip, her largest area.
- The eye also wants to *repeat color, line or value.* A black scarf or necklace worn with the above outfit would cause the eye to immediately go to the portrait area. Without the scarf, the eye would immediately go to the waist where the black and white meet. The eye will go to the *brighter* color. A red, white and black print or solid red scarf and earrings worn with the above outfit would also bring the eye quickly up to the face. And, of course, the look is completed by the addition of the accessories.

The major emphasis should always be on the face. The eyes and the mouth are the source of our major communication. Every other emphasis should be minor by comparison.

No fashion design emphasis should ever be greater than one's own visual design, e.g., a big, chunky necklace looks out of place when worn by a petite, soft-featured Summer woman.

Lines can create illusion.

Our eyes are trained to read from left to right horizontally rather than vertically. They move from top to bottom. The eye will go to every line and will release to the stronger contrast, (e.g., a jabot on a blouse or a double wrap hip belt; a stripe or border) and it will move most quickly along a line. The eye will move along straight lines faster and more directly than along curved lines. It will go to grouped structural details such as surplice ruffles, rows of stitching, or a pleated flounce. The eye will go to decoration, such as Faire Isle designs or printed borders. Grouped structural detail or decoration should, therefore, be used only in those areas that you are willing to emphasize.

• **Vertical lines are slimming and elongating.** You can diminish width and look taller by keeping the eye of the observer looking vertically. If you lead the eye into the center of the body, it will also look less wide. Any space divided will appear smaller than one that is not divided. Some tricks to keep the eye of the observer looking vertically include: lifting the collar of a shirt or jacket, pushing up sleeves, dividing an area with vertical lines, such as a tie, scarf or lapels, having buttons from hemline to neckline (leave buttons at top and bottom unbuttoned for maximum vertical line), wearing vertical stripes, long necklaces, etc.

Avoid using horizontal lines in unflattering places. Horizontal lines are created not just by the traditionally unacceptable horizontal stripe for the heavy woman, but by borders, boat necklines, flounces, ankle strap shoes and cuffed pants. These will not only emphasize the area where they are worn, they cause the observer to look from left to right horizontally. However, a horizontal line can create an illusion of length if it is placed either just below or above the middle of the body, e.g., empire waistline or drop waist.

Diagonal lines can have a slimming effect if they are long lines. However, if they are short diagonal lines, they can create a horizontal effect instead.

• The eye is drawn to lines that are **brighter, wider, longer or repeated.** These dominant lines should be restricted to those areas that one is willing to emphasize.

Texture can create illusion

• Texture is the quality of roughness or smoothness. It is the surface appearance of a fabric that the hand can feel and the eye can see. Bulky or shiny textures (those that reflect light, such as satin) tend to increase apparent size. Dull or matte finishes (those that absorb light, such as nubby cotton gauze or raw silk) tend to diminish apparent size. And there are some textures that both reflect and absorb light, such as velvet or corduroy.

Proportion and Balance

Proportion is a matter of balance of space/size relationships. According to the standard body proportions used by artists, the entire height is equivalent to eight times the length of the head, and, ideally, mid-body or four head lengths is at the top of the thigh. Very few people have ideal proportions. (Recently a customer who had attended a *Scientific Dressing* workshop came in for a fitting and laughingly exclaimed "The only thing on my body in the right place is my knee caps!" This was not particularly apparent by her appearance. It isn't important. What *is* important is that one's clothing provides the camouflage or the balance to create the *illusion* of more perfect proportions.

In terms of clothing this means that if you make one area look larger, another will look smaller. A good example is the exaggerated shoulder look of the mid-'80's: large shoulder pads not only make the shoulders appear wider, they cause the hips to look narrower in comparison. Another example might be that of the belt the same color as the blouse, worn with a contrast color skirt, causing the upper torso to appear longer and the lower torso shorter — ideal for the short-waisted person. A long jacket or overblouse will achieve a similar effect. An exceptionally long waisted person could achieve the opposite effect by wearing a pair of high-waisted pants with a wide belt of the same color intensity. This would cause the legs to appear longer and the upper torso shorter.

Some Specific Tricks of the Trade — Camouflage and Illusion

• **Heavy Hips** are the bane of the majority of women. It is not by accident that manufacturers started producing related separates. Being able to buy separates is a godsend for the large numbers of women, whose skirts and pants sizes are one to two sizes larger than that of their blouses and jackets.

Obviously, keeping the observer's eye aimed for the portrait area of the woman with large hips is advisable and anything that broadens the shoulder area will diminish the apparent size of the hips, e.g., shoulder pads or epaulets. Interesting, attractive blouses with shoulder treatment or focal points near the face will draw the eye away from hips. Dark and cool colors will recede, so darker and/or cool colored skirts with lighter tops will minimize the hip area.

A full cut garment such as a tent, float or caftan that hangs from the shoulders hides a multitude of sins. Boxy jackets, tunic length jackets, vests and even overshirts worn to end just below the heaviest part of hips may conceal what's underneath, while a too short blouse will end at just the wrong place, actually accentuating the negative. Fitted jackets or skirts cut on the bias or ones with excessive fullness or in large plaids and horizontal stripes are also apt to emphasize the hip area.

Remember that the eye goes to where there is color change as well as to horizontal lines. The eye will also go to every detail, so be careful of pocket placement and drop waist detail.

Don't over-emphasize smallness of waist. Be certain that belts are not cinched too tightly as that will only serve to emphasize what is above and below the belt!

Appropriate styling of a skirt depends on hip *placement,* as well as size. A high, square hip becomes large just below the waist: this person will need front gathers or darts with smooth lines at the sides, concealed pockets, and her belt should be worn a little loose; an alternative might be to wear her waistband an inch or so above her natural waistline.

Other good advice for the woman with heavy hips is to adjust the shoulder strap on her bag (or better yet, carry a clutch) so that it doesn't bounce on her heaviest area. Remember the eye goes to just such focal points.

She should also avoid a too tight look, creating horizontal lines (wrinkles) and unattractive bulges. It's also a good idea for her to avoid shapeless tops with shapeless bottoms. A full top can be most attractive, but it should have a fairly narrow pantleg or slim skirt beneath. Pleats in pants and skirts should never slant outward as they create short diagonal lines, which are broadening. She should choose, instead, ones that are pleated straight from either a yoke or a band.

• **Protruding tummy or thick middle** is the most common problem, next to heavy hips. Keep belts the same value and intensity as the outfit; avoid having light and dark colors meet at the waistline; contour belts are best for tummy bulge; and the very best way to disguise a thick waist is to cover it up with a tunic or a chemise. A well-cut jacket, vest, etc. will break the line and conceal what is underneath. A contrasting blouse worn under an open jacket or vest divides the area, creating a vertical line, which is slenderizing. Jackets are best worn open. A long scarf tied loosely round the neck and extending to below the waist will also create a vertical line.

A-line skirts or ones with inverted pleats or pleats that are sewn down to about four and a half inches, almost creating a girdle-like effect, as well as those with soft pleats or gathers at the sides would be good choices. Side gathers and side-slash pockets tend to divert the eye. Trousers should have soft pleats at the waistline. Avoid front zippers on skirts or pants, as well as tight belts. Be careful that pocket linings do not show through.

Dresses without waist emphasis, such as dropped waists or A-line, shift or tent silhouettes, will flatter a thick waist.

• **Prominent bust.** Darker, cool colors worn on the top will diminish apparent size. A well tailored jacket, somewhat unstructured, that doesn't hug the body or nip in at the waist will camouflage a prominent bust. Collarless V-neckline jackets are probably the very best. Avoid the clutter and bulk of patch pockets and/or wide lapels.

The person with a prominent bust should avoid figure hugging clothes in clingy fabrics, as well as too fitted jackets or coats, double breasted or belted jackets, boleros, wide lapels, ruffled collars, raglan sleeves, cowl neck sweaters, square or round necklines, clinging tops, tight fitting sleeves or puffed sleeves. They should also avoid a too pinched in waistline; it may make the waist look small, but the bust and hips will look larger by comparison.

This person will also want to avoid flounced or low-flaring skirts, which tend to emphasize the prominent bustline.

Be sure there is no pull at bustline in either blouses or jackets. To avoid gaposis be sure the blouse is the correct size and that buttons are at the apex of the bust. If individual's bust placement varies even a little from that of the fit-model (i.e., the model a designer uses for fitting during the design process), ready-made blouses may gap. A customer who finds this to be a common problem is always pleased to discover that there are a couple of solutions: 1) to determine by trial and error which designers use a fit model closest to their proportions, and then buy only that brand of blouse; or 2) to be sure button placement is adjacent to the apex of her bust. A style with a little shirring off a yoke will alleviate a potential problem or sometimes it may be possible to add a snap. Another obvious solution to the problem, of course, is a blouse that buttons down the back. The right bra may also eliminate gaposis and at the same time minimize a prominent bust.

How to find Correct Bra Size: Hold a tape measure snugly just under breast. Take that number and add five inches. This is *bra size*. Measure loosely around the fullest part of breasts. If the number is one inch more than the original measurement, the cup size would be an *A;* two inches more a *B;* three inches more a *C;* four inches more a *D,* etc.

- **Narrow or sloping shoulders:** When one has very narrow shoulders and larger hips, it is often not possible to get a good fit, i.e., if the shoulders fit, it is too small at the hips; if it fits at the hip, it falls off the shoulders. Sometimes, in order to accommodate a larger hip or bustline, it may be necessary to go to a larger blouse or dress size, producing a too-large look at the shoulder. It may be possible to incorporate shoulder pads. But there also is a fairly simple alteration that may solve the problem: you can take two or three small tucks at the shoulder line, in both the front and the back, creating a little shirred effect, which takes up the excess fullness at the shoulder line. Or you could use a little inconspicuous gathering line on both sides of the shoulder seam to accomplish the same end result.

- It should be noted that sometimes figure problems are based on *old realities*. Sometimes a woman who heard as a teenager that her shoulders were *broad* has now grown into her shoulders. Her hips have increased in size, making her more perfectly proportioned. Her image of herself, however, often has not kept pace with reality. She may still be utilizing techniques for what she perceives to be *too broad shoulders,* e.g., "No padded shoulders for me. My shoulders are already too broad." Analyzing either a tracing or a photograph of both front and side view of her figure is often enlightening, bringing her idea about herself more into line with the facts. Most women seem to have enough feelings of insecurity about their bodies, aging, etc., without the additional burden of out-dated perceptions that are now misconceptions and distortions of the truth.

* * *

BOOKS that go into great detail about proportion, illusion and balance that I have used with my students and can personally recommend include the following:

Marilyn Curtin describes in her book *Scientific Dressing* (Ro-Lyn Publishing, Sacramento, California) useful techniques to compare an individual's own personal proportions with those of the *ideal,* as well as some ways to create the ideal once the deviations are known.

Pinckney and Swenson include in their *New Image for Women* (Reston Publishing Co., Inc. Reston, Virginia), not only ways to choose best styles for your own figure challenges, but what alterations need to be made to correct a variety of fit problems, e.g., such as the wrinkling which may occur just under waistband and again just below the buttocks in the case of the swayback figure.

• **Losing weight doesn't always eliminate figure problems** or *challenges* as we like to call them. In our Image/Style seminars, as a part of figure analysis a drawing is made of each student's body, both front and side views—sometimes before and after weight loss. While overall size changes with weight loss, actual proportions seem to change very little. If one has an hour glass figure before weight loss, she will still have those proportions after. If she is shortwaisted, she will remain shortwaisted. Whether she be topheavy, pear shaped; whether she have broad, narrow or sloping shoulders, etc., these figure challenges will remain even after losing desired weight. So for the multitudes who have less than the perfect proportions of today's ideal, illusion is a very useful tool. For those same multitudes, it is also healthier to concentrate *less* on what you don't like about your body and *more* on what you do like.

Use illusion to draw the eye to those parts of your body which you do like. It creates higher self esteem to think about all of those areas of your body which you like and then choose to emphasize them, rather than to always be a Negative Nellie, deploring something you simply cannot change. With tricks of illusion it is possible to direct the eye of the observer away from one area and to another.

16
The Ideal Image — Reflective of the Inner You

It seems to be generally agreed by the various authors of fashion magazine articles, as well as numerous books that:

"Style comes from *within,* while fashion is imposed from *without.*" It has been said that "one *has* style — and *uses* fashion." One who has style integrates the influences of fashion with her own individual body proportions and personality to emphasize her assets, while minimizing her liabilities, and at the same time expressing at a glance her inner self. In addition, one with personal style has a harmonious finished look.

A well-defined self-image seems to go along with personal style. That makes perfect sense, doesn't it? How can one express at a glance one's inner self, unless the self-image is well-defined? The individual with personal style usually dresses to please herself with no apparent need to conform to either current fashion or fad. Expressing herself almost always seems more important to her than the approval of others. She may lack confidence in other areas, but in at least this one area — her own unique clothing style — her self-confidence shows through.

For some this comes easily and naturally. For others, perhaps The *Color Connection* will provide the missing clues to what has long seemed such a mystery.

Color Analysis — Can You Do It Yourself?

When one needs a new wardrobe, it sometimes seems like an extravagance to spend money on a color analysis. But, of course, that really is the perfect time to have it done if there is any lingering doubt as to one's ability to select personal colors.

Color analysis often reveals new colors which you might never have thought to wear — or which you would never have purchased because of your uncertainty as to whether they were flattering to you. You may find yourself especially uncertain since the onslaught of books and magazine articles about color and color analysis — all talking about *sabotage colors.*

There has been a hint in many of the books on color that you can do it yourself. Occasionally a customer comes into Tarika, carrying *her page* of colors from such a book. Those colors which I have seen reproduced in the do-it-yourself books have rarely been *true* to the ones named, and therefore seem to lack credibility as a reliable personal color palette. Color in this book has been limited to photos of clients for the very reason that it is difficult at affordable prices to reproduce color on paper which has much relationship to that of fabric.

Furthermore, it is extremely difficult to be objective enough to identify correctly all of one's best colors. To see all of the subtleties and nuances of one's own coloring is next to impossible even under the best of conditions. The accuracy of color separations and reproductions in most books is limited and often flawed, making it particularly impractical for accurate analysis.

A few people seem to have a talented eye for selecting colors and are able to choose their own best colors intuitively. If you are determined to attempt self-analysis, you would do well to team up with one of those people — a friend who has an artistic eye.

Instead of using the colors from a book, make a trip to a fabric store — one with a mirror near natural daylight. (This may already be an impossible situation for you! Natural daylight and a mirror in a yardage store!) Wear no make-up and a blouse in a neutral color, preferably off-white. Find a bolt of your favorite red — the one which always gets you compliments. (See page 251 for another way to determine your related reds — ones which relate to your personal coloring. Select several others, including a yellow-red (coral, rust, orange-red) and a blue-based red (berry, azalea pink, rose). Hold these colors up to your face. Concentrate only on your face, including your eyes. What happens? Do you look more lively? Do you look more tired? What about wrinkles, lines, and dark circles? Do they become more or less apparent? Do you look more or less yellow?

Is your best red yellow-based or blue-based? After you have determined this, you may put away all but your very best reds. Select several — a light, medium and dark value at the very least, and preferably any you can find in between from the very lightest to the darkest. Now you will want to hold each of these up to your face. Observe how light and how dark you can go before there is a color change in your face, e.g., at what point in the value change do you begin to appear washed out or gray-looking. Do the very light values look as good as the medium values? How about the darkest values?

Once you have selected your very best reds, you can go on to other colors. Let's assume you have decided your skin has blue undertones, since you look the best in reds which are blue-based. You are either a Summer or a Winter. Is your best red a *true, clear* red or is it more of a watermelon red? Is your best pink more like a hot pink? Or is it more rose-like? Does your best red seem dramatic or soft?

Is your whole look more dramatic looking? Or gentle and romantic? Do you think you have much contrast in your visual image? Or is your contrast softer?

If you are leaning toward the more dramatic, vibrant colors, with contrast in your visual image, you are probably a Winter; if toward the softer look, you are no doubt a Summer.

Similarly, if your related reds seem to be yellow-based, (e.g., cherry or poppy red, shrimp or coral, rust or brick red, terra cotta or tangerine), you are either a Spring or an Autumn.

Now compare the results of the cherry red fabric with a brick red; and the shrimp with tangerine, the poppy red with terra cotta, etc. Does your skin change? Is your visual image more light/bright? Or rich looking? Do you feel your skin is enhanced more by pastels or by the richer tones?

If your look and feel is more perky and your colors are lighter and brighter, you are probably a Spring. If you feel better and look more alive in the richer colors, then you are probably an Autumn.

(Note: It has been theorized in an earlier chapter that the seasonal types are on a continuum. Often there seems to be such a fine line between, for instance, an Autumn who is almost a Winter...and the Winter, who is almost an Autumn. The real difference is what happens to the skin and the eyes when the colors change from blue- to yellow-base, and with some that change is so subtle that it can only be seen by the very discerning. Occasionaly there is one who can wear yellow-based and blue-based reds equally well. This woman is extremely difficult to identify season-wise. Personality will surely be the deciding factor in this instance.)

If you are one who is *on the cusp,* season-wise, you may have an even more difficult time *diagnosing* your own season. However, you may be able to achieve a fairly accurate result if you use the color comparison tests in combination with the personality and yin/yang characteristics. But do take plenty of time to get acquainted with your related reds before you go on to the next step.

Once you have zeroed in on your season, buy an eighth of a yard (or the smallest amount your yardage store will sell) of each of your related reds from the lightest to the darkest. Get acquainted with these *best reds.* Let your family and friends help you decide if they are better than the ones you already have in your closet. Try them with your current wardrobe. Are your related reds harmonious with your favorite colors in your current wardrobe? Set aside items in those colors which do not harmonize with your best reds. Are these items that you enjoy wearing? Do you wear them alone? Or do you always add another color in the form of a scarf or a piece of jewelry to make it more pleasing to the eye? If the latter is true, this may not be one of *your colors.*

From what you currently have in your closet that *works with your red,* and that you wear with confidence, you probably have the foundation for a color palette. Check all those colors by using the *mirror test* — in natural daylight with no make-up, etc. Once you have determined which colors are in harmony with your best reds, take a little snip from a seam allowance if you can. Tape or staple it to a 3x5 card.

Next make up your composite, which is determined by your very own coloring, i.e. your hair color (and almost everyone has several different shades), your skin tones, and your eye colors. Pick out a group of fabrics at the yardage store which seem to be as near your hair colors as possible, the beiges, the taupes, the grays, the browns, blacks, etc. which seem closest to 1) the overall appearance of your hair, that which is seen from 3 feet away, and 2) the various gradations of colors seen up close. It is from these colors that you will select your best neutral, your *basic* color. (If your hair has been dyed or bleached, get someone to assist you in examining the roots underneath the hair at the back of the neckline to determine the natural hair color. The fabric color that you match to your natural hair color is your very best neutral. (Usually Winters with very dark brown hair will use black as their best neutral, because from a distance, their hair appears almost black.) Once you have selected this color, take it as light and as dark as is flattering on you personally, just as you did with your reds.

Again, you can purchase an eighth of a yard of each of these fabrics. You should also be looking at texture and how that affects your visual image.

You may be thinking: "This is a complicated process. The fee of a competent color analyst is beginning to seem like a bargain." By the time you have collected 50 to 150 color samples, it is true you will have made a bit of an investment in both time and money — enough probably to have treated yourself to a good color analysis!

If you wish to persevere, you can now move on to other neutrals, your eye color (see page 251), your complementary colors, etc. Remember to look at all parts of your eye, including little flecks, the outer rim, etc. Your primary color is your eye color, the generalized color that is seen from three feet away. You will want to find a fabric swatch which matches this general color as closely as possible. Some shades of that color may change the color of your eyes, e.g., even if your eyes are a soft blue, some soft blues will make your eyes appear almost gray, while another shade of blue may make them appear a vibrant blue. The goal of color analysis is to find colors for your palette which enhance your skin and make your eyes appear lively and bright.

You will repeat the process for each of the primary, secondary and tertiary colors around the color wheel, excluding those colors which do not enhance your appearance, such as yellow for many Winter and most Summer types. (This is not a hard and fast rule. Some Summers and Winters may have a perfect yellow.) Find the best values and intensities of each, whether clear or softened, etc.

When you have your full collection of colors, you will want to organize them so that they will be easy to use when shopping. You can use uniform clear acetate strips or card stock, attaching the fabric swatches with double-stick masking or carpet tape. Group colors from each color family together, so that they can be easily used.

Some color analysts prepare a color fan for the use of their clients; others hand out pre-packs. Still others believe it is a good opportunity for the client to experience and get acquainted with her *new best colors* by making up her own color fan. Sometimes your color analyst will provide extra fabric or a second fan for a small fee. Your favorite shop may welcome having your colors on file so that they can call you when anything in your color comes in.

• *Remember to write your name, address, telephone number on your color swatches,* and whether you will pay a reward if your colors are returned to you if lost. It's always good insurance, of course, to make a duplicate.

Learn to Use Your Colors

• *Take your colors with you when you go shopping.* Try to match as nearly as you can, of course, but be aware that your colors were made up with the fabric swatches which were available at the time your colors were done. Any color that blends, or is between two colors on a wand of your fan, should be perfectly acceptable. If your color samples are paint chips, it is even more difficult to match to fabric exactly. It is not intended that you match your wardrobe to the limited selection of pre-packs provided by some color analysts. The pre-pack merely provides a general idea of the values and intensities, etc. of that particular seasonal harmony.

Each year, there are new fashion colors available from which to choose. Were you to have your colors done this year, and if your color analyst happened to have those colors in her limited collection, you might be given this new color.

When you are shopping and find a color that you like — one that is not on your color fan — decide whether the color looks good on you...or more importantly, you look good in it...then open the fan of your colors against the color. Is it pleasing with the majority of colors on your palette? Does it blend well? Or does it stick out like a sore thumb? If it blends well, you can feel perfectly safe in making the purchase even though the color does not appear on your palette. If it blends with your palette, you will be able to use it easily with the rest of your wardrobe. Remember to add the color to your palette if you make the purchase.

- **Use a color wheel** to expand your color horizons. Try new combinations of your colors, using the guidelines outlined in your season's chapter.
- **Keep a shopping "wish" list** in your closet. When you think of something you wish you had, (e.g., a yellow belt for a violet dress...and maybe a scarf or a pair of earrings which would combine the two colors, tying the whole outfit together), jot it down! Make a hash mark behind the item every time you wish you had it. If a wish keeps recurring, you may decide it's a *need* rather than a casual wish. This kind of shopping list will give you purpose and direction when you go shopping, perhaps preventing unnecessary impulse buying, while adding meaningful things to your wardrobe.
- **Plan Your Wardrobe**

A basic wardrobe should include, depending, of course, on your life style:
- *a basic coat* — one which is simple, classic, uncluttered, and in your best neutral color, most often your hair color, which is usually your dressiest neutral.
- *a raincoat* — a raincoat in your high shade is a *cheerer-upper* for everyone. And, if it is has a bit of a sheen, it can even be worn for evening.
- *a basic suit* — again, a timeless style in your best neutral, one which is simple enough to accessorize and wear for many different occasions.
- *a dress* — also in your best neutral, and in a style which is simple enough to be dressed up or down by changing accessories.
- *shoes, handbag, clutch, wallet, gloves* if you wear them, and a *briefcase* if you need one — all in your best basic neutral color.
- *a dressy jacket* — one which skims the hip area, ending at mid-hip, to wear with dreses and skirts. Have you ever found yourself dressed perfectly for a special occasion, praying that it is either warm enough so that you won't have to wear a coat or that it will rain because you have a decent

Mothers and Daughters

Winter

Winter

Spring

Spring

Autumn

Winter

Spring

Autumn

Illus. 306

raincoat? If so, you need a dressy jacket — and your best neutral will be a good choice.

Your second and third neutrals will be less formal looking and more suitable for everyday wear. If fabrics are compatible, you will be able to mix and match the two neutrals, as well as your neutrals with your colors, e.g., a black jacket with a gray blouse and gray skirt, worn with an accent of color in scarf or jewelry.

For further wardrobe suggestions, turn to Chapter 14, *Color and How to Use It*.

• **Update your color palette** with samples from your new purchases or with new fashion colors which blend. It is especially helpful to carry fabric swatches of your prints and plaids. Take them from a seam allowance or from hemming scraps. A little snip of a print or plaid is invaluable if you are trying to match to a belt, scarf or blouse. It's worth a thousand words to a sales clerk who may be trying to help you.

• **When you shop with your mother, sister, friend, etc.** remember that your style may not be her style and vice versa. It is not at all uncommon for there to be conflict between mother and daughter during shopping sprees. These conflicts are often in direct proportion to the amount of variance between the mother's seasonal type and that of the daughter. For example: a Spring mother will be much more understanding of a Spring daughter's natural wardrobe choices than will a Winter or an Autumn mother. And an Autumn or Winter daughter will often say, "Ycchhh!" to the choices of a Summer mother.

Friends may be more subtle than mothers and daughters, but they also are often very influential. Our greatest number of returns are as a result of a friend encouraging a customer to buy something which really isn't quite right. "It looks great on you. It is just darling. You ought to get it!" are encouraging words for the moment. At home, sometimes a clearer head prevails. And, at home, there is sometimes a husband, who may be of a different seasonal harmony. He may have an opinion which is not in accord with the choices of his distaff side.

And sometimes one is tempted to try the colors and/or styles of others whose looks we admire. It is not uncommon for a Spring or Summer type to try to wear the striking color combinations and sophisticated looks of a Winter sister or friend. It rarely works to borrow someone else's style.

- **Pay Attention to Your Own Feelings.** If you feel like you're playing dress-up in someone else's clothes, even though the sales clerk, your mother, friend, husband and everyone around exclaims how wonderful it looks on you — pay attention to your own feelings! That feeling you're having is a good signal that those clothes are not reflecting that 'essential you'. These are the kinds of purchases which either get returned or hang in your closet, which you put on time and time again, taking them off each time because the occasion is just not quite right.

On the other hand, if you try something and are a little intrigued, even though you've never worn anything like it before. Think about it. This may be something that is expressive of a part of you that you are just beginning to be aware of — a part of you that you may wish to develop. It may be an image that you'd like to project even if you don't feel totally identified with it yet. And sometimes you may say, "No, this really isn't me. But I don't care. I want to look out of character just this once for the fun of it."

Surprisingly often, the clothes that you choose like this often turn out to be favorites — and reflective of you, after all. Often a customer will return to the store after just such a purchase to say: "Joan, you know that outfit I bought for my class reunion? I just love it. I feel so good in it. I received so many compliments on it. I didn't think it was 'me,' but I sure love wearing it!" Such a customer may find that she is in the process of developing a new style or a new image. A success like that may give her the courage to continue.

It is at once challenging and exciting to be the sales clerk in that kind of personal style evolution. It is rewarding to help a customer discover the *technique,* to watch her style evolve and grow as she does. Each individual, of course, has to take the primary responsibility for her own style. Otherwise, it would not be her style.

You can profit from gathering ideas from a variety of sources — family, magazines, color analysts and wardrobe consultants or even the sales clerk in your favorite store. But in the end, true personal style is something you alone can develop. It's not something that you can find already bottled, packaged and ready-to-wear.

True personal style evolves through being true to yourself — through expressing your own inner essence. It is a process. And it is rarely ever complete. Most people change their look, even if only in subtle ways, when they get tired of wearing the same old thing or when something new fires their imagination.

"Style is natural, never contrived. It's that special something that makes things look so easy. It's a positive, confident attitude toward life and self-expression. It's the freedom of being at peace with yourself and the way you appear to others..."
— Henry Grethel.

Comparative Seasonal

	WINTER	**SPRING**
Overall:	Striking, with high contrast, often even features, high cheekbones and heavy dark eyebrows.	Light, bright, animated, golden, radiant, buoyant, rounded features, bubbly personality.
Skin:	From light to dark olive, nearly white, champagne, alabaster, light peach.	Light golden, ivory, light peach, may or may not tan.
Eyes:	Sparkling charcoal, gray-green, jade green, light blue-green, pine green, lapis blue, navy blue, or icy blue.	Sparkling blue, green, blue-green, blue-gray, green-blue, purple-blue, yellow-green, sometimes brown (but brown-eyed blondes are often autumn!).
Hair:	Black, charcoal brown, platinum, salt & pepper, dark brown. May gray early.	Golden, flaxen, golden brown, ash, lighter values of red as in strawberry blonde.
Colors to Wear:	Strong intensity or icy pastels; value contrast in same outfit.	
Express:	Dramatic, high fashion, sophisticated, elegant.	Bright, fresh, energetic, animated, cute, trendy.
Textures:	Drapable, smooth, not bulky.	Crisp: pique, denim, cotton, linen, silk, gabardine, knits, eyelet, crisp lace.
Prints:	Abstract, geometric, dramatic, unusual, large space division, paint brush streaks, uncluttered.	Small, dainty, scattered. Ginghams, calicos, hearts and flowers, fun, cute prints, polka dots, stripes, plaids, butterflies.
Lines:	Symbol: Oval Uncluttered, simple, classic, dramatic. Relaxed S-curves, undulating lines with no abrupt beginnings or endings, as in hills and valleys.	Symbol: Circle Rounded lines, Peter Pan collar, rounded notched collars, middy look, small details, e.g., little buttons, exposed zippers, piping, scallops.
Jewelry:	Silver, white gold, bone, ivory, real jewels, glitter, rhinestones, dramatic and overscaled.	Gold, brass. Can also wear fun trendy plastic, ceramic, and light woods, painted, small in scale, charm bracelets, flowers, beads, white jewelry.

Harmony Chart

	SUMMER	**AUTUMN**
Overall:	Soft, gentle, romantic, meticulous, well cared for, feminine, graceful.	Flamboyant, rich, bold, dramatic, dashing, dynamic, energetic, exotic with strong features, often angularity of face and body.
Skin:	Pink, peach. Blue or lavender undertones; usually does not or should not tan.	Ranges from cafe au lait, amber, yellowish brown, ruddy, brushed with copper or bronze; may be ivory, cream or peach in tone.
Eyes:	Misty blue, gray-blue, powder blue, gray-green, blue-green, hazel or brown.	Green, gray-green, yellow-green, topaz, hazel, olive, blue-green, brown with rust flecks. (Very intense in color.)
Hair:	Strawberry blonde, ash blonde, grayish brown, light brown, gray.	Red, dark auburn, copper brown, metallic blonde, brown with reddish or copper highlights.
Colors to Wear:	Blended, weaker intensity, muted, sun-bleached, faded, lighter values.	Darker earthtones, the colors of fall leaves, strong intensity, rich, no blue based reds, no pastels, black only as background in prints. Cool colors will intensify personal coloring.
Express:	Softness, iridescence, dreaminess, romance.	Confidence, drama, flamboyancy, naturalness, ethnicity, tawniness, forcefulness.
Textures:	Pliable, soft and fine-grained, soft lace, no nubbiness, delicate.	Textures you can see as well as feel; corduroy, handloomed, suede, tweeds, basketweaves, primitive fabrics.
Prints:	Blended florals, roses, fluid, flowing designs, medium size.	Plaids, paisley, leaf shapes, herringbone, houndstooth, geometric, exotic floral, animal skins, jungle motifs, stripes.
Lines:	Symbol: Oval Medium sized, S-curves, subtle, highly finished, well tailored, cascading limp ruffles, soft bows, embroidery.	Symbol: Rectangle or any part thereof. Angularity, asymmetrical, swift lines, pointed collars and details, v-necks, notched collars, color blocking, intarsia (especially leaf shapes), V-shapes, impact lines.
Jewelry:	Silver and white gold, floral designs, ovals, cameos, pearls, soft romantic looks.	Bold heavy jewelry, bangles, hardware look, baroque pearls, multiple strands, turquoise, heavy metals, angular shapes, oxidized metals, brass, copper, bronze, gold, pottery, macrame, stones that glow rather than sparkle.

Index

accessories 33, 248
Allyson, June 116
amethyst 54, 129
ample fit 21, 67
analogous 28-29, 74, 121, 151, 250
Andress, Ursula 145
Andrews, Julie 116
angularity 75, 153, 163
animated 27, 29, 74-75, 81, 101, 113
  (See Spring)
Aphrodite 205
applique 33, 135
aquamarine 54
ascot 37, 52, 61
asymmetry 59, 155, 161, 163, 224
authoritative 105, 139, 248
Autumn seasonal harmony 15, 20-21, 24, 35-39, 139, **149-177**, 195, 204, 210-211, 225
  analogous colors 151, 250
  bags 159
  black 151
  bridal 155, 160, 169
  brown 150-151, 248-9
  buttons 161
  coats 171
  coloring 149
  colors 29, 33, 150-151, 211
  continuum 37-38
  design lines and detail 33, 49, 153
  dresses 163
  earth mother 38
  earth tones 24, 29, 151, 248
  eyes 74, 149
  fabric 33, 49, 155
  famous persons 176
  fit, ample 21, 33
  formalwear 169
  gray 248
  Grecian 48-49
  hair 149, 151
  hair styles 159
  hats 159
  jewelry 158, 210
  knits 175
  men 176
  navy blue 248
  necklines 161
  pants 165
  personality 149
  physical characteristics 150, 153
  prints 158
  professional 167
  shoes 173
  silhouette 155
  skin 28-29, 149
  skirts 161
  skiwear 103
  sleeves 163
  swimwear 175
  texture 49, 150, 155
  visual design 150
  walk 149
  what to wear in summer 155, 157, 211
  white 151, 248
  word portrait 178

Bacall, Lauren 177
bags 54, 91, 159, 256
balance 256
Ball, Lucille 177
Banana Republic 205
beige 248
Belafonte, Harry 70
belts 224
Bergen, Candace 145
Black, Shirley Temple 116

black 63, 73, 151, 248
  shoes 109
Blacks 43, 249
blonde 11, 74
blue-based colors (See colors.)
blue-green, universal complement 31, 249
blush 249
Bogart, Humphrey 177
boots 67
bra, how to find correct size 259
braid 111, 129
bridal 46, 84, 122, 160
bright colors 254
brocade 169
brown 3, 150-151, 249
Brynner, Yul 71
buckles 224
Burnett, Carol 177
buttons 55, 93, 127, 161, 224
  placement 227
buyer (see retailer) 5-7, 21, 219
buying error 7, 213
buying skills 21, 223

caftans 59
cameo 33, 39, 129, 139
camouflage 256
capes 67
Capra, Fritjof 179-180
cascading lines 24, 39, 48, 125, 139
Caygill, Suzanne 8, 17, 29, 31, 43, 150
ceramic 54
Chamberlain, Richard 145
Chanel 61
Channing, Carol 116
Cher 70
Chesterfield 111
chic 55
chignon 54
circular 81
classic 31, 47, 55, 59, 61, 67, 133, 137, 200
closet consultation 222
closet — mistakes 207-8
coats 66-67, 111, 141, 171
cocoon 45, 59, 67
collarless 47, 55, 61
collars (see design detail) 47, 55, 85
Collins, Joan 70
color 7, 25
  basic principles 247
  consistent with guidelines 205
  creates illusion 254
  designer choice 205
  has energy 247
  hue 247
  science 17
  sensuous and romantic 249
  true colors 28
  warm colors 11, 13, 28
color analysis 2-4, 14-15, 17-18, 27-33, 200, 203, 262
  accuracy 17
  do-it-yourself 261-2
  pre-packaged 16, 29
  primary method 28
color analysts 1-2, 137, 238, 250
  licensure 14, 18
color base 11, 13
color blocking 51, 65
Color Connection 20-21
Color I Associates 16
coloring, correlation to style and personality 20
color palette 3, 14, 31
colors 20, 73, 121, 150-151
  analogous 28-29, 74, 132, 151, 250
  blended 151
  blue-based 11, 13, 18, 28, 208, 263
  clear 28
  complementary 249-250
  cool 11, 13, 28, 121

cross-colors 15
dusty 28, 137
earth tones (See Autumn)
elegant 250
hard to find 210
high visibility 250
  in prints 250
monochromatic 68, 250
muted 27-28, 137
neutrals 47, 73, 247
sabotage 2, 250
secondary 247
skin tone 31, 63, 249
split-complementary 250
tertiary 247
triad 74, 250
understated 249-250
universal 31
white 74, 248
yellow-based 11, 13, 18, 28-29, 208, 263
Color, The Essence of You 17, 43
Como, Perry 145
comparative illustrations 10, 12, 20, 32, 198, 218
comparative seasonal harmony chart 34, 43, 197, **272-273**
concealed pockets 59, 61
consumer 3-5, 261
  value service 222
continuum **34-39**, 68, 79, 105
contrast (See Winter) 25, 29, **41-72**, 114
copper 153
Cosell, Howard 177
cowl 137, 143
Crawford, Joan 177
crisp 49, 74
cross-season 15
crystal 54
Curtin, Marilyn 260
customer
  loyalty 22
  records 243
  returns 22

dark or middle value colors 254
Day, Doris 116
denim 86
design 6-7
  detail 51, 79, 83, 99, 125, 153, 206
  should relate to season guidelines 225
  error 6, 8-9, 19, 21-24, 77, 207, 211, 215, 217, 223
  lines 19, 23-25, 45, 83, 85, 123, 153, 203
  create shapes 224
design-on-design 227
designer/retailer/consumer relationship 5, 212, 217
designers 5, 19, 23-25, 155, **203-218**
  annotation re:separates coordination 216
  annotation re: seasonal harmony 216
  Autumn color and style availability in spring 155-157, 211
  benefits of adhering to guidelines 200
  critique by objective consultant 214-215
  design detail 206
  fabric, of 19, 206
  fashion colors 207
  prints, of 208-209
  questions to ask yourself 205-206
  silhouette 206
  standardized sizes 216
  target seasonal type 205, 216
diamonds 54
dirndl 57, 81
discount stores 220, 223

dolman sleeves 55
dominant harmony 15, 39, 68
  seminars 222
Donahue, Phil 145
dramatic 24, 37, 52, 249
dresses 58-59, 99, 133, 163
dressmaker
  detail 79
  suit 105
drop shoulder 55

Eastwood, Clint 177
earrings 54
earth child 38
earth mother 38
earth tones (See Autumn)
elegance 24, 43, 54, 61, 68-69, 107, 250
emeralds 54
encrusted look 169
environmental influences 239
epaulets 171
ethnic 153
Etidorpha 204-205
exotic 153, 158
exposed backs 55, 59
eye contact 249
eye colors in clothing 249
eyes 2, 15, 43, 74, 121, 149

fabric 7, 20, 24-25, 49, 53, 61, 63, 87, 126, 131, 141, 143, 155, 157, 205
  crisp 49
  fine-grained 123, 143
  pliable 24, 49, 126, 137, 204
  shimmery 49
face
  major emphasis on 254
Falk, Peter 177
falling lines 45, 49
famous men and women 22, 70, 116, 145, 176
fantasy 214
fashion colors 209
fashion coordinators 210
  application of theory 210
Fawcett, Farrah 145
feminine 18-19, 114, 121, 133, 135, 150, 195-196
  tailoring 141
  knits 65, 113, 143
figure challenges 37, 57, 246, **253-260**
fit and flare 45
flamboyant 149
flamestitch 158
flange 55
floats 59
Ford, Harrison 177
formalwear 63, 107, 139, 169
Fox, Michael 145
freckles 119
fresh 74
frustrated shoppers 213
futuristic 45, 51, 54, 67

gabardine 61
Gable, Clark 70
Gabor, ZsaZsa 116
gaucho 165
generalizations 16, 20-21, 43, 75, 203
genetic 239
gentle (See Summer) 15, 27, **119-148**
Gere, Richard 70
gifts 22
graceful 121
grainline 7-8
Grant, Cary 70
gray 248
Grecian 45, 48-49, 59
Griffin, Merv 145
gross profit 220
guidelines, style 2-3, 20, 38, 47, 205, 213

Index

basic recipes, as 200
evolved over time 29, 38, 203

hacking jacket 61
hair 74, 89, 139, 149
　color 42-43, 119
　gray 43, 151
　red 149
　styles 2, 15, 54, 125, 159
Hamel, Veronica 70
Hamilton, George 70
handwoven 49, 155, 171
Hawn, Goldie 116
harlequin 51
harmony 15, 39, 68, 139
Harrison, Rex 177
Hartman, David 145
hats 54, 91, 159, 199
Hayes, Helen 116
Hepburn, Audrey 70
Hepburn, Katharine 177
herringbone 37, 158
Heston, Charlton 177
high fashion 51, 55, 63
high visibility colors 249
hip placement 256
hips, heavy 256
Holliday, Judy 116
homespun 49, 155
Hope, Bob 116
horizontal lines 257
Horn, Lena 70
houndstooth 37, 53, 158
hue 247
Hurt, William 145

illusion 13, **253-260**
image 13, 37, 75, 105, 137
impact lines 153, 175
increased sales 21
individual style 15
inner style 7, 15, 18, 239, (See personality)
intensity of color 247
iridescent 121

jabot 52
jade 54, 158
Jackson, Glenda 177
jeans 57, 79, 101, 135
　jacket 111
jet 54
J. G. Hook 205
Jessica McClintock 305
jewelry 54, 91, 129, 158, 209

Kaye, Danny 177
Kelly, Grace 145
Kennedy, Caroline 145
kimono sleeves 55
knickers 101
knits 65, 113, 143, 175

lace 33, 39, 137, 139, 155
ladylike 121
Lansbury, Angela 116
lapels, wide 155
leather 21
light colors 254
light-bright (See Spring) 15, 27, 29, 73-118
leaf shapes 153, 158
leather 153, 161, 171, 175
lines create illusion 255
lingerie 249
Little, Carole 77
lizard 173
long-waisted 256
Loren, Sophia 177

macrame 153
maintained markup 221
make-up 249

mandarin 55, 59
mannerisms 21, 75, 121
man-tailored 155
manufacturers (see designers) 5, 157
manufactuers' representatives 217
markdowns 8, 79, 213, **219-221**, 223
Martin, Mary 116
masculine 18-19, 195-196,
Mason, Marsha 116
Matthau, Walter 177
McLain, Shirley 116
men 14, 69, 115-116, 144, 176
Merrill, Dina 145
metals 54,
meticulous 121
monochromatic colors 68, 151, 250
Monroe, Marilyn 116
Montalban, Ricardo 70
mood dressing 139, 210
Munsell Color System 8, 17
muted colors (See Autumn) 27-28, 137
nail polish 249
narrow shoulders 259
nautical 74-75, 83, 111
navy blue 248
natural preferences 1, 7, 20, 31, 39
naturalistic 155, 158
necklines 55, 85, 93, 127, 161
Nethery, Betty 238
neutrals 47, 67, 109, 137, 150-151, 247-248
　rules for wearing neutrals 248
New Image for Women 260
Newman, Paul 145
Nolte, Nick 145
non-Caucasians 43, 249
notched collars 137, 153, 155, 255

off-price 220-223
Onassis, Jacqueline Kennedy 70
onyx 54
opulence 169
Orientals 43, 249
Osmond, Marie 70
outer style 7, 18, 200
oval 37, 45, 52-54, 67, 141
oversized 153

paisley 158
pants 57, 101, 135, 165
peacoat 111
pearls 33, 54, 158
Peck, Gregory 70
peplum 107
personality 15-16, 18, 20, 25, 43, 67-68, 75, 119, 121, 149
personal style 13, 241
physical characteristics 18, 25, 43, 68
Personal Style Counselors (PSC) 17
Pinckney, Gerrie 8, 238-239, 260
platinum 54
Pleshette, Suzanne 70
pockets 33, 61, 165, 226
pointelle 113
predictability 20, 204
preppy 105, 111, 113
primary colors 247
prints 19-20, 53, 68, 74-75, 77, 87, 141-143, 158, 209, 250
　combining 251
　designers of 208-209
　paisley 158
professional look 39, 61, 105, 137, 139, 167
prominent bust 258
proportion 256
protruding tummy 257
purchase orders 232

Queen Elizabeth 145

raglan sleeves 55

rayon/linen blend 24, 204
rectangular form 153, 175
red 13, 29, 63
　for business 249
　selecting reds 249
　related reds 249
Redford, Robert 126
Redgrave, Vanessa 177
red haired 11, 74, 150
refined fabrics 141, 143
relationship of coordinates 216
released lines 45, 49
"rep" (see manufacturer's representative)
retail buyers 1-9, 78-79, 211, **219-237**
　balanced mix of merchandise 227
　annotate lines by season by color 230
　Autumn styles for Spring/Summer delivery 155, 157, 212
　benefits of adhering to guidelines 200
　emotions 233
　generalizations useful 43
　identifying seasonal harmony of item 230
　imperfect detail may be removed or altered 225
　purchase orders 232
　rating the styles 230
　remembering what you've seen 228
　Spring/Summer styles for fall delivery 157, 212
　total market picture 232
　vendor meeting criteria 229
　whose style? yours or your customers 235
retailer 1-27, **219-237**
　discriminating shoppers 213
　staff training 235
Reynolds, Debbie 116
rhinestones 54-55
rich (See Autumn)
romantic (see Summer) 24, 129, 139, 205
rope 153
round 81
rubies 54

sabotage colors 2, 250
safari look 33, 153, 157, 165, 171
sales associates 21-22, **235-251**
　client's records file 242-243
　customer
　　concerned about expense of clothing 244
　　figure challenges 244, 353-260
　　keep in touch with 243
　　requests 243
　　wishes to look younger 244
　figure challenges 245, **253-260**
　generalizations 43
　honest feedback 237, 245
　phone tag 243
　soft-sell approach 246
　solving the riddle of customer preferences 238
　some specific questions to ask 241
　take an interest in customers 240
sapphires 54
sarong 57, 59
scarves 61
Scientific Dressing 256, 260
S-curves 45, 49, 123, 126
　relaxed 53
scallops 113-114
Seasonal Color Harmony **1-39**, 69, 203
　advantages for sales associates 235
　as it applies to men 69
secondary colors 247
secondary harmony 15, 19, 34-40, 53, 68, 79, 200, 208, 213,
self-image 13, 261

separates 256
service 4
shapes
　are created by collars, sleeves, etc. 226
shirring 135, 141
shoulder pads 259-260
shoulders
　narrow or sloping 259
silhouette 6-7, 20, 39, 45, 81, 123, 155
sizes, standardization 216
shoes 67, 109, 141, 173
Shore, Dinah 116
shoulder pads 123, 137, 155, 163
silhouette 20, 81, 155, 206
silver 54, 129
Sinatra, Frank 116
single focal 51, 54-55, 61
Skelton, Red 177
skin 2, 15, 18, 42-43, 74-75, 119, 149, 150
　non-Caucasian 43, 249
　olive 28
　sallow 28
　translucent 74
　undertone 13, 15, 28-29, 150
　Winters misidentified as Autumns 150
skirts 57, 81, 97, 130-131, 161
skiwear 103
sleeves 55, 95, 127, 163
slickers 111
slimming lines 255
sloping shoulders 259
small detail 79
Smith, Jaclyn 70
socialization 11, 18
soft (see Summer) 19, 27, 49, 135, 143, 150
Songer, Joan 8, 196
sophisticated 54-55, 68
spaced designs 53
split complementary colors 250
Spring type 15, 19, **73-117**, 157, 195, 200, 204, 210, 225
　bags 91
　black 109, 248
　bridal 84
　buoyancy 63, 73, 85
　buttons 93
　casual looks 79
　coats 111
　colors 29, 73
　collars 85, 93
　contrast 29, 38, 114
　design lines 83, 85
　dresses 99
　earth child 38
　elegance 107
　eyes 74
　fabric 33, 87
　famous personalities 116
　Floral 200
　formalwear 107
　gentle 37
　Golden 200
　Grecian 48-49
　jewelry 91, 209
　hair 74, 89
　hats 91
　knits 113
　men 115-116
　navy blue 248
　necklines 93
　neutrals 73
　outside contour 81
　overall look 114
　pants 101
　personality 75
　prints 74, 77, 87
　professional look 105
　scale 107

Index

shirtwaist 32-33, 99, 107
shoes 108-109
silhouette 81
skin 28-29, 74
skirts 97, 130-131
skiwear 103
sleeves 55, 95
  unusual combinations 86
white 74, 248
word portrait 117
younger version of Autumn 38
Stallone, Sylvester 70
standardized sizes 216
stark 51
Stewart, James 145
stock tie 52
straight skirt 57
Streep, Meryl 145
Strickland, Eloise 204-205
striking (See Winter) 19, 24, 37
stripes, uneven 53
style 13, 15, 20, 47, 52, 200, 261, 271
  natural preferences 38-39
stylized 51, 53-54, 68
success-oriented 13
suede 155
Summer types 15, 19, 24, 27-28, 33, 38, 47, **119-147**, 157, 195, 204, 208, 210
  analogous colors 250
  bridal 122
  buttons 127
  coats 141
  colors 28, 121, 123
  continuum 38-39
  design lines 123
  detail 33, 125
  dresses 133
  eyes 121
  fabric 33, 123, 126, 143
  famous personalities 145
  formalwear 139
  gray 248
  Grecian 48-49
  hair 119, 125-126, 139
  hats 126
  jewelry 129, 209
  knits 143
  mannerisms 121
  men 144
  necklines 127
  overall look 143
  pants 135
  personality 119, 121, 127
  prints 77, 126
  professional look 39, 137-138
  S-curves 49
  shirtwaist 32-33
  shoes 141
  silhouette 123
  skin 28, 119
  skirts 131
  skiwear 103
  sleeves 127
  suede 21
  swimwear 142
  symbol 119
  undertones of skin 119
  voice 121
  walk 121
  white 248
  word portrait 147
Suzanne (See Caygill)
Swenson, Marge 8, 238-239, 260
swimwear 64, 76, 142, 174

tanning 119
tapestry 169, 171
target market 205
Taylor, Elizabeth 70
technique 22, 239
tent dresses 45, 59
tertiary colors 247

texture 155, 161, 167, 173, 175
theory, (See Seasonal Color Harmony) 3, 7-8
  applicable to more than clothing 209
Thomas, Betty 177
Tiegs, Cheryl 145
tone-on-tone 53, 69
top stitching 93, 97, 111, 114
Tracy, Spencer 177
trench coats 171
trendy 57, 75, 101
triad 74, 250
true colors 28
tucks
tunics 59 .CU
Turning Point, The 179
tweeds 155, 171

ultrasuede 155
uncluttered 51-52, 55, 61, 67-68
understated colors 249-250
undertones of skin 13, 15, 119, 150
uneven stripes 53
unknown customer 21
unusual combinations 86

value 247
value of clothing 244
vertical lines 255
video 22
visual design 16, 21, 43, 52, 68, 75, 105, 121
V-necks 153, 161
voice 16, 21, 43, 75, 121

walk 16, 21, 43, 75, 121, 149
warm colors 11, 13, 28
weeding out process 5, 214, 219, 223
weight loss 260
"What if...?" 214
wide lapels 155
Williams, Andy 145
Winger, Debra 70
Winter 15, 20, 24, 27-29, 31, 33, 35-39, **40-71**, 150, 195, 204, 210
  bags 54
  black 248
  boots 67
  bridal 46
  buttons 55
  casual 57
  clear colors 28
  coats 66-67
  collars 61
  colors 28, 42
  contrast 15, 27-28, 42, 51, 53, 65, 68
  design detail 33, 52, 61
  design lines 45
  dresses 58-59
  elegance 63
  eyes 43
  fabric 33, 51, 53, 63
  features 43
  formalwear 63
  gray 248
  Grecian 48-49
  hair 42-43
  hair styles 54, 57
  hats 54
  high fashion 51
  jewelry 54, 209
  knits 65
  lustrous 49, 52-53, 69
  men 69
  metals 54
  navy blue 248
  necklines 55
  overall effect 68
  pants 57
  personality 42-45, 45
  pockets 61

  prints 53, 68
  professional look 36-37, 61
  scarves 52, 61
  serenity 68
  shirtwaist 32-33
  shoes 67
  silhouette 45,
  simplicity 61
  single focal 51, 54-55, 61
  skin 28, 42
    misidentified as Autumns 150
  skirts 57
  skiwear 103
  sleeves 55
  striking appearance 15, 19, 27, 52
  style 42, 52
  swimwear 64
  true colors 28
  uncluttered 51-52, 55, 67
  values 28
  voice 43
  walk 43
  white 248
  wrinkled look 33, 61
  yellow 42
wood 153, 161
work clothes 13
Wyman, Jane 177

yang 18, 19, 79, 155, 179-183
yellow-based (See colors)
yellow 42, 121
yin 18-19, 79, 99, 179-183
yin/yang 18-19, 21, 25, 35, 37, 53, 179-183 200, 238
  profile chart 182
Young, Loretta 145

zircon 54